JOHN TAVENER

JOHN TAVENER

GLIMPSES OF PARADISE

Geoffrey Haydon

VICTOR GOLLANCZ

LONDON

First published in Great Britain 1995
by Victor Gollancz
An imprint of the Cassell Group
Wellington House, 125 Strand, London WC2R 0BB

A catalogue record for this book is
available from the British Library.

ISBN 0 575 05703 3

Photoset in Great Britain by
Rowland Phototypesetting Ltd,
Bury St Edmunds, Suffolk
Printed in Great Britain by
Mackays of Chatham plc, Chatham, Kent

In memory of my son Tom

Contents

Illustrations

(Following page 130)

John aged five

The Tavener family in 1953

Lady Birley (*Valerie Finnis*)

John with Rachel Davies

Rachel Davies in the National Youth Orchestra (*Michael Peto*)

Stravinsky greets Rostropovich at the Royal Academy of Music (*Eric Auerbach*)

John rehearsing *The Whale*

Rehearsing *Celtic Requiem* with the children of Little Missenden village school

Sunday Telegraph magazine: 'Party people and their party clothes' (*Robin Saidman*)

John with Mia Farrow at Little Missenden, 1972

Vicky Maragopoulou

John with Mother Thekla during the filming of *Glimpses of Paradise* (*Mike Coles*)

With Steven Isserlis in Finland (*Heikki Tuuli*)

Archbishop Gregorios officiates at the wedding of John and Maryanna (*Sarah Fitzgerald*)

Maryanna, Theodora, John and the ikon of the Protecting Veil (*Malcolm Crowthers*)

Patricia Rozario as Mary of Egypt (*Malcolm Crowthers*)

John at Paleochora on the island of Aegina (*Malcolm Crowthers*)

Preface

During the summer of 1992, I made my second film about John Tavener, aware that room would not be found for many of the ingredients which make him fascinating. When the filming was finished, I invited him to become my subject once again, in the less pressurized circumstances of a book. Neither of us suspected how long this new project would take.

The first interviews were done in the early spring of 1993, in his garden, and in his favourite mode: reclining on a sun-lounger, eyes closed, face exactly angled to receive the vital rays. During the filming I had argued against his sunbathing, because the saturated colour of his flesh was not viewed kindly by the camera. He used to smile in apparent agreement, then soak up the ultra-violet just the same. Now, there was just me with my tape-recorder, so it did not matter. Nor did the technical quality of the sound, so nothing was lost when March winds buffeted the microphone; or when John knocked it, as he often did when adjusting his position to stay in line with the sun.

To prompt his recollections, I used a chronological list of his works. The music was obviously what mattered to him most, but his religious beliefs came a close second. He also saw an opportunity to confess his sins. The ups and downs of his emotional life and the failings of his flesh were described to me with extraordinary candour and a keen sense of the ridiculous.

These free-wheeling sessions went on from March until June, when I travelled to Athens to see him honoured for services to Greek culture. While I was there I met his first wife, and did a reconnaissance of his favourite island haunts.

Back in England, I approached his family, his musical associates, and some of his enormous number of friends. The list of those who were patient with my questions and generous with their time is printed in Appendix C. Key witnesses, like Mother Thekla, were examined on more than one occasion. Some of those closest to John handed over private letters and diaries.

Meanwhile, his publishers, Chester Music, greatly obliged me by shipping to my home, in huge batches, the scores of his published works. By no means all of the 120 Tavener compositions could be woven into my narrative, but the most important and distinctive are there, and a comprehensive list is printed in Appendix A.

Through the winter of 1993/4, I got to know the music really well, and had a second series of meetings with John, based on the scores. The winter weather was in my favour. On most days it was impossible to sit outside, so he would spend hour after hour at the piano, singing and playing his way through the answers to my long questionnaire. He seemed particularly gratified by my attention to his use of Russian and Byzantine tones. Amazingly, he had never been grilled before on this crucial aspect of his later work. A guide to the Byzantine tones is provided in Appendix D.

During 1994 my chronicle settled into its final shape, on a firm foundation of archival research. For the thoroughness of this, I am extremely grateful to my wife, Mary, who trawled with a fine net through the records of Highgate School, the Royal Academy of Music and the Royal Opera House; spun through miles of microfilm at the British Museum; and foraged tirelessly in the Public Lending Libraries of Barnet, Camden and Westminster.

All the quotations from Tavener compositions are with the permission of the copyright holders, Chester Music, where James Rushton and Jane Williams provided indispensable support.

GH
London, Christmas 1994

PART ONE

The Sacred Grove

§

Nymphs and shepherds come away!
In this grove let's sport and play,
For this is Flora's holiday,
Sacred to ease and happy love,
To music, to dancing and to poetry.

These words by Thomas Shadwell, set to music by Henry Purcell, have achieved folk song status, thanks to a recording made during the 1930s by a choir of 250 Manchester schoolchildren.

When John Tavener is asked to list his favourite records, this invitation to Arcadia is the one with which he starts. He became devoted to it in 1947, when he was three years old and his mother went into hospital to give birth to his baby brother. While she was gone, he made his nanny wind up the gramophone and put on 'Nymphs and Shepherds' for him. Then wind it up again, and put it on again. And again. And again and again and again.

It is possible to argue that John's tastes have not changed. He remains in love with the sound of high, pure voices, and continues to yearn for the paradise promised. Another constant has been the fondness for ritual and repetition. It showed in the first, childish entertainment he devised, soon after the arrival of his brother. His inspiration was the sales literature for the motor trade which had been brought home by his father. He would arrange the pamphlets on the floor, then dance from one to another, chanting 'Big car, little car, big car, little car' until rewarded with family applause. But before we pursue these straws in the wind, some genealogy is in order.

★

A beautifully penned scroll headed *The Ancestry of the Taverner Family* has been circulating among the members for thirty-five years. It was drawn up by John's uncle Alec, and it seems to show that our John is in a line of descent from his Tudor namesake, John Taverner (with a middle *r*), who wrote some of the finest music in the English inheritance, then 'repented him very much that he had made songs to Popish ditties', abandoned composition, and served King Henry VIII by persecuting Catholics.

Since his teens, our John has taken it for granted that he is a descendant of the illustrious Tudor musician, but a recent examination of the document has shown up some flaws. In particular, there is a break in the line around 1760. Further research, by John's cousin Jenny, has cast more doubt: the Tudor composer is buried in Boston, Lincolnshire, whereas the Tudor John Taverner on the family tree, whose dates are the same, lies in the church at Brisley, in Norfolk.

The disappearance of the middle *r* is less problematic. It has been demonstrated to cousin Jenny's satisfaction that towards the end of the eighteenth century her branch of the Taverner family dropped that *r* because they were devout non-conformists living near a pub, and they wanted to make it clear that they had nothing to do with the retail liquor trade.

The evidence for direct descent may be shaky, but there could be no more fitting heir than John. Like his presumed ancestor, he has enriched the English choral tradition with outstanding writing for voices. And he too has dramatically switched his religious allegiance.

★

After the shadowy early centuries comes the solid ground of the nineteenth. In 1846 the firm of C. Tavener and Son, builders and undertakers, was established in St John's Wood, North London, by Charles Tavener from Hatfield Peverill. Charles chased and won some juicy contracts: the underpinning of the Adelphi Arches, for example, and the reconstruction of Hertford House, in London's West End, the home of the Wallace Collection. Here, C. Tavener and Son created the most sumptuous museum interiors in London, including top-lit galleries upstairs and, on the ground floor, a Minton-tiled smoking room.

By the 1920s, when John Poole Guthrie Tavener, grandfather of our composer, was in charge, the undertaking side of the business had been dropped, and the firm had come to specialize in the building and restoration of homes for gracious living. Sarum Chase, for example, a mock-Tudor pile on the fringe of Hampstead Heath, was put up by the Taveners for royal portrait painter Sir Frank Salisbury.

Another important client was Sir Oswald Birley, also a portrait painter to the nobility, whose house and studio were in Acacia Road, St John's Wood. In 1930 Sir Oswald and his young wife, Lady Rhoda, bought themselves a country property in Sussex: the beautiful but decaying Charleston Manor. The firm of Tavener was called in to carry out the restoration.

To accommodate his expanding business and growing family, John P. G. Tavener moved from St John's Wood to Swiss Cottage, where he bought three of the tall houses on the Finchley Road. He lived with his family in one, while he demolished the other two and replaced them with a block of flats, christened Mullion Court. From the mid-1930s Mullion Court was his headquarters. He lived in a roomy apartment on the second floor, with his wife Gertrude, sons Alec and Kenneth and his daughter Brenda. A private staircase led down from the family home to the firm's showroom: a lofty studio, lined with samples of the wooden panelling available to clients. In an alcove, John P. G. installed a two-manual pipe organ, built by Holt: one of the very best. He was not an organist himself, but he loved the sound the organ made. His own instrument was the viola, and this he played in the West Hampstead Orchestra. Under the baton of the local bank manager, they rehearsed and performed the light classics in West Hampstead Congregational Church hall.

John and Gertrude had been married in the Congregational Church in 1908. They remained devout non-conformists all their lives. Gertrude loved to sing. Her distinctive mezzo gave the church choir its character, and she was a regular recitalist: at women's meetings, and for family and friends in her own home. Her repertoire was parlour ballads and gems from the oratorios. 'Nothing highbrow', as her daughter Brenda puts it.

All three children were musical. Alec took lessons on the double bass. Brenda studied piano. Kenneth did well on the cello and even better on the organ. Brenda remembers his style: 'Very emotional, using lots of swell. People liked it very much.'

The courses of the boys' lives were set for them. Both joined father in the West Hampstead Orchestra, and both prepared themselves to enter the family business. Brenda, too, was pressed to be relevant. She graduated as an architect, although she would have preferred to study music.

Alec joined C. Tavener and Son as soon as he left school. Kenneth was first articled to a firm of quantity surveyors. By now he was the regular organist at the Congregational Church. As well as playing the hymns, he would pipe the congregation in with Introits by Bach, and send them on their way with something rousing by Karg-Elert. At Easter time, the church might put on Stainer's *Crucifixion*, or Maunder's *From Olivet to Calvary*.

In 1938 Kenneth got married. The wedding was in the Congregational Church, although his bride was a Christian Scientist. She was Muriel Brown, daughter of Ernest, the Taveners' dentist and long-time family friend. After a honeymoon on the south coast, the newly-weds moved into a brand-new, detached, four-bedroom house with garage and nice garden: 15 Greenhill, in the rapidly spreading North London suburb of Wembley Park.

The next year, the war came and Kenneth was drafted into the Royal Engineers at Woolwich, where the army made use of his skills as a surveyor. This posting meant he would continue to live at home, making the elaborate journey daily from Wembley to Woolwich by underground and main line train. At eight o'clock one morning, his train was hit by a bomb as it was pulling out of Charing Cross station. Kenneth escaped from the wreck with a cut arm, grateful that his organ-playing had not been impaired. By now it was in demand at St Andrew's Presbyterian Church, in Frognal. The Tavener family, and all the other members of West Hampstead Congregational Church, had been obliged to transfer to this socially superior place of worship at the outbreak of war, when their own minister suddenly left London.

Suburbs like Wembley Park were not exempt from the bombing. The house at the back of the Taveners was demolished. In the evenings, Kenneth and Muriel watched from their front window as families from the neighbourhood streamed past, carrying blankets and provisions, on their way to the station. The Bakerloo line carried them into town, and nights were spent on the tube platforms deep underground. The Taveners preferred to stay at home and rely for shelter on the reinforced roof of their garage.

By the beginning of 1944, the blitz was long over but there was still the occasional raid. On the night of 28 January, with bombs exploding in the distance and search lights raking the sky, Muriel gave birth to a son: John Kenneth. His Wembley Park birthplace was to be his home for the next forty-seven years.

★

John's fondness for 'Nymphs and Shepherds' and his invention of 'Big car, little car' have already been described. Next came his discovery of the piano, on which he used to imitate rain, wind and thunder. These studies of events in the natural world were hugely appreciated by his maternal grandfather, Ernest Brown, the dentist and Christian Scientist, whom John remembers as an unfailing source of applause. Ernest also sticks in John's mind as a flamboyant role model: hair worn long; flower in buttonhole; fingers covered in showy rings. He smoked Havana cigars and, best of all, always arrived at Greenhill behind the wheel of his latest sensational American car. Buick and Cadillac were his favourite makes. White was his favourite colour. And now he was young John's number one fan, determined not to be outshone by rival grandfather John P. G. Tavener.

John P. G. was normally aloof, but he outdid Ernest at Christmas times, when he closed his Mullion Court studio for business and converted it into a children's wonderland with a towering Christmas tree. Carols were sung, with John's father Kenneth playing the pipe organ.

When he was five years old, John became a pupil at St Christopher's, the local primary school. He was also taken for a piano lesson once a week to the little music school in Wembley Park run by Franklin Taylor. It was Franklin Taylor who alerted Kenneth and Muriel to their son's talent, and told them he had perfect pitch.

In September 1952, when he was eight years old, John became a day boy at Arnold House Preparatory School, St John's Wood, where great emphasis is laid on the formation of character. The headmaster, George Smart, was not noted for his interest in music, and young John was lukewarm about everything else. Fortunately there was a kind and attentive music teacher, a Scots lady called Margaret Kain, who could see what John had to offer. More than forty years later, she still recalls him with great clarity, as an extraordinary pupil in every way. He was extraordinarily tall and skinny (the only boy allowed to wear long trousers), extraordinarily polite and extraordinarily gifted. He had a nice singing voice. He sang in the choir. He won a school competition singing 'The Lass with the Delicate Air'. But the truly remarkable thing about him was his ability to improvise at the piano. 'He could improvise in the style of Bach, Beethoven and Mozart,' says Margaret Kain. 'You name it!' When the other boys in John's class wanted a treat during music lessons, they would shout 'Come on, Tavener! Let's have Tavener!'

Margaret Kain got to know John's father after he played the organ for the school's Christmas carol service. When he tackled her about the prospect of John winning a music scholarship to Highgate School, she had to speak frankly. Almost as strange as John's brilliance was his ignorance of even the rudiments of music theory. Whoever had been responsible for his instruction, she said, had failed miserably. She recommended he be sent to one of the teachers at the Academy on Saturday mornings. She remembers she was 'absolutely flabbergasted' by what happened next. 'Two nights later, Kenneth rang me and said would I take him on! So he came to me for two hours every Saturday morning, and we started off with an hour's theory. I used to say "Let's do the bad thing first." Then we had an hour's piano. He was absolutely brilliant at that.'

The plan was for Margaret Kain to give John private lessons right up to the time he sat the music scholarship at Highgate, but that plan came unstuck when her husband got a job in Toronto. John's father did everything he could to induce her to stay behind until the end of the school year. She was flattered, but she felt she just couldn't. John was desolated. 'I cried and cried my eyes out,' he says. To fill the breach, Kenneth talked nicely to Guy Jonson, Professor of Piano at the Royal Academy of Music. Jonson lived in Hampstead, and the Tavener firm had done renovation work on his house. He took John on.

*

By 1956, thanks to grandfather John P. G. Tavener, news of the boy's prodigious talent had reached Lady Birley, who sent for him to come and stay with her at Charleston Manor in the summer holidays. Rhoda Birley was widowed – Sir Oswald died in 1952 – and her own children had grown up. She developed a rapport with her young protégé which stayed strong for the next twenty years. Charleston Manor became John's second home. The grand piano in the Long Room was always at his disposal. For quiet reflection, he had the use of the Elizabethan Tithe Barn. For spiritual refreshment, he could wander the avenues of the secluded grounds. He took to referring to Lady Birley as his godmother, and has fond memories of her 'extraordinary blend of eccentricity, mad humour, and serious feeling for spirituality'. But what struck him first, when he was twelve and she was fifty-six, was her beauty. He had heard her referred to as 'one of the greatest beauties who came out of Ireland', and when he met her he could see why.

Rhoda Birley was not particularly musical, but she was a shrewd enabler. Not far from Charleston Manor was Glyndebourne, where her friend John Christie had built himself an opera house. One of her first initiatives was to take her protégé to the Glyndebourne production of *The Magic Flute*. It was one of the most memorable evenings of John's life, and the excitement began long before he reached the opera house. He was staying in the guest cottage at Charleston, and was sent to get changed. Evening dress was a novelty to him. While he was studying his appearance in the mirror, he heard Lady Birley calling. He walked towards the Manor House to meet her, and saw a vision approaching him, lit by the low sun. 'I was staggered. I had never seen anybody so striking and so beautiful. She had a genius for throwing clothes together. She loved scarves and liked to call herself an Irish gypsy. And she wore a characteristic perfume. I worshipped her from that moment.'

At Glyndebourne, young John was entranced by the glamour of the occasion, the mysterious landscape of symbols presented on stage, and the unearthliness of Mozart's music. And there was more magic on the night drive home, with Lady Birley at the wheel of her open-topped Alvis, head-scarf and neck-scarf flying. She didn't bother to turn on the lights, relying instead on her homing instinct, plus a little bit of moonlight.

More than thirty years after that visit to Glyndebourne, when he was writing his opera *Mary of Egypt*, John kept the score of *The Magic Flute* beside him. In his view, Mozart's late masterpiece is the only opera that leaps the bounds of the eighteenth century and 'enters the realm of the primordial'.

*

To fall under the spell of *The Magic Flute* at the age of twelve is not surprising, particularly when the opera is discovered under such romantic circumstances. To become besotted at that same age with Igor Stravinsky's *Canticum Sacrum* is altogether more unlikely.

Stravinsky wrote this piece specifically for St Mark's, Venice, where it was given its first performance on 13 September 1956. The composer by now was seventy-four years old, and just starting to make use of the serial techniques pioneered by Schoenberg and Webern. *Canticum Sacrum* is for tenor and baritone soloists, chorus, orchestra and organ. It is in five movements, corresponding to the five domes of St Mark's. The texts are in Latin, from the Vulgate Bible. No one would describe this as easy listening. *Time* magazine reviewed the first performance as 'Murder in the Cathedral!' And yet young John Tavener fell in love with it at once. He talks of it today as 'the piece that woke me up, and made me want to be a composer'. And he still regards this eighteen-minute composition as 'the pinnacle of twentieth-century music, which brings together Webern, organum and Gregorian and Byzantine chant. The nearest Western man can come to creating a sacred work of art.'

Quite how he first heard it is a mystery. With the passing of the years, he has come to see himself inside the Basilica of St Mark in Venice for the first performance, conducted by the composer. It is true that there were family holidays on the continent around this time. His father remembers a stay in Montreux, where they went to a concert conducted by Karl Böhm. 'That was the night,' says Kenneth, 'when I felt John had taken off.' Memories of Venice are much hazier. There certainly was a trip there, which might have included a tour of St Mark's Basilica, but the music of Stravinsky was outside Kenneth's range and he is sure he can take no credit for leading John to the *Canticum Sacrum*. Perhaps the boy heard it on the radio and was transported back to Venice in his imagination. John thinks that must be it.

When the *Canticum Sacrum* was issued on a French LP, John acquired it immediately. He became particularly enamoured of the second movement, 'Surge, aquilo' ('Awake, O north wind'), a tenor aria accompanied by flute, English horn, harp and double basses. The words are from the Song of Songs. The tenor line is based on a twelve-note row, but not far from tonality. The John of today identifies the atmosphere of this music as strongly Byzantine, and points to a sustained, drone-like note in the ensemble, which underpins the melismatic tenor part. John the boy just found it all strangely and compellingly beautiful. The three minutes of 'Surge, aquilo' got the 'Nymphs and Shepherds' treatment on his gramophone.

PART TWO

'I know'

§

1 : Credo

John's new music teacher, Guy Jonson, did not encourage the boy's interest in contemporary music. Jonson had been a pupil of Tobias Matthay and Alfred Cortot, and stood for the old-fashioned virtues. He remembers John was 'not very avid to imbibe the great piano repertoire'. Nevertheless, Kenneth Tavener's immediate goal was accomplished. The honours board at Arnold House shows that his son John was awarded a scholarship to Highgate School in July 1957.

John's start at Highgate was less than happy. His long, thin frame made him a target for bullies, and the playing fields were a constant source of anguish. The redeeming feature was the music master, the late Edward T. Chapman, an awesome figure who trained his school choir to be the best and the most sought after in London. Whenever boys' voices were needed, for a recording, or a broadcast, or a big occasion, then they were provided by Chapman. John's treble voice was among them from his very first term. As a matter of routine, he would find himself present at the BBC or in a concert hall, contributing his part to Mahler's Third, for example, or Carl Orff's *Carmina Burana*, and listening while these works were rehearsed by the world's top musicians.

Highgate School was brimming over with music. As well as the school orchestra and the famous choir, there were instrumental and choral groups within each of the houses, which were regularly pitted against one another in formal competitions. Although John's talent was obviously exceptional – he played Beethoven's Fourth Piano Concerto with the school orchestra on speech day at the end of his first year – he was certainly not the lone star. Other pupils of the extraordinary Chapman during John's time at the school included at least half a dozen who went on to make reputations in the world of music: the composer Brian Chapple; David Cullen, composer-turned-chief orchestrator for Andrew Lloyd-Webber; John Rutter, another composer, famous for the sweetness of his carols; Howard Shelley, the concert pianist; Nicholas

Snowman, founder of the London Sinfonietta and now Chief Executive
of the South Bank Centre; and Francis Steiner, who tours the world as
one half of the popular piano duo Rostal and Schaefer.

John developed particularly close friendships with Brian Chapple,
John Rutter and Francis Steiner, all of whom were welcomed into the
Tavener household and invited to share Tavener family holidays. There
was also a bond between the Taveners and the Snowmans, cemented
when the firm of Tavener renovated the Snowman family home in
Hampstead.

Pupils with keyboard ambitions could take individual lessons with
Chapman, both on the piano and on the organ. Tavener, Rutter and
Steiner all seized this chance. Edward Chapman had been organ scholar
at Pembroke College, Cambridge. His composition teacher was Charles
Wood, who succeeded Stanford as Cambridge Professor of Music, so
those taught by Chapman were being granted entry to the great tradition
of English composer-organists. John remembers the Chapman organ-
playing style: 'Very thick, using every sub-octave possible. Super legato:
chords held together with glue. And incredibly slow.'

According to Rutter, 'John was a very gifted musical mimic. He would
mimic the playing of Edward Chapman to the life.' Nevertheless, John
insists on the huge importance of Chapman to his musical development.
Most precious of all were those moments of revelation during the private
lessons, when Chapman would talk with religious fervour about the
essential mystery of music. Once, Chapman discoursed on the slow
movement of Bach's Italian Concerto, which John was preparing for a
concert performance. To this day, says John, no one has matched the
profundity of Chapman's insight. John Rutter remembers John's
performance of the Italian Concerto as quite outstanding. It was given
in the Recital Room next to the Festival Hall on London's South Bank.
Another Tavener performance which has stuck in people's minds was
of the Shostakovich Second Piano Concerto, played as a duet, with
Edward Chapman taking the orchestral piano part.

When describing Chapman's qualities, none of his pupils has
mentioned kindness. Here was no Margaret Kain. Chapman, in John's
memory, was 'a bit like Wagner: fierce face and long hair, going back.
A rather short man, and very short-tempered.' During the piano lessons,
a stick was always on standby, and often in use. John's sensitive friend
Brian Chapple says he took years to get over Chapman, who had a
genius for sarcasm, ridicule and making people feel small.

Chapman's deputy, Arthur, played the organ for the choral rehearsals.

Poor Arthur. Brian Chapple and John both remember Chapman's demolition job on him. 'Thank you, Arthur! You played that with a great deal of feeling – [long pause] around in the dark!'

When John was sixteen, Chapman decided to send him up to Trinity College, Cambridge to sit for an organ scholarship. Far more traumatic than the examination itself was the briefing which preceded it, when Chapman sat him down at the school organ. The scene haunts John's dreams:

CHAPMAN: To begin with, they'll probably ask you to play from a full score.
He has never before asked John to transpose from a full score at sight, but now he puts a Brahms symphony up in front of him.
CHAPMAN: Play it.
John struggles.
CHAPMAN: Going for an organ scholarship tomorrow and can't read from a full score!
Chapman sniffs.
CHAPMAN: They'll probably ask you to do a paper on counterpoint. Do you know anything about strict counterpoint?
Silence from John. Sniff from Chapman.
CHAPMAN: Going up to Cambridge tomorrow and doesn't know anything about strict counterpoint!
Pause and sniff.
CHAPMAN: They'll probably ask you to play the scale of C sharp minor on the organ pedals. Play it.
John makes a stumbling effort, but he has never bothered with scales.
CHAPMAN: Going up to Cambridge for an organ scholarship tomorrow and can't play the scale of C sharp minor on the organ pedals!

John left the school chapel in tears. Up at Cambridge the next day, the examiners were impressed as he sailed through his improvisation, but less enthusiastic about what he did with his theory paper. When they gave him a piece of chant to work in strict counterpoint, he simply filled in the spaces as his ear dictated. The examining committee, chaired by Raymond Leppard, suggested he come and see them again in two years' time. He never went back.

He was leading a full life, and had more or less decided he was going to be a composer. A year earlier, he had considered becoming a poet and was bold enough to send his writings to no less a judge than T. S.

Eliot. The poems have not survived, but John still has Eliot's friendly letter of reply, which points out that poetry is hard work and urges him to get on with his music. Next term, as Francis Steiner remembers, John came to school one day walking with a stoop. 'When we asked him to tell us what had happened, he said he saw Stravinsky last night!' John thinks this must have been when Stravinsky conducted the concert version of his opera *Oedipus Rex* at the Royal Festival Hall. Jean Cocteau spoke the narration. John remembers that Cocteau took up a dramatic pose, stage left, wearing a dashing black cape and sweeping the audience with majestic looks. Stravinsky, hunched on the conductor's podium, seemed far from pleased when Cocteau left meaningful pauses between the receipt of his cues and the delivery of his lines. Sometimes the conductor's baton had to be pointed at Cocteau several times before any words were forthcoming. The man of letters had a lot of style, but it was the little bent-backed composer with whom John identified.

His own compositions began to appear at a prodigious rate. To make sure his music was heard, John also took the role of impresario, organizing concerts in the studio at Mullion Court. The printed programmes were home-made by some willing slave on the Mullion Court typewriter. One has come down to us. It advertises the start time as 7.45 p.m. John thinks he pinned it to the street door, hoping to catch the eye of passers-by. The twenty-five items on the bill were played or sung by John and his friends from school, including Brian Chapple and John Rutter. Handel, Mozart, Haydn, Beethoven, Chopin, Sullivan, Debussy, Vaughan Williams, Stravinsky and Gershwin were all represented, and from the current hit parade came 'Elizabethan Serenade', by Ronald Binge, and 'Forgotten Dreams', by Leroy Anderson. Spread throughout the evening were compositions by John: a Gavotte in B flat for instrumental ensemble; a *Pater Noster* for vocal quartet; and three pieces for solo piano, including *Suite Moderne (à Igor Strawinsky)*.

Like the other aspiring composers at Highgate, John used to show Edward Chapman what he had written. The flavour of late Stravinsky was not to Chapman's taste, so he was inclined to restrict himself to practical advice on workmanship. With missionary zeal, John took his record of the *Canticum Sacrum* to one of his lessons and played Chapman his favourite bits. Chapman had a stock response to such impositions. It began 'The trouble with modern music is . . .'

None of the Tavener pieces performed at Mullion Court has survived – they were probably not written down – so Opus One in the catalogue has to be his Trombone Sonata, or, to give it its proper title, the *Duo Concertant* for trombone and piano. The manuscript is in the neat hand of John Rutter, who was much more confident than John with the theory of notation. The work is in three movements, lasting about ten minutes altogether, including repeats. John wanted it performed at a Highgate School concert, and it was fashioned with that end in view. The first two movements lean less on Stravinsky's serial music than on his neo-classical pieces. The closing movement, marked *Scherzando*, has the sunshine and the raggy syncopation of Percy Grainger's *Handel in the Strand*. Most importantly, the *Duo Concertant* was playable by local talent: John himself and another Highgate schoolboy, Stuart Harding, who was something of a trombone virtuoso.

Edward Chapman agreed to it being played in front of the school during the Easter term of 1961, and John had the diplomatic flair to dedicate it to the headmaster, Mr Alfred Doulton, who was himself a keen trombonist. After that, life at Highgate was one of cloudless pleasure. No need to study for any A levels. No need to play games. Even music lessons became optional. On a typical day, John might start by playing the organ for the morning service in the school chapel. Then he would pop across the road to St Michael's Parish Church and enjoy himself on the much louder instrument in there. Back to school for lunch, then perhaps an hour or so making use of a piano to work on his compositions, before a final burst on the St Michael's organ. Once he got home, there would be more composing and piano playing, while his mother hovered to anticipate his every need.

Two of the other young composers at Highgate, Brian Chapple and John Rutter, showed a more academic turn of mind. Both studied A level music. Tavener remembers he was impressed by Rutter's intellectual brilliance. Rutter remembers he was in awe of Tavener's natural gifts:

He had perfect pitch, and a very analytical ear for musical colour. You could play a ten-part chord to him, horribly dissonant, and he'd pick out every note, just like the colours in the rainbow. His natural musical equipment was so formidably tuned that whatever he heard, whatever appealed to him, was instantly absorbed.

Rutter did not share Tavener's fascination with the sound world of late Stravinsky, but the two Johns agreed on Broadway musicals. They devoured the song books of Gershwin, Kern, Richard Rogers and Cole Porter. When *The Sound of Music* opened in London, Rutter booked them seats.

By now, John's brother Roger was also at Highgate. He too became a member of the school choir, but his musical gifts were not exceptional. Life at Wembley Park as the younger brother of a genius was not a comfortable one. The domestic chores, he remembers, were assigned exclusively to him: the washing-up, the errands, and all the odd jobs that needed doing in house and garden. Whenever he complained, he was told that John couldn't be expected to do such things. If he persisted in his complaints, his mother used her clinching argument: 'In any case, dear, John would only do it badly.'

In July 1961 John auditioned at the Wigmore Hall for the National Youth Orchestra. He played the Shostakovich Second Piano Concerto and received an invitation to the summer course in Canterbury, as concerto soloist. This was his first time away from home. His parents, against all the rules, turned up in Canterbury to see how he was getting on. They were right to be worried. At the age of seventeen, John was in love. The object of his affections was eighteen-year-old Rachel Davies. She was dark-haired and beguiling, from a romantic Welsh background, and she played the harp. He remembers he told his parents he wanted to marry her. 'They hit the roof.'

Kenneth Tavener was now concentrating on getting John into the Royal Academy of Music. To improve his understanding of theory, it was arranged that he should have private lessons from Margaret Hubicki, Professor of Harmony at the Academy, who was recommended by her colleague and friend Guy Jonson.

Margaret Hubicki was a war widow, living in St John's Wood. She remembers when John's father brought him to her door. 'John's very first words were "What do you think about Stravinsky?" In the nicest possible way. But it was a testing question, because if I'd made some derogatory remark, I think we should have lost contact.'

She said the right things about Stravinsky, then concentrated on the assignment, which was 'to help John be clear on the basics'. At the same time, she was deeply impressed with the spirituality of the boy, which chimed in with her own preference for the other-worldly. John remembers her gratefully because 'she cared more about the why of music than the how of music'.

On 7 October 1961, with his father standing over him, John filled in an application form to sit the entrance examination at the Royal Academy of Music. Against *Principal study* he wrote, 'piano'. Against *Secondary study* he wrote 'organ and composition'. In answer to *Recent exams passed* he put down his distinction in the Grade VIII Examination

of the Associated Board, for which he had played a Beethoven piano
sonata, Ravel's *Tombeau de Couperin*, and the Shostakovich Second
Piano Concerto. Under *General education* he listed five GCE O levels:
English Literature, English Grammar, French, Latin and History. In
the space beside *Professional musical aspirations* he wrote 'Mus. Bac.,
concert pianist, organist and composer.'

The application form was accompanied by a letter from his headmaster, Mr Doulton:

> I have no hesitation in commending this boy to you unreservedly. He
> is one of the most promising musicians we have had for a number of
> years . . . and has done much for the musical life of the School . . .
>
> He bears a good character, is notably modest despite his public
> appearances, and is very hard working at his specialist interests.

The examination was held on 23 October 1961. Guy Jonson was the
examiner. His findings are on the Royal Academy file.

Piano:	Ravel – beautiful sounds, sensitive playing. Most musical.
	Beethoven – Good technical control and excellent positive qualities.
Organ and composition:	Produced some remarkably interesting compositions. Lovely harmonic sense. Very good, lyrical clusters.
Extras:	Wonderful ear.
General impression:	Really wants to be a composer.

Two days later, the Secretary at the Academy, H. Stanley Creber,
wrote offering John a place from the beginning of the next term, 8
January 1962.

*

John's first opportunity to write something for public performance came
when news of his Trombone Sonata travelled with his father to
St Andrew's Church. The minister there, the Revd Copland-Simmons,
remembered by Kenneth as 'a real go-getter', had plans to put
St Andrew's on the cultural map with a series of monthly Musical
Services. Copland-Simmons could see the publicity value of featuring
music specially written for his choir by a seventeen-year-old Highgate
schoolboy. He commissioned John to write something for the November
Musical Service, and made sure the local papers knew about it.

John decided to make a setting of the *Credo*. To do it justice, he felt he needed more than just the choir and the organ of St Andrew's. In the end, his score was for solo tenor, chorus, organ, three oboes, three trumpets and two trombones. Kenneth agreed to pay for the brass players, who would be seasoned professionals. Two of the oboists were from the National Youth Orchestra, the third was John's schoolfriend Nicholas Snowman. John Rutter wrote out the parts. Francis Steiner would conduct, since John would be playing the organ.

Taking his cue from Stravinsky, John set his *Credo* in Latin. Then it occurred to him to add a spoken text in English, and here was his opportunity to involve Rachel Davies. Since she was fluent with words, he asked her to write and speak the English narration. To Rachel this looked like a wooing tactic rather than a genuine invitation to collaborate. Nevertheless, she wrote as she was bid and posted the result to Wembley Park. John wrote back gratefully, enclosing a short piece for harp, organ and violin, dedicated to her and entitled *Portrait d'une Jeune Fille et l'Harpe*.

> Oh, you must think it very presumptuous of me to paint your portrait, considering all you know about me is that I have written a rather second-rate trombone piece! Please lay it aside until we can try it with the violin and organ.
>   Your narration is wonderful, so slick, and I like the literary style. I'm going to write an opera next year, probably based on 'The Doctor and the Devils' by Dylan Thomas. It was unfinished, but since I know Caitlin Thomas, and since I know you! (you really are talented) I'm sure we can do something with it.

Rachel says now that from the very beginning she was out of her depth in this relationship. Nevertheless, her diary entry for Sunday, 12 November 1961, the day of the *Credo* performance, coolly records that she spoke her narration 'rather well'.

Rachel's narration has not survived, but the score was eventually published. *Credo* is a bold mixture of styles. The first notes, on the trombone, are a quotation from the *Canticum Sacrum*. Then come joyous echoes of Verdi and of William Walton – it seems John was temporarily under the spell of *Belshazzar's Feast*. Eventually, the oboes return us to the world of the *Canticum Sacrum*, and we end with highly decorated Amens in the Byzantine manner.

By the time of the performance of *Credo*, John and Rachel were seeing each other virtually every day. On the days when they did not meet, they wrote to one another. John's letters abound in references to his music, from which we can tell that the surviving compositions are just the tip of the iceberg. He describes a cello sonata, for example, and a 'Latin-American symphony'. He also talks of recitals he was being asked to give, on the piano and the organ.

Shortly before Christmas 1961, when he was still a seventeen-year-old schoolboy, he was appointed organist and choirmaster at St John's Presbyterian Church in Kensington. It was a position he valued highly. He held it for the next fourteen years.

2 : Genesis

John began at the Royal Academy of Music in January 1962. He was assigned to four professors, two of whom he already knew: Hubicki for harmony and Jonson for piano. His organ professor, Douglas Hawkridge, was no Edward Chapman and made no impression. The exciting novelty was his composition teacher, the composer Lennox Berkeley. He loved Berkeley not for his music, which has never meant much to him, but for his human qualities: his eccentricity, his gentleness, and his famous modesty. The upper-class Englishness was also very much to John's taste. Berkeley did not enjoy the bustle of the Academy buildings, so lessons took place at his elegant home in Maida Vale. He was unfailingly polite about the compositions brought to him by his students, but his mind was often elsewhere, as John noticed. 'When Lennox was a little anxious about his music, he always used to cock his eye towards the manuscript in the corner, and I could feel he was itching to get back to it.'

Berkeley had spent five years in Paris, studying with Nadia Boulanger. If ever John came to a lesson with no new composition to be discussed, Berkeley brought out the scores of the Bach Cantatas he himself had used as a student, and took John through them at the piano, stopping to read aloud whenever they came upon words the *grande dame* had added in the margin.

Sometimes the lesson would be agreeably interrupted by Berkeley's wife, Freda, who was a good friend of Rhoda Birley. She would come in with tea, and quiz John about the latest carryings-on among the students, while Lennox glided away gratefully towards the drinks cabinet. Freda was very warm. Lennox was very shy. It was a winning combination.

The Berkeleys became extremely fond of John, and accepted an invitation to visit the Tavener family at home. They found John's parents awfully nice and terribly conventional. In Freda's words:

Both Ken and Muriel were amazed that they'd got this extraordinary son. It was very difficult for them to come to terms with it. It must have been astonishing for them to produce John. He's so unexpected in every way.

Lennox Berkeley had been a fervent Catholic ever since he was converted by Nadia Boulanger, so when John developed leanings towards the Catholic Church this brought them even closer. Freda remembers John bringing communion bells to his lessons. The Catholicism did not please John's parents, but it was less bothering than his continuing associations with Rachel Davies. The more they opposed it, the more John found Rachel attractive. Freda Berkeley was his confidante: 'He was terribly unhappy over his girlfriend, and he came and cried on my shoulder, literally. He was very caught up with her.'

Rachel had started at the Academy one term before John. She was studying harp with Osian Ellis and harmony with Hubicki, but she and John rarely met on Academy premises. John's favourite rendezvous was the tall, rambling house in Westbourne Park Road, Notting Hill, where Rachel lived with her widowed mother. Mrs Davies made ends meet by providing board and lodging for foreign students, many of whom were Roman Catholics, studying at the London language schools. Everyone ate together, at a long table in the kitchen. John loved the meal-time chatter. He also loved to hear stories about Rachel's extraordinary father. The late D. R. Davies had been a Welsh coalminer at the age of twelve before becoming a university scholarship boy, then a Congregational minister, a tramp, a socialist, an author, a music critic, an attempted suicide, and finally an Anglican clergyman. John borrowed the D. R. Davies autobiography, *In Search of Myself*. He still has that book on his shelves.

Directly opposite the house in Westbourne Park Road was St Stephen's Church. Rachel's mother had a key. Rachel remembers John spending countless hours in there, playing the organ:

I used to wander in and out, go home, practise the harp, go back, and find him still playing, improvising, and singing away at the top of his voice. All the stops out. John liked volume . . . I was deeply admiring of his music. It was coming out of his every pore, all the time.

John revelled in the atmosphere at Rachel's home, so different from his own, but Rachel was never in doubt about the strength of his attachment to his mother. She remembers a particularly awful evening. She had bought tickets for John, Margaret Hubicki and herself to see *The Caucasian Chalk Circle*. John and Hubicki came to her house for supper first. When they were all seated at the long dining table, with the foreign students, John announced that his mother had ordered him to be home by eleven o'clock. Rachel protested. She had warned him when she bought the tickets that *The Caucasian Chalk Circle* was a long play. For all at the table to hear, Hubicki gave her a stiff lecture about the immorality of leading John astray. Well before eleven o'clock, while *The Caucasian Chalk Circle* was still in full swing, John stood up and led his party from the theatre. Next day, Hubicki sent Rachel a note recommending the virtue of self-sacrifice.

Rachel stayed besotted with John, in spite of his unique interpretation of the role of lover. For their next outing together, he borrowed his mother's Triumph Herald. Rachel was taken to the offices of Faber & Faber, publishers of T. S. Eliot. While she sat outside in the car for what seemed like hours, John attempted unsuccessfully to gain access to the eminent poet, who was in there somewhere. Rachel was given to understand that John had been in long correspondence with Eliot, and needed to clinch permission to use the poem 'The Rock' in his next major composition, an oratorio called *Genesis*.

★

To Rachel it was clear that John's vocation was composer. Playing the piano and the organ were just means to an end. However, this was not the view of John's father, who saw composing as no kind of profession. He and the rest of the Tavener family still thought John had a glittering future as a concert pianist. When the firm of Tavener was called in to renovate the St John's Wood home of Solomon, John P. G. Tavener took the opportunity to ask the legendary pianist if he would lend an ear to his talented grandson. John remembers that first audience. It did not go well. He was a few minutes late, and the rage which met him was all the more terrifying because it could not be expressed in words (Solomon had suffered a stroke in 1956, which had destroyed his career and his power of speech). When the fury subsided, John played excerpts from Beethoven's Fourth Piano Concerto. Afterwards, Solomon managed to get out just one word: 'Wonderful.' Gwen Byrne, Solomon's secretary, who later became his wife, warned John 'I shouldn't get too excited. That's one of the few words Mr Solomon can say.'

Nevertheless, John became a regular visitor to the house in Loudoun Road, and developed a warm friendship with the stricken maestro, who was born Solomon Cutner in the East End of London in 1902. When he was eight, Solomon made his debut at the Queen's Hall, playing Tchaikovsky's First Piano Concerto. He was admired for his soulful eyes and white sailor suit, as well as his consummate virtuosity. John would have liked to sit with him listening to the profound recordings he had made for HMV shortly before his illness. But Solomon was unable to face them. The memories upset him too much.

Master and pupil attended a ballet performance of Stravinsky's *Agon*. They sat in a box together. Solomon paid attention to the music for a while, but clearly did not like it. He stared at the word AGON on the front of his programme, then took out his pen and added the letter Y. John remembers 'I was very offended. I loved that piece.'

*

The composition of *Genesis* progressed. In July 1962, John wrote to Rachel:

> 'Genesis' is having a peculiar effect on me. The creative stimulus takes its physical toll. It is a singularly 'unplatonic' work.
>
> This afternoon, my second cousins are coming to stay. All have the 'I love you Cliff' mentality. Perhaps I shall play them my latest pop song, 'If it's love, then it might as well be Rachel'!! Please, please don't take offence at that. If you knew how it went on I'm quite sure you wouldn't. After all, it's only a pop song and not a profound document on the nature of my feelings towards you!

Rachel did not mind the pop song, but she was hurt by her exclusion from Tavener family life. She was hardly ever invited to Wembley Park, and when she did get there it seemed to her she was received coldly. She wrote John a farewell letter, accusing him of being too weak to speak up for her. He wrote back enclosing a new piece of music, dated 2 August 1962.

> You are a very wonderful person, Rachel, and when you say 'Goodbye' to me I shudder because I know what I am losing . . . You have given me much more than I deserve, helped me more than you realise in my latest work, 'In Memoriam Frank Salisbury'. I would love you to hear this, for without you this never could have been written . . . I have not written a note of 'Genesis' for days. Just 'In Memoriam' . . .
>
> If we have to part, it is my wish we part through this piece I love more than any other. It is written for violin solo and string quartet.

The *Elegy In Memoriam Frank Salisbury* is a gem, with a dreamy melodic line and lush, Ravelian harmonies. It was originally intended to salute the passing of the portrait painter, but it served equally well to effect a reconciliation with Rachel.

The première of *Genesis* was set for Sunday, 11 November 1962, in St Andrew's Church. After continued pressure from John, T. S. Eliot had conceded that his poem 'The Rock' could be quoted free of charge. John then pressed him to attend the performance. Eliot didn't exactly say no, so the local paper had its headline:

T. S. ELIOT MAY HEAR JOHN'S ORATORIO

John had promised Rachel that she should speak the narration, but shortly before the performance he had to inform her that he had been overruled by the Revd Copland-Simmons, who was insisting on a male speaker. As a matter of fact, Copland-Simmons was going to speak the narration himself. Rachel was far from pleased, but agreed to sing in the choir instead.

Genesis is more ambitious and difficult than *Credo*, so John felt he should add a warning note to the typewritten programme which was handed out to the audience:

The music of 'Genesis' is eclectic, but it is unified by a twelve-note theme, presented in seven different guises during the work. The treatment of the series is by no means strict, and there is no hesitation, for instance, in using the notes harmonically, however much this may be the antithesis of what Schoenberg intended.

The score is for narrator, tenor solo and chorus; brass; timpani, piano, organ and string quartet. John Rutter again copied out the orchestral parts, and sang with the basses of the choir. Brian Chapple played one of the violins, but most of the instrumentalists were hired professionals.

*

Genesis begins with a brass fanfare and a unison statement by the chorus of the first verse in the Bible, set to a twelve-note theme. The second verse, about the Spirit of God moving upon the face of the waters, is sung by the tenor soloist, while the strings drone mysteriously. The third verse, shared by the tenor and the chorus, ends resoundingly: *And there was light!*

The next sixteen verses of the Book of Genesis go mainly to the narrator, with interjections from the chorus, and orchestral figures which sometimes echo Stravinsky's *Agon*, sometimes the *Canticum Sacrum*.

After God has divided the light from darkness, John digresses to describe in music the Great Monsters of the Sea: a subject which eventually inspired him to write another, much more famous piece.

Back to the Book of Genesis, where John applies his musical ingenuity to what for him is the key line:

> Male and female created He them.

The word 'male' is attended by furious triplet figures in the brass. 'Female' is swathed in the soft, *legato* folds of the strings. This must be what John meant when he wrote to Rachel that *Genesis* was 'a singularly unplatonic work'.

We are now at the end of the sixth day, and the music rests while the narrator reads from 'The Rock': T. S. Eliot's poetic gloss on the Book of Genesis, with the refrain:

> Waste and void. Waste and void. And darkness on the face
> of the deep.

After the words of Eliot, the music returns quietly and briefly: a simple setting for tenor soloist and organ of the opening of the Gospel according to St John, sung in Latin.

> In the beginning was the Word
> And the Word was with God
> And the Word was God.

*

Back home after the concert, John found a note on his pillow. It was a fan letter from his brother Roger, which read 'I want you to know how much I admire your 12-tone music. *Genesis* is your first great work, at the start of your life. Perhaps your last great work will be *Revelation*.'

This should have been John's hour of triumph, but all was ashes in his mouth. He took to his bed and wrote Rachel a furious letter, headed in big letters HEART WARNING. It began 'How nice of you to help out with the singing tonight, your presence was felt if not heard.' Then, after declaring he was so ill he would probably have to go to hospital, John came to the point.

> Why did you have to pour your wet grease all over the Tenor, is he
> more deserving than me? He had hardly entered the room, and you

had poured ointment over his head, and kissed his feet. I, the one who needs you most, ignored.

If the battle does not stop I promise you I will fall under the sheer physical blow . . .

For the next three days, John felt too unwell to attend the Academy. On the fourth day, 15 November, he went in but collapsed on arrival with acute pains in the chest. An official note on his Academy file shows that a doctor had to be called. No medical reason for the attack was recorded.

Rachel denied any interest in the tenor, and there were moves towards another reconciliation. John offered to help her with her harmony. She let him see the work she had been doing. He wrote her a rather chilly note.

> I looked at your harmonisation of 'O Perfect Love'. You seem to have a sense for parts, but your ideas of sonority seem contrived, and falsed by a desire not to be ordinary. You can't be different unless you know how to be ordinary . . . Believe me, I can help you. I shall be so happy, since I appear unable to do this in any other way whatsoever.

A few weeks later, his pride in his musicianship took a nasty blow. He failed the LRAM: the Academy's end-of-first-year theoretical and practical test. It was the theory, of course, which caught him out, and this was a serious embarrassment to Margaret Hubicki. 'I had to stick some pins in him rather sharply,' she says. She had sensed there was trouble brewing. He would never do his exercises. And it was hard to defend him when he failed to appear at official Academy functions because he was involved in performances of his own music elsewhere. She had been happy to give him technical advice on how to get *Genesis* down on paper, but sometimes she felt she had been reduced to the role of mere scribe.

John passed his LRAM easily at the second attempt, and tried to become a good student. His end-of-term reports from Lennox Berkeley were always warm with praise for his 'remarkable natural gift', his 'splendid ear' and his 'real creative imagination'. For Guy Jonson, he polished his performances of Mendelssohn's *Variations Serieuses* and a Bach/Busoni prelude and fugue. Jonson assessed his piano playing as 'very good average, perhaps average plus'.

On 19 July 1963 John was honoured with a letter from the Secretary of the Academy, saying he had been awarded the William Wallace Exhibition, which entitled him to free tuition for one year. His parents were proud, but this institutional approval left John feeling hemmed in. His family had to bear the brunt of his frustration. One evening, he cut short his practice of a Beethoven piano sonata and hurled the book across the room, shouting that all he wanted to be was a composer, and that the music he wanted to play hadn't been written yet.

He wrote to Rachel, signalling the approach of the end of their relationship, and getting in a dig at sonata form while he was at it.

> Rachel, if you go in the mist, I shall not battle to get you back, I shall let you go. I will believe that God willed it . . . I do not regret the past. I know now that we must not go back . . . I warn you, I hate Development – the section I deplore in symphony and sonata, the section I always miss out, the trite and boring devices, the unsubtle harmonic changes, the improvisatory wandering style . . .

The letter ended with a scathing attack on the cult of the virtuoso: 'those ephemeral prize-winning finger muscles that can draw as much from the bank as they can from their instruments', and there was a dark hint that virtuosity was what Rachel really admired.

As his crisis deepened, he wrote again to Rachel, trying to crystallize his beliefs.

> Darling, I will try to explain. A long and serious illness of mind has led me to doubt my own sincerity, purpose and personality . . .
>
> I put mùsic first, because of some weird notion of mine that I owe to GOD what He has given me. I don't pray, I don't fast, I cheat and lie my way through HIS world, without any real aim except to try to create music which must come from me alone – a personal sacrifice, a burnt offering if you like . . .
>
> I must not see you so often, I want to work harder, I want to develop a routine.
>
> Must be honest with myself, give up the organ and the piano as studies at the Academy. Oh but I can't, I'm frightened of hurting my professors' feelings, frightened of disillusioning friends, frightened of losing, and yet I recognise a 'truth'.

During August 1963, on holiday in Italy with his parents, John continued the debate with himself. Before the start of the new term at the Academy, he wrote to the Warden, Myers Foggin, announcing that it would be wrong for him to continue piano lessons.

> My attention is entirely focused on composition. I have completed a concerto for orchestra in five movements this holiday and begun a lute sonata. The desire to play the piano exists only for trying out my

own music. It would be very wrong of me to waste Mr Jonson's precious time . . .

It is rare that I make so positive a decision. I do hope you will understand.

Myers Foggin wrote back, with best wishes, enclosing a timetable from which the piano had been excluded.

John also made the final break with Rachel, or rather, he orchestrated things so she would make the final break with him. She still has the silver cross he gave her.

3 : I am a little world

Ironically, the next composition on which John focused his energy was a piano concerto. He looks back on this wildly eclectic work as 'Youthful high spirits, coupled with lessons from Lennox Berkeley: very dapper, very unsentimental, quite jazzy. And it has the influence of late Stravinsky in his more vital mood: pieces like *Agon*.'

The fifteen-minute concerto – for piano solo, three French horns, timpani and strings – is in three movements. Both the outer movements have plenty of zip, and hints of Gershwin, Rachmaninov and Prokoviev. The slow movement is the *Elegy In Memoriam Frank Salisbury*, expanded and revised, with the dreamy melodic line now given to the piano.

John believed he had written a winner. He demonstrated it to Harry Blech, the conductor of the orchestra at the Academy, hoping to talk him into including it in a student concert. Blech liked what he heard, but was put off by the look of the manuscript. To increase his chances of a performance John would have to smarten up his written presentation.

His local retailer of manuscript paper and composer's accessories, Stan Kitchen, advised that if he wanted a conductor's score and orchestral parts that looked really classy, he should go to Marcel Gardier, a top copyist who lived in Chorley Wood. The price was steep, but John's father agreed to foot the bill and Marcel Gardier's immaculate handiwork was set before Harry Blech. A performance of the Concerto, with John as soloist, was scheduled as part of a concert in the Duke's Hall at the Academy in December.

The first rehearsal was in mid-November. Kenneth Tavener was there. He wrote to Myers Foggin, the Warden of the Academy, thanking him profusely for giving his son this great opportunity, and asking for twenty-four tickets.

Guest of honour in the Duke's Hall for the concert was Solomon, to whom the Concerto is dedicated. Guy Jonson was notably absent. Among the Academy students in the audience was sixteen-year-old

Philip Pilkington, a precocious pianist, who liked modern music and became one of John's lifelong friends. This is his recollection of John's piano playing:

> John didn't study the classics or do his scales and arpeggios, but he had a natural ability to make a very good sound. He could make the piano percussive and he could make it sing. He made a noise on the piano which was very much his own.

As for the Concerto itself, Philip Pilkington can see now that 'it already had salient Tavener features: the striking sense of orchestral colour, the feeling for dramatic gesture'.

Also in the audience in the Duke's Hall was Francis Steiner, a friend from Highgate School and another outstanding pianist. He loved John's Concerto, went away and learned it, then gave a public performance in Hornsey Town Hall.

*

Now he was no longer obsessed with Rachel, John relaxed into student life. His Highgate friend Brian Chapple was now at the Academy, studying with Lennox Berkeley. Francis Steiner was not far away, at the Royal College, where he had formed a partnership with another pianist, George Barbour. Francis and George were in a party led by John to Portofino on the Italian Riviera, which for a time was his favourite holiday resort. Other members of this party were Brian Chapple, Philip Pilkington and John's brother Roger. Alcohol and tobacco were among the delights. Brian Chapple remembers a trip to sea in a hired boat, which, for him, nearly ended in disaster. He couldn't swim and he fell overboard. In the end, he was rescued by Roger, 'the only one on board with any sense'. After the rescue, says Chapple, John was heard to announce in solemn tone, 'If this boat goes down, it will be a tremendous loss to English music.'

Philip Pilkington remembers that John insisted they frequent only the smartest waterfront bars, designed to lure millionaires from their yachts. As the boys sat nursing their fabulously expensive drinks, John would smoke a cheroot and point out that Stravinsky was a well-known *bon viveur*. He kept a Stravinsky dossier, in which he stored all kinds of facts about the great man: what kind of whisky he drank, which brand of cigars he smoked, what his wife looked like.

*

Most of John's friends talk of the welcoming warmth of the Tavener household. Everyone, apart from poor Rachel, was made to feel at home in Wembley Park and invited to come on family holidays. A favourite watering hole for the Taveners *en famille* was the Seaford Head, an eccentric and faded seaside hotel in Sussex. John's friends, Roger's friends and the friends of their friends, were all entertained here by Kenneth and Muriel Tavener. The hotel liked having musicians on its guest list. John tells a story which captures the flavour of the place.

The fire alarm rang one night and this seemed urgent, so he jumped out of the bath and made his way along the corridor wearing no clothes. As he came down the open staircase, he could see flames shooting from the bar at the far side of the lounge. While he hesitated, the hotel owner came forward and called up to him, 'Ah, Mr Tavener, I'm glad of the chance to have a word with you. We're thinking of starting a concert season here, with the Eastbourne Symphony Orchestra.'

Just a few miles inland from Seaford, sheltering in the Cuckmere valley, is Charleston Manor. Sometimes the Taveners and their friends were invited to stay in the guest cottage. Brian Chapple was struck by the beauty of the place, and the 'charismatic, extraordinary personality' of Lady Birley.

Each year, Rhoda Birley put her energy into the running of a summer festival of music and the arts, centred on her Tithe Barn. Among the attractions for 1964, she was delighted to list a new work by her young protégé, John Tavener. This was *The Cappemakers*, based on two New Testament stories, as dramatized by the medieval guild of cape-makers for the York Cycle of Mystery Plays. Above his signature at the end of the score, John has written 'Wembley Park and Allington Castle, Kent.' This calls for an explanation.

*

Family friends of the Taveners, Dr Frank Cosin and his wife, kept a houseboat on the river Medway. Their mooring was beside Allington Castle, which was used by the Carmelite Friars as a retreat and Christian centre. Head of the Carmelite order there was Father Malachy Lynch, who combined Irish whimsy with a firm sense of purpose. The Cosins were impressed by Father Malachy. They knew young John Tavener felt drawn towards Catholicism, so they suggested to Kenneth and Muriel that he should visit the castle. At this time, John was taking instruction from Father Christopher Pemberton, a priest at Westminster

Cathedral recommended by Lennox Berkeley. Father Malachy Lynch had a much more lasting influence.

Painting, pottery and weaving were all practised at Allington Castle, which was plastered with notices in medieval script: 'Keep the medieval spirit of Art alive'. The choice of *The Cappemakers* as a subject owes as much to Father Malachy's feeling for medieval tradition as it does to the musical precedents: Benjamin Britten's *Noye's Fludde* and Stravinsky's *The Flood*.

John admits *The Cappemakers* is 'very Stravinskian in many ways'. It is written for solo voices, chorus and instrumental ensemble. Before the music begins, words spoken in Latin introduce the *dramatis personae*: Jesus Christ, two of his apostles, the woman taken in adultery, and the Jews who accuse her.

In the first scene, the Jews (tenors and baritones) describe the adulterous woman as a 'false stud-mare and stinking stray . . . worthy that she be doomed to death this day'. The rhythmic punch, the melodic spikiness and the sparseness of the texture are all from Stravinsky.

The entrance of Christ brings a new and beautiful musical element, distinctly Tavener. Christ's gentle words are sung canonically by a three-part male chorus, with the bass part trailing half a beat behind the others: an ancient device known as the *hocket*. With a memorable melodic line, centring on a minor sixth, Christ weaves his spell and delivers his judgement:

> He that from sin is free
> He first shall cast a stone.

The subject of the fallen woman, by the way, is to become a Tavener favourite.

A passage of spoken narration introduces the second drama: the raising of Lazarus. It opens with Mary and Martha singing a lament, whose lyricism seems to stem from Lennox Berkeley or Benjamin Britten. 'Too soft,' says John in retrospect. But toughness reasserts itself when Christ summons Lazarus back to life. Flute, trumpet and piano combine to produce an astringent fanfare, and the three voices form hollow chords to call Lazarus from the tomb. Then there is an effect of pealing church bells, created on the piano, which echoes the music of the rising waters in Stravinsky's *The Flood*.

★

For the performance of *The Cappemakers* at Charleston, students from the Royal Academy and the Royal College were bolstered by professionals. Rehearsals needed to be in London, so the Taveners' Mullion Court studio came into its own. John conducted, and Francis Steiner took the prominent piano part in the ensemble, which consisted otherwise of woodwind, horn, trumpet, harp and string quintet. The chorus was the St Christopher Singers, who also provided the male trio to sing the part of Christ. One solo tenor and one baritone shared the parts of Lazarus and the four Jews.

In a volume of Stravinsky's conversations, John had read the great composer's description of the part of Satan in his opera *The Flood*: 'a high, slightly pederastic tenor'. Having no idea what 'pederastic' meant, but assuming it was a musical term, and loving the sound of Satan on the recording of *The Flood*, John urged his soloists to sing more pederastically. One of them 'turned the colour of an orange', he remembers. During the next break in rehearsals, someone explained to John what a pederast was.

The Charleston première of *The Cappemakers* was on Sunday, 14 June 1964. Although this was only a semi-staged performance, preparations in Lady Birley's Tithe Barn were elaborate. The set was designed by John's glamorous new girlfriend, Susan Vaughan, an aspiring young artist, as well as a fashion model. Susan was the daughter of wealthy friends of the Taveners. John had met her through her brother Simon, one of his contemporaries at Highgate. The narration for *The Cappemakers* was written by another Highgate schoolfellow, Nicholas Snowman.

Lady Birley's Festival coincided with the more famous one up at Aldeburgh, and it so happened that *The Cappemakers* première was during the same weekend as the first performance of Britten's *Curlew River*. Nevertheless, Monday's *Daily Telegraph* found prominent space for John's 'very moving work'. The review was headed COMPOSER, 19, BRINGS BEAUTY TO BIBLE PLAY. It ended

> The highly gifted Tavener belongs wholly to the present and his music
> is full of novel ingenuities of sound and rhythm. His aim, the poetic
> blending of words and music, was beautifully attained.

As a matter of fact, 'the highly gifted Tavener' was twenty, not nineteen, and already obsessed with mortality. Philip Pilkington says that as long as he has known him, John has made gloomy references to Mozart and indulged thoughts of his own premature demise. Other lifelong friends say much the same. This preoccupation with death, which was to become one of his trademarks as a composer, showed as early as his settings of *Three Holy Sonnets of John Donne*, which he finished while writing *The Cappemakers*, but began while he was still at school. Today he looks back on those settings of Donne as

> The first real sound of me. The only music I really love out of that period. It has gravity, it has something of all the pieces I've written since. So much of my music has been influenced by the death of people close to me.

The score is headed 'In Memoriam D. B.' Daisy Brown was John's maternal grandmother. He thinks it was his mother's brother, Eric, who introduced him to Donne's poetry. From the nineteen Holy Sonnets, he chose 'Spit In My Face', 'Death Be Not Proud' and 'I Am a Little World'. Their themes are sin, death and the corruption of the flesh.

The music is for baritone solo, accompanied by French horns, trombones, timpani and strings. The absence of woodwind has since become a Tavener characteristic, and several more features of the *Three Holy Sonnets* are still found in John's music today: the very slow tempi, the long-held notes, the sense of drama, and the fine feeling for the voice.

'I Am a Little World' was the sonnet set first, for organ and voice, while John was still at Highgate. He wrote it to be sung by his friend Simon Vaughan, Susan's brother, who had a good strong baritone voice. The first performances were at Mullion Court, accompanied by John on the organ. No record has been kept of that organ accompaniment. The reworking for brass and strings is bleak and fierce.

The setting of 'Spit In My Face' is the one which stands out, because of its grave and austere beauty. The opening lines

> Spit in my face, you Jewes, and pierce my side,
> Buffet, and scoffe, scourge, and crucifie mee,

are fitted with a slow-moving twelve-note row, supported by muted phrases on violins and violas, and long-held notes on the cellos and basses. As the drama develops, there is subdued activity from the horns, trombones and timpani, but at the end it is the baritone and the strings who are left with the burden.

> God cloth'd himself in vile mans flesh, that so
> Hee might be weake enough to suffer woe.

*

At the end of June 1964, Igor Stravinsky arrived in this country to take part in the English Bach Festival. He was to conduct his *Symphony of Psalms* and his Variations on the Bach Chorale *Vom Himmel Hoch* in Oxford Town Hall. Even more excitingly, the rehearsals were to be in the Duke's Hall at the Academy. Once Stravinsky was in London, John hovered and hoped. A chance nearly fell his way to give his idol a lift back to the Savoy Hotel, when travel arrangements made by the Academy seemed to have broken down. He came forward to announce that his mother's Triumph Herald was standing by, but at the very last moment the official Stravinsky transport rolled into view.

A photo taken of Stravinsky during those Academy days shows him greeting his Russian friend, Rostropovich. Fuzzily visible in the background are two tall thin boys: the ever-attendant John, and his faithful brother Roger. In the end, John's patience and persistence had their reward. Through the good offices of Madame Ruffina Ampenoff, Stravinsky's publisher, he was invited to a reception in Stravinsky's honour. Madame Ampenoff introduced him to the great man, who, John remembers, was sitting down. The score of John's *Three Holy Sonnets* was thrust into his hands. He looked at it, then stared up at John for what seemed a very long time. Finally, without saying anything, he inscribed the score with just two words: 'I know.'

A few days later, still ecstatic about the mystical inscription, John was driven up to Oxford by Susan Vaughan to hear the *Symphony of Psalms* and *Vom Himmel Hoch*. After the concert, heaven sent him an opportunity to do his master a service. He found Stravinsky stranded outside Oxford Town Hall, with nobody doing anything to help him down the steps. John offered his arm. As the two of them made their descent to the pavement and the waiting crowd of autograph hunters, the stooped 82-year-old composer confided to the sky-scraping one of twenty, 'Up to heaven, down to hell.'

*

On the recommendation of Lennox Berkeley, the *Three Holy Sonnets* were taken to Paul Steinitz, a professor of harmony at the Academy who was also the founder and conductor of the London Bach Society. Might this new music be appropriate for a Bach Society concert? John remembers standing nervously while Steinitz opened the score. 'He was quite an abrupt man. He looked at the first page and he said, "I want to do it."'

The première of the *Three Holy Sonnets* was at a concert of

new music, which Steinitz conducted in the church of
St Bartholomew-the-Great, Smithfield, on Monday, 20 July 1964. The
baritone soloist was John Noble. The rest of the programme consisted
of a nocturne by Nicholas Maw; Benjamin Britten's *Rejoice in the Lamb*;
and Anthony Milner's *Salutatio Angelica*.

For John this was a thrilling and unforgettable occasion: the first fully
professional performance of his music. Music, moreover, which had
received the imprimatur of Stravinsky himself. When it was over, he
was deflated by the senior composer present, Anthony Milner, who
seemed immensely elderly, and wanted to know if John always wrote
such morbid stuff. But William Mann, the music critic of *The Times*,
also attended that concert, and it was the Tavener piece that he chose
to review. He found the vocal line 'compelling and highly expressive',
and praised John for using 'sensuous beauty of sound to focus attention
the more strongly'. He also complimented Mr John Noble on his 'warm
tone and expressive delicacy'. John Noble remembers, and can confirm
from his account book, that he was paid directly for his performance
by Mr Kenneth Tavener. His immaculate records also show when he
sang the *Three Holy Sonnets* again. It was 7 January 1965, in the Guild
Church of St Andrew, Holborn, as part of a programme by the London
Bach Society which also included three Bach cantatas. Mr Noble's pay
cheque this time came from the BBC, from which it can be deduced that
John had become a broadcast composer.

On 28 January 1965, exactly three weeks after the broadcast performance of his *Three Holy Sonnets*, John Tavener was twenty-one-years
old. His father threw a party for him at the Dorchester Hotel in Park
Lane. Family and friends, colleagues and teachers were all there,
including Lennox and Freda Berkeley. The evening was not an unquali-
fied success. John drank too much and had to be sent home early in a
taxi.

PART THREE

An extraordinary creature

§

1 : Cain and Abel

John was now in his last year at the Academy. Myers Foggin, the Warden, who was also Director of Opera, decided to mark his departure by mounting a fully dramatized production of *The Cappemakers*. John overhauled the score, replacing Nicholas Snowman's spoken link with a bridge passage for orchestra, and there were two stagings, on the 7th and 8th of July 1965. John conducted. He also wrote an explanatory note, to be inserted into the programme:

> The difficulty has been to supply a short piece of music, linking the two miracles. The embryonic 'serial style' of the music composed when I was nineteen is very different from what I am writing at the moment. The piece linking the two episodes is based strictly on the material of the rest of the music, but is much more compressed.

The better to understand this switch to unremitting serialism we have to go back two years, to John's first meeting with a mature student at the Academy who was to have an enormous influence on him. The student's name was David Lumsdaine.

Their meeting took place in May 1963, at a concert celebrating the sixtieth birthday of Lennox Berkeley. As a surprise tribute to their teacher, each of Berkeley's students had written a variation on the aria 'I Do Not Like My Looking Glass', from the Berkeley opera *A Dinner Engagement*. Most of the variations were good-humoured. John's was radical. It took the light-hearted Berkeley tune and used it as a kind of *cantus firmus*, stripping away the flippant rhythms. The notes came evenly and very slowly from the oboe, while high cellos and organ provided a solemn atmosphere. After the performance, David Lumsdaine took John aside and congratulated him. John responded with enthusiasm for Lumsdaine's variation, which had banished tonality completely. Tavener and Lumsdaine felt themselves to be men apart.

The next thing that happened, as John remembers it, was that

Lumsdaine offered to give him free lessons. Lumsdaine says it was not quite like that. Although he was twelve years John's senior, he was in no position at the Academy to teach him officially. He prefers to think of what occurred as an engagement of like minds. However that may be, he became massively important to John's development as a composer.

David Lumsdaine was born in Sydney in 1931. After university in Australia he came to London in 1953, to study composition with Matyas Seiber. He became immersed in serial music and then, surprisingly, entered the Academy and became a pupil of Lennox Berkeley. In recognition of Lumsdaine's seniority and commitment to modernism, the Academy put him in charge of its library of contemporary music. This curatorship brought in a little money.

Philip Pilkington suspects that what brought John Tavener and David Lumsdaine together was the attraction of opposites. David had the range of technical skills and a rigorous mind. John lacked both technique and the power of analysis, but 'maybe David saw in John those rather more fundamental qualities that he himself was in need of'.

John became a regular visitor to Lumsdaine's home in the Surrey countryside. During peak periods, when he was giving birth to a new composition, he would drive down there from Wembley Park three or four times a week. He admired Lumsdaine's own 'enormously complex' compositions and he gives him great credit, not just as 'the one who opened the doors to Boulez, Ligeti, Stockhausen, Messiaen', but also as a visionary who spoke of music's magic and mystery:

> He had a vision which was beyond the system. More so than Peter Maxwell Davies. More to my liking than Birtwistle. Nearer a kind of spiritual vision. But his music is very rarely played. Whenever I do hear a piece of his, I'm very stimulated by it still . . . As a teacher he was quite extraordinary.

Like Messiaen, Lumsdaine was a passionate ornithologist. His recordings of bird-song were meticulous. John remembers being allowed to join him on a field trip to the estuary of the river Cuckmere, not far from Charleston. 'It was a great inspiration, seeing his love of the stillness of Cuckmere Haven, on an incredibly quiet day.'

Lumsdaine remembers John as 'urgently in need of technical advice on how to build and extend temporal structures. He could hardly get anything down on paper'. He let John into the secrets of canons and isorhythms. They shared a commitment to Stravinsky's *Canticum*

Sacrum, and Lumsdaine ignited John's enthusiasm for Messiaen by lending him his record of the *Turangalîla Symphony*. John became hooked on the slow movement, 'Garden of Love': a long thread of dreamy melody, played sweetly on the electronic *ondes martenot*, attended by soft strings and fluttering piano. Lumsdaine says John played that track 'until he wore it out'.

Beyond Lumsdaine's range was John's obsession with *The Sound of Music*. By 1965 the film version had opened in England. Lumsdaine remembers John went to see it 'countless times'. It contained a new number not included in the stage show: a ditty sung by Julie Andrews called 'Somewhere in my youth or childhood, I must have done something good'. John could not get it out of his head. Francis Steiner and his partner George like to reminisce about a visit they received from John during those days. 'He sat down at the battered old piano, and he played "Something Good" from *The Sound of Music*. It was so gorgeous, so tender and sensitive. We have never forgotten it.'

Meanwhile, bolstered by regular visits to the cottage in Surrey, John was writing his toughest piece so far: a purely orchestral and relentlessly serial chamber concerto. No concession to a tune anywhere. At the time, John was proud of it; looking back on it today, he sees it as a mistake. The piece he identifies as the first important fruit of his association with David Lumsdaine is *Cain and Abel*: a cantata for four solo voices and orchestra, with a text drawn from the York Mystery Plays and the Latin Bible. It won the Prince Rainier of Monaco International Award for composition in 1965.

*

Now that John's time at the Academy was up, Lennox Berkeley was keen he should continue his studies in France, with Nadia Boulanger. Berkeley had never lost touch with his old mentor. She was president of the jury which gave the Monaco award to *Cain and Abel*.

Stravinsky was known to admire the teaching methods of Nadia Boulanger, so she seemed an ideal choice to bring out the best in John. He travelled with his parents to visit the Boulanger conservatory at Fontainebleau. The grand old lady impressed him greatly, but the rest of the set-up did not. It seemed to be dominated by wealthy American students, all writing the same kind of music. He hurried back to Wembley Park and continued his commuting to the Lumsdaine cottage. Lennox Berkeley was very disappointed. He felt John needed to get away from home. Nevertheless, the Academy awarded him the Charles

W. Black Fellowship for a year, to help support him while he found his feet as a composer.

*

Cain and Abel received its first public performance in St Andrew's, Holborn, on Saturday, 22 October 1966, at a concert given by the London Bach Society. The programme began with four Bach cantatas, conducted by Paul Steinitz. Then John himself conducted his new work. The soloists were Gregory Dempsey (tenor), as Cain; Christopher Keyte (baritone), as Abel; and Maria Stader (soprano) and Barbara Robotham (contralto) singing the words of the angel. The orchestra was the English Chamber Orchestra.

Cain and Abel was broadcast by the BBC, and widely reviewed. Anthony Payne in the *Daily Telegraph* declared: 'Peter Maxwell Davies was the last composer to make such an impact, with his "Second in Nomine Fantasia" last year.' Payne went on to praise Mr Tavener's 'acutely perceived instrumental sonorities, often put to superb dramatic use'. *The Times* was similarly complimentary, and in the *Financial Times* Andrew Porter concluded: 'The strong character of Tavener's vocal writing, his exuberant rhythmic sense, the boldness and vividness of his aural imagination all proclaim him a composer to watch.'

After its success in Monaco, *Cain and Abel* was entered for another competition. This one was held at the Royal College of Music on 21 November 1966, and *Cain and Abel* won first prize. The composer Malcolm Arnold, who was on the panel of judges, sought John out afterwards to tell him personally, 'My boy, I think this is a work of genius.'

John wrote an article about *Cain and Abel* and the thinking behind it for the October 1966 issue of the *Musical Times*.

> *Go jape thee ribald jangle on, I list not now to bend or groan . . .*
> It was sounds like this quotation from the York Play, and my persistent inclination towards Biblical texts, which led me to compose *Cain and Abel*. Any 'moral' or 'amoral' undertones are coincidental.
> The work falls into five main sections, descending in pitch as the drama unfolds. This 'falling' in the music is marked by four-note brass chords which act as pivots . . .
> The story is treated ritualistically. All the four solo voices have their share to do, characterizing in medieval English and narrating in Latin. Cain has an ejaculatory and very high vocal line; Abel is calm and always legato. The family resemblance is a rhythmic one. The music

for the Angel, sung by the two female voices, is very simple . . . The orchestra is used in families. Brass and percussion have rather more to do than anyone else.

Influences? Perhaps the bouncing rhythms of 'The Quarrel' were suggested by the first movement of the Fifth Brandenburg. The recent serial works of Stravinsky have made a great impression on me. I might also add that the sound of church bells is more moving to me than any 'written-down' or 'unwritten-down' music that I have yet heard.

Cain and Abel is among a number of works on Biblical subjects. *The Whale*, which I have been working on for some time, is the climax of this group. All these pieces share extravagance, which I may not be capable of when I grow older.

In November 1966, John received a letter from the Secretary of the Academy, saying that his tenure of the Black Fellowship had been extended for a further year. He wrote back to say he was thrilled, and to ask if it would be possible to receive the money in a lump sum, rather than in instalments. The Secretary replied promptly, enclosing a cheque for £450. Just as promptly, John went to a vintage car dealer in Harrow and bought a ten-year-old Armstrong Siddeley Sapphire. This stately saloon, with its thoroughbred look, was the first in a long line of similar purchases.

2 : Marine mammal of the order Cetacea

John's trailer for *The Whale* at the end of his *Musical Times* article was hardly adequate warning of what was looming.

It had never before been of interest to him that Wembley Stadium was close to his home, but while working on the new extravaganza he used to hover within earshot on Saturday afternoons, drawing musical inspiration from the rise and fall of the roar of the crowd. A set of Sanctus bells, bought on a whim, produced random pitches which fitted his musical scheme. A great idea for a beginning came to him one night as he lay soaking in the bath. It sent him rushing downstairs in a towel, to look up the entry for 'whale' in Collins Encyclopaedia:

> Marine mammal of the order Cetacea. They comprise three groups (1) 'Archaeoceti', believed to have been derived from the Credonta, the primitive fossil members of the Carnivora . . .

and so on for nearly a column of boring close print. Perfect. This would be his overture. He would have it read on stage in a dry, pedantic voice, which would gradually become engulfed in orchestral noise: the approach of an extraordinary creature, and then a musical swallowing.

He hit upon a musical motif which was like an opening maw: a rising four-note phrase, each note shorter than the last – first four beats, then three, then two, then one. This same phrase worked equally well at the end of the piece, where it suggested the whale spitting Jonah out.

Deeply implicated in this flurry of creativity was David Lumsdaine. As well as receiving two or three weekly visits, he was bombarded with telephone calls by day and night. And this went on more or less non-stop for over a year. John remembers requiring Lumsdaine to come to the phone, 'even when the poor chap had the measles'. He has always believed in his right to call on people at any hour to service the demands of his creative process. He still does it, without apology. Over the years, the endurance of many collaborators has been sorely tested. David

Lumsdaine was one of the first to find that the gentle charm of the Tavener manner is dangerously misleading.

After visiting Lumsdaine for what they called their 'brainstorming sessions', and leaving him exhausted, John often drove on down to Charleston Manor to find spiritual refreshment. The dark, cool interior of the Tithe Barn became his composing room. In there, he could imagine himself inside the belly of the whale. And there it was, in the middle of a heat wave, that the score was finished.

By chance, on the very day that John wrote the last note, David Lumsdaine dropped in to see him. He happened to be passing on one of his birdwatching expeditions. He made his way straight to the barn, where he found John in euphoric mood. Sounds of congratulation and celebration reached Lady Birley in the Manor House. Deeply incensed, she hurried over to the barn and called John outside for a private word. He remembers her stern lecture went something like this: 'When you are here, you really must leave the boys and gals alone totally and give yourself entirely to your Art. You don't want people coming down and interfering. And you certainly don't want people like him around you when you're trying to compose.' Perhaps it was the Australian accent that put her off. She never did understand the importance of David Lumsdaine.

*

During the London season, John's gifts as a musical mimic were a regular feature of Lady Birley's St John's Wood soirées. Once they discovered what a big draw he was, other hostesses clamoured for him too, but Lady Birley's large studio and full-sized concert grand gave her an edge over her rivals. John remembers the parties in that studio, peopled with extraordinary characters, 'who looked as though they'd stepped off the set of *Rosenkavalier*'. What they liked to do was to call out the title of some simple tune – 'Three Blind Mice' was a popular one – and hear it played, to start with, in a way they could all follow. Then they would shout out the names of famous composers – Mozart, Chopin, Rachmaninov – and marvel at John's instant variations in all those styles. An even more popular game was called 'society portraits'. For this one, guests would be brought in front of John, to have their characters described in music. He remembers his musical portrait of Lady Diana Cooper went down very well, but his summing up of an aristocratic Frenchwoman and her pampered poodle was too candid. She removed her pet from the party and took to her bed.

*

The score of *The Whale* is 'affectionately dedicated to Lady Birley', but to get the piece put on, John had to look elsewhere. Myers Foggin, who had staged *The Cappemakers* at the Academy, remained a supporter. As well as being the Academy's Head of Opera, Foggin ran the Croydon Philharmonic Society. He was keen to commission something for that Society along the lines of *Cain and Abel*, or better still like *Belshazzar's Feast*, and he was hoping *The Whale* would be it. When he saw the score he had a nasty shock. This would never do for Croydon. First of all, the style was extreme. Avant-garde touches included five minutes of aleatory music, where players and singers were invited to do their own thing: 'choose any low note', 'choose any high note', et cetera, on the off-chance that good might come of it. Then there was the instrumentation. The orchestra included no violins, but all the rest of the strings were there, plus woodwind and brass sections, and no fewer than eight percussion players, responsible for a big battery of drums and gongs and bells, as well as extras like a football rattle, two amplified metronomes and an amplified sheet of glass. The keyboard line-up included glockenspiel, xylophone, marimba, celeste, grand organ, Hammond organ and amplified grand piano. The choir was of modest size, but members were called upon to neigh, grunt, snort, yawn and make vomiting noises. On top of that, there was another choir on tape, singing fast permutations of the syllables in 'swastika'. And then there was a second tape, carrying fire alarms and pop songs. To complicate the logistics still further, six male performers were armed with loudhailers.

Myers Foggin bowed out.

Enter John's old schoolfriend Nicholas Snowman, and a bright young conductor Snowman had met at Cambridge, called David Atherton. These two were plotting to form a brand-new orchestra, which would specialize in contemporary music. Snowman was working at Glyndebourne and Atherton was on the music staff at Covent Garden, so the creation of the London Sinfonietta was a spare-time activity. It succeeded because of Snowman's genius for raising funds. David Atherton took the title of Musical Director. Nicholas Snowman became General Manager. What was needed to give the Sinfonietta its launch was a headline-grabbing piece of new music. Snowman turned to his old pal from school, who happened to have the very thing. Once they had seen the score of *The Whale*, Snowman and Atherton looked no further. To take care of the choral part, the London Sinfonietta Chorus was set up at the same time as the orchestra. The job of chorus

master went to Clive Wearing, who was to become one of John's closest
friends.

*

The personality chosen to deliver the opening reading from Collins Encyclopaedia was Alvar Lidell, the senior announcer from the BBC whose
voice had been heard by the nation reading the news of the abdication
of King Edward VIII and the outbreak of the Second World War. Lidell
delighted John by dressing with immaculate formality even for the
rehearsals. He wore a flower in his buttonhole as a matter of course.

The job of the six men with loudhailers was to warn the audience
that a storm was coming. John wanted the effect of 'hysterical orders
shouted in confusion'. The men were to be positioned strategically
around the auditorium, and armed with fragments of text:

> it is my duty to
>   wash after
>   mines reported in the
>   vipers who hath warned
>   and cause suffocation

Midway through the score comes another *coup de théâtre*. Here, John
decrees orchestral and choral silence, while Jonah cries unto the Lord and
hears in return only the sound of his own voice. The manner in which this
is to be staged is exactly prescribed. First, while the orchestra is still
playing, the singer is to walk unobtrusively to the piano. Then, while the
pianist silently depresses large clusters of keys with his forearms, the singer
is to shout, 'loudly but not roughly', into the instrument, using the French
vowels sounds *é* and *o*, repeated seven times. Finally, there is a long pause,
while the singer remains motionless, bent over the piano, listening until
the reverberation dies away. For greater audience involvement, it is
directed that a contact microphone should be placed inside the piano, to
feed the voice and the harmonics to loudspeakers around the hall.

This scene was to become a big talking point, with opinion divided as
to its meaning. Some critics assumed Jonah was testing the acoustics of the
whale's sonorous belly. Others thought he was being violently sea-sick.

*

The inaugural concert of the London Sinfonietta Orchestra and Chorus
was at the Queen Elizabeth Hall on Wednesday, 24 January 1968.

Although Nicholas Snowman was entirely new to this kind of thing, he had telephoned the papers and sold them a good story: about a new orchestra; a new conductor, just twenty-four years old; and a new work, written by a composer even younger than the conductor. There was a photo-call, where John posed for action shots, 'rehearsing' with David Atherton and the two soloists, Anna Reynolds and Raimund Herincx. One of the pictures headed a preview splash in the *Guardian*.

On sale at the Queen Elizabeth Hall on the night of the concert was a well-produced programme booklet, announcing the London Sinfonietta. Inside were capsule biographies of key people. The entry on John listed his 'profoundest influences' as 'late Stravinsky, Messiaen, late Richard Strauss, Cage and hymns'. There was also a note by John about the piece (reprinted below).

THE WHALE   *First performance*   *John Tavener*

Anna Reynolds
Raimund Herincx
Alvar Lidell
John Constable
John Tavener

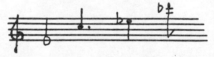

This was the first idea which came to me; these notes and the rhythmic interversions form the basis of a fantasy on the Biblical allegory 'Jonah and the Whale'. A fantasy which grew around the text from the Vulgate, and at times moved so far from it that I decided to call the piece 'The Whale'.

Sanctus bells was another sound from out of which the piece grew, and a chance purchase of some bells proved their pitches and intervals to be relevant to the music.

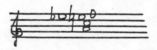

Ideas were very abundant in the first stages of 'The Whale', and I owe a great deal to the constant enthusiasm and encouragement shown at this and at all times, by David Lumsdaine.

At the performance, John played the Hammond organ. The concert was a sensation. As Nicholas Snowman puts it today: 'The Sinfonietta was launched for ever, just on one night.' And on just one piece. There was hardly a word in any of the papers about the other items on the programme: the Symphony for Wind by Richard Strauss and Henze's *Apollo and Hyazinthus*. Oddly enough, the solo harpsichord part in the Henze piece was played by Raymond Leppard, who had chaired the panel of examiners facing John at Cambridge.

The Whale triumphed because it was modern music without tears. As the *Guardian*'s Edward Greenfield put it: 'First and foremost, Tavener's score is remarkable for providing such joyful music.' Stanley Sadie in *The Times* described *The Whale* as 'one of the most exciting works by a young composer I can remember hearing'. R. L. Henderson for the *Sunday Telegraph* called it 'a thoroughly enjoyable work of immense skill and exuberance'. Stephen Walsh in the *Observer* hailed 'A great victory for those who recognise that modern music is not simply a matter of solemn incantations in the sacred name of tedium.'

The Whale received its first BBC broadcast on 19 April 1968. Then in June it was back in the Queen Elizabeth Hall, on a double bill with John's uncompromising Chamber Concerto. This concert was Meirion Bowen's chance to catch up with *The Whale*, for which John again played the Hammond organ. Bowen wrote in the *Guardian* that Tavener was the musical discovery of the year. 'An extraordinarily gifted and imaginative composer, he is also one of the most colourful sights on the concert platform.'

3 : A musical love-in

Two months after the première of *The Whale*, another new Tavener work created a stir. Commissioned by the London Bach Society, the *Introit for March 27* was performed on that date at the Queen Elizabeth Hall, in a concert to celebrate the Society's twenty-first anniversary.

This was a composition which fell into place quickly, without any reference to David Lumsdaine. To find a text, John simply looked up the date of the concert in the Catholic Church service book. March 27 happened to be the annual Feast of St John Damascene. He took the Latin words in praise of that saint, although he had no idea what they meant. Today, he could not bear to treat the life of a saint in such cavalier fashion, but then it was sufficient that the Latin text provided a religious atmosphere. The important thing was the source of musical inspiration: the *Kyrie* from Johann Sebastian Bach's Mass in B Minor, on which the whole composition is based, and which emerges serenely at the end.

The *Introit for March 27: the Feast of St John Damascene* opens with the astonishing sound of a long-held high B, played *pianissimo* on the French horn. John was prompted to begin in this way by the theme music from the James Bond film *Goldfinger*, where a wild whooping on French horn introduces the vocal by Shirley Bassey. He discovered that the French horn for *Goldfinger* had been played by Alan Civil, and he made sure the Bach Society booked Alan for 27 March.

The horn note at the start of *Introit* is followed by a twelve-note row, played simultaneously forwards and backwards on two trumpets. After that, the Latin text is carried forwards spasmodically by a chorus and two soloists – soprano and contralto – while the orchestra, with piano very prominent, provides embroidery distantly linked to Bach's *Kyrie*. The composition is almost in the form of a palindrome, with a sustained high D for the soprano soloist at its centre. Towards the close, the members of the chorus are instructed to stamp their feet and clap their hands in strict quavers. At the climax, reminiscent of *The Whale*, the basses have a sequence of vowels to shout. And then the first four bars of Bach's *Kyrie* emerge, played softly and serenely by the strings of the orchestra.

At the first performance the piano part was taken by John himself. Paul Steinitz conducted and his wife Margaret sang in the chorus. She remembers the *Introit* as fiendishly difficult to learn, but immensely rewarding to perform. For her, the final surfacing of Bach's *Kyrie* was a master-stroke, and John's presence in the orchestra was an inspiration. 'He's so marvellously caught up in the music, it rubs off on everybody else.'

Not all the participants shared her enthusiasm. While the audience was applauding at the end of the performance, one section of the chorus was booing, according to a report by Gerald Abraham, who covered the concert for the *Daily Telegraph*. Also in the audience was George Rizza, managing director of Chester Music, who had recently signed John to an exclusive publishing contract. Rizza noticed that the eminent lady who sang the soprano part refused to acknowledge the applause and would not shake hands with the conductor. He assumed this was because of her distaste for *Introit*'s modernisms. John has a fuller story.

During rehearsals, the soprano said she would not strain her voice by singing the top D lasting sixteen seconds which marks *Introit*'s centre. Instead, she would sing that note an octave lower, even at the performance. John did not argue with her, but was reluctant to have the shape of his music spoiled. He knew there was a girl in the chorus who could sustain that high D with ease, and he talked to Paul Steinitz about her. Without a word to anyone else, it was arranged that this girl should sing the top D at the vital moment, leaving the *prima donna* down below.

In spite of the ructions on the platform, the *Introit for March* 27 was a huge critical success. Gerald Abraham summed it up as 'a richly inventive fabric of sonorities'. In *The Times*, under the headline BACH SOCIETY STRIKES GOLD, Stephen Walsh wrote that John Tavener's *Introit* was 'a work which only instinctive caution deters me from proclaiming here and now a masterpiece'. The final breakthrough of the Bach felt to him 'indescribably serene'. John Warrack in the *Sunday Telegraph* declared the fifteen-minute *Introit* the work of a true composer. 'Here is the keenest sense of how unusual musical devices may give dramatic sharpness to a religious piece,' he said. 'Bach would not have rejected the principle.'

*

Nineteen sixty-eight was looking like Tavener's *annus mirabilis*, and there was more to come. William Glock, Controller of Music at the BBC, had commissioned a piece from him for the 1968 season of Henry Wood Promenade concerts – and this was a commission with a difference. Glock had decided to conduct an experiment, which became notorious as 'the ballot Prom'. New works were invited from three composers: Don Banks, Thea Musgrave and – twenty years their junior – John Tavener. All three compositions would be performed during the first half of the concert. During the interval, the audience would use the ballot papers provided to vote for the one they would most like to hear again in the second half.

When he was commissioned, John was made aware of the identity of the other two composers. He remembers he felt it likely they would both write 'serial music of a rather grey, angst-ridden kind', so decided to do something completely different.

For his text he chose lines by the French visionary poet Charles Péguy, beginning '*L'espérance est une petite fille de rien du tout*' ('Hope is a little girl of no importance'). Péguy was a favourite of the Revd Cameron Joyce, the minister of St John's Presbyterian Church in Kensington, where John played the organ. By now, John had been organist there for seven years, and had drawn extremely close to Cameron Joyce and his wife Jane. The new work was dedicated to them, and set out to express in musical terms the yearning the Joyces felt for a world of sweetness and light. To the lines of Péguy, John added a second text:

> *Spem in alium nunquam habui*
> *Praeter in te, Deus Israel*
> I have hope in no other
> But in thee, O God of Israel.

This church responsory – once set by Thomas Tallis into a monumental forty-part motet – gave John's new work its title: *In Alium*.

It is written for high soprano, strings, piano, grand and Hammond organs, bells and gongs, and a four-track tape-recorder feeding loudspeakers stationed in the four quarters of the Albert Hall.

The first section is a setting of the lines by Péguy, which the soprano sings 'live', while taped sounds circle the hall, moving from loudspeaker to loudspeaker. These sounds on tape include children at play; romantic piano music; and hymn for children's voices plus wheezy harmonium.

The second section includes the most sensational material in the piece:

a cloying melodic line, pitched stratospherically high, which the soprano sings 'live', over a lush carpet of sound laid by the Hammond organ and the strings. The debt to Messiaen's 'Garden of Love' is confirmed by a barrage of amplified kissing sounds and heavy breathing.

The third section is entirely pre-recorded: six-part chords, all sung by the soprano, emerge from the loudspeakers in canon, producing an effect like church bells.

The last section unfolds as a canon for soprano in sixteen parts: one 'live' and fifteen pre-recorded. Also on tape are the voices of four small children, saying their prayers in Latin, French, German and English, and gradually falling asleep.

To achieve complicated effects on tape, John had come to rely on the assistance of David Lumsdaine, but Lumsdaine had nothing to do with *In Alium*: John was sure he would have disapproved. Fortunately, since this was a BBC commission, he had access to Auntie's engineering division, where a senior staff member called Eric Dougharty was put on his case.

To John, at twenty-four, Dougharty seemed immensely old and wise. He took a careful note of the requirements as John blurted them out. When it came to the sounds of little children falling asleep after saying their prayers in Latin, French, German and English, he said, very slowly, 'We shall have to see what we can do about that.' It took time, but John eventually got the call saying that four sets of parents with suitably qualified children had been found. He remembers going with Dougharty and a BBC recording engineer to family homes, where stereo microphones were rigged in children's bedrooms. The little French girl, who was only three, really did fall asleep while saying her prayers. The others were coaxed into pretending to do so.

The rest of the pre-recorded elements were put together in a BBC studio. John himself played the flamboyant piano solo. The BBC singers made kissing, clicking, popping and heavy breathing noises. The soprano soloist had a huge amount of multi-tracking to do, and some very high notes indeed to sing, including a sustained top F sharp, well above the D that had been required for *Introit*. The singer was June Barton, who had impressed as the Queen of the Night in *The Magic Flute* at Sadler's Wells. She made it all sound easy. John was thrilled with her.

His experience with the conductor was much less happy. Norman Del Mar was the man who had been selected by the BBC to conduct all three new works, and he was hostile to *In Alium* from the start. John

went to a preliminary meeting at Del Mar's house, where he found the
atmosphere far from pleasant. Was Del Mar rude about the piece
because he found it beyond him? Whatever the reason, he withdrew
from conducting it before the first rehearsal with the BBC Symphony
Orchestra, which John had to take himself. For the performance, the
BBC rushed in David Atherton, who became, at twenty-four, the
youngest conductor ever to take the podium at the Proms. He was not
invited to conduct the whole concert: just *In Alium*, leaving Norman
Del Mar in charge of the pieces by Musgrave and Banks.

This most unusual of Promenade Concerts was staged and broadcast
on Monday, 12 August 1968. It began with Thea Musgrave's Concerto
for Orchestra. Then came *In Alium*. Then a new violin concerto by Don
Banks, with Wolfgang Marschner as soloist. During the tense thirty-
minute interval, voting took place and then the counting of the votes.
Norman Del Mar packed his bag ready to leave, fearing the worst. He
was right. *In Alium* was the winner. David Atherton and June Barton
rejoined the orchestra on the platform. So too did John, who once again
sat with an engineer at a mixing desk, controlling the flow of taped
sounds to the heavy-duty loudspeakers.

The music critics added their commentaries to the outcome of the
ballot. John Warrack in the *Sunday Telegraph* praised 'the fascinating
skill with which Tavener controls all his resources' and his 'welcome
gift for producing pleasure and excitement in a world all too full of
grim experiment'.

Edward Greenfield in the *Guardian* confessed he had voted for Thea
Musgrave's Concerto for Orchestra, but accepted as inevitable a win
for *In Alium*: 'a work specially written with the enormity of the Albert
Hall's acoustic in mind'. While it was being performed, he had observed
the behaviour of the audience:

> This was a musical love-in – literally, for one saw old couples suddenly
> compelled to hold hands as uninhibitedly as the youngsters in the
> Promenade.

Peter Heyworth in the *Observer* praised Tavener's 'striking ability to
gauge imaginative effects with precision and dispose them in space',
but complained that the ideas were 'basically static, and non-developed
mentally'.

Andrew Porter in the *Financial Times* expressed no such reservations.
For him, *In Alium* was 'a skilful, formally controlled, warm-toned fresco

of appealing and arresting sounds, which, like *Cain and Abel* and *The Whale*, reveals Tavener's rich and original imagination'.

*

In the autumn of 1968, BBC2 launched a monthly magazine programme devoted to current affairs in music. It was edited by John Drummond, who called it *Music Now* and announced that each edition would carry a film profile of a newsworthy British composer. Not surprisingly, the composer profiled in the first edition was John Tavener.

The little film about him was made by this author. It opened with Sunday evening service at St John's Presbyterian Church in Kensington. John was at the organ, sporting a light grey suit and an early Beatle haircut, and radiating pleasure as he led the way through a distinctly unhurried version of 'O Worship the King'. In his commentary, he paid tribute to the choir for helping him with his experiments. At a recent choir practice, he said, 'There were guns pointing from all the three galleries, and the members were equipped with toy pistols and whistles.'

Later in the film, seated at the piano in the picture window of the lounge in Wembley Park, he divulged more secrets.

> Many of my recent pieces are built up as a kind of collage. I use a tape-recorder and with this way of writing I am able to use anybody to come in and make a noise, however limited their musical training. Working at home, I have often asked my mother to come in and hum something, or blow a whistle. I also dished out parts to the church choir of a fifty-part canon, and of course I haven't got fifty in the choir. But I was able to superimpose afterwards, with myself singing and playing the organ and the piano.

It was a memorable film debut. Television viewers marvelled at the strangeness of his creative ways and the enormous length of his limbs.

What John did not reveal was that the fifty-part canon was for a mammoth psychedelic opera, based on *Our Lady of the Flowers* by Jean Genet, French poet of perversion and the criminal mind. Corruptions of chorales by Bach were being amassed on tape, alongside distorted fragments of Genet blasphemies and obscenities. The ambition was to create a religious shocker in sixteen tableaux, lasting more than two and a half hours.

Our Lady of the Flowers had existed in embryo since the early days of *The Whale*, but completion was still some way off and the prospect of a performance looked remote. From time to time John recycled lumps of it, and one of these spin-offs became a minor *succès de scandale*. *Grandma's Footsteps*, for five groups of instrumentalists and five musical boxes, was premièred at St Pancras Town Hall on Thursday, 14 March 1968, as part of the Camden Festival. Modelled on a traditional children's game, it was a staged 'happening', where the 'live' performers were enslaved to the whims of the automata, which started and stopped at random. It fitted the mood of the late sixties and was enthusiastically reviewed in *The Times*, but John did not see it as very important.

*

For a time, the poet and art critic Edward Lucie-Smith worked on the Genet opera as librettist. Before they split up, he and John fulfilled a little commission from BBC Schools Radio. The requirement was for three songs to brighten a broadcast to schools about surrealism. Colour slides of paintings by René Magritte, Max Ernst and Salvador Dali would be projected in school classrooms, while the songs came over the air. Edward Lucie-Smith's words were set by John for mezzo-soprano, piano, bongo drums and pre-recorded tape.

The first song, 'To René Magritte', tells of a giant comb, a strong man's brain and an invasive apple. Over a note-cluster on tape, the bongos and the piano take it in turns to argue with the mezzo-soprano.

The second song, 'To Max Ernst', is about a barking man trapped inside a nightingale. To portray this circumstance, John has created a hauntingly beautiful melodic line. His instruction in the score is that the soprano should first pre-record the complete song, then duet *ab lib* with her pre-recorded self. For both the live and pre-recorded performances she should keep her head 'inside or very near the inside of the piano'.

The third song, 'To Salvador Dali', is about sleep and dreams. The mezzo-soprano sings in strict canon with her pre-recorded self, while the piano provides live and taped decoration.

A recording session was set up by the BBC, and after the excellent service he had received during the preparation of the *In Alium* tape John looked forward to exploiting Auntie's resources once again. The first pre-recorded sound required was a cluster of notes on the organ, held for exactly two minutes and fourteen seconds: the duration of song number one. The BBC music producer assigned on this occasion was Albert Chatterley. He took John to the Concert Hall of Broadcasting House, where the BBC organ and a BBC recording engineer were standing by. Mr Chatterley had been advised that young Tavener was of striking appearance and had something of an aura about him, but he was not prepared for what happened next. The tape-recorder was started; John depressed his chosen cluster of notes; everyone watched the BBC clock, which was fixed on a perch in front of the organ pipes. After two minutes, the vibrations set up by the Tavener cluster had infected the clock with a feverish tremble. At two minutes and ten seconds, just before time was up, the clock sprang from its moorings, crashed to the floor, and rolled on its rim. The Tavener legend suffered no harm at all.

The *Three Surrealist Songs* were beamed to schools in the autumn term of 1968. They also became a popular recital item. In October, they formed part of a star-studded Oxfam Concert at the Royal Festival Hall, which consisted mostly of celebrity soloists riding operatic warhorses. John's was the only original musical contribution, and it came with a bonus denied to the radio audience: the spectacle of mezzosoprano Honor McKellar with her head inside the grand piano. In the *Guardian* next day, Hugo Cole praised Tavener as 'that delightful and rare find, a contemporary composer who can be enjoyed (and by anyone) at first hearing'.

The Whale, Introit, In Alium and now these songs: such huge success for a composer so young provoked envious muttering in the dank recesses of the music business. The bile found a conduit in the journal *Music and Musicians*, disguised as a review of the charity performance of the *Three Surrealist Songs*. The reviewer was Ates Orga. 'Profusion of styles', he said, 'is no substitute for artistic integrity.' Tavener was 'a fashionable composer rather than a committed creative artist'. Worst of all, he was someone 'finding a platform through no merits of his own'.

This *ad hominem* assault was spotted by the respected composer Richard Rodney Bennett. His response, which headed the letters page of the next issue of *Music and Musicians*, began 'I feel very strongly that Ates Orga's attack on John Tavener should never have been printed in your columns.' The nub of Bennett's vigorous rebuttal was this:

A malicious and destructive attack of this kind, from which Mr Tavener emerges with, in theory, only a 'prolific mind' to his credit, seems to me unforgivable. If this were a criticism of one specific work, it might be partially justified, but Mr Orga has surely grossly overestimated his function in dismissing the artistic integrity, the creative personality, the level of self-criticism, indeed the whole talent of a composer of 24. The article aroused much greater doubts in my mind

as to the integrity of your critic than to that of the very talented Mr
Tavener.

★

By now, John's brother Roger had finished his apprenticeship and joined
the family firm. These were the days of Swinging London, and word
started to spread among its trend setters that if you wanted your home
improved you should engage Roger Tavener, the swinging builder. He
sported a Beatle haircut and an American wife, kept up with the music,
even sang lead vocals with a beat group for a while, and was at home
among the beautiful people in the smartest clubs. His heroes, the Beatles,
were now a multi-million-pound business called the Apple Corporation,
with offices in Savile Row. Roger was summoned to a conference there
by Brian Epstein, the Beatles' manager. John, Paul, George and Ringo
all attended. As a result of that meeting, the Tavener firm was invited
to add some luxury touches to the private rooms reserved for the Fab
Four at Apple HQ. Then there were little jobs to be done at George
Harrison's place in Henley and at the Lennon mansion at Ascot. A lot
of work was needed on Paul McCartney's house in St John's Wood, but
the Taveners' biggest Beatle client was Ringo Starr, who spent hundreds
of thousands of pounds on his home in Highgate. Roger remembers
going to breakfast there with Ringo and Maureen every day for about
two years. 'I'd have a cup of coffee with them, and a slice of toast and
marmalade, and we'd talk about what we were going to do next.' Things
done included a rear extension, a snooker room and a private cinema.
Early in the history of these friendly breakfasts, Roger introduced the
subject of *The Whale*, his brother's number one hit in the world of
concert music. Ringo seemed intrigued. Roger took him a tape of the
performance broadcast by the BBC. Would it not be a good idea, he
suggested, to issue *The Whale* on the Beatles' Apple label?

In a separate development, John Lennon and his Japanese girlfriend,
the conceptual artist Yoko Ono, were introduced to John and his Black
Mass, *Our Lady of the Flowers*. The meeting place was the Kensington
home of a wealthy American, who invited the Johns Lennon and Tavener
to dinner and a sharing of ideas. The American's cook had prepared a
sumptuous feast, but Lennon and Yoko arrived in their white Rolls
Royce bringing their own macrobiotic diet. They ate sitting on the floor,
and played tapes of their latest experiments. John played them his Genet
opera. He remembers that Lennon and Yoko were not in the least bit
interested in its religious message, but they were fascinated by the way

the effects had been produced. The next day, Lennon called John from his car phone and said the resources of Apple were at his disposal.

★

The Whale, meanwhile, had gone international. UNESCO in Paris gave it a prize for best work by a composer under twenty-five. There were performances in Warsaw and Copenhagen, and, in November 1968, a North American première in Vancouver, where John was received as a celebrity. To coincide with his arrival, the *Province* newspaper printed a large picture of him, and a lengthy syndicated feature, under the multi-decker headline:

WHO IS JOHN TAVENER?

★ he's a mod-styled young composer
★ he's a friend of John Lennon
★ he's a swinging Presbyterian

Canadian readers were told that the 24-year-old Tavener 'towers above the crowd at six-foot-six, wears his hair shoulder length and his clothes modern – flared jacket, broad shirt cuffs, purple tie'. But he 'doesn't exactly fit the picture of the swinging Londoner ... He likes hymns, even the Victorian hymns rejected by some with-it parsons.' The articles went on to identify two strands – pop and religious – running through Tavener's music. *The Whale*, it explained, brought the strands together, and included a part for electric organ, which would be played in Vancouver by the composer himself. It quoted Tavener as believing that the electronic inventiveness of pop music signalled the end of the symphony orchestra.

The hype was exemplary, but the concert-goers of Vancouver were set in their ways. The morning after the performance, the *Province* ran another Tavener picture and story. This time it was an action shot of John feeding a leaping whale in the Vancouver Aquarium, captioned

THAR SHE BLOWS!
– THERE THEY GO

The review beneath it began 'For the first time in memory people walked out of a Vancouver Symphony Society concert – and not in order to catch the last bus. It was John Tavener's dramatic cantata *The Whale* which prompted the rush for the exits.'

John's memory of that evening is that the audience was too old for music so loud. He can still see the pained expressions on the elderly faces as he played the Hammond organ with all the stops out, while the notoriously fierce North American brass players gave it all they had got. The decibel level would not have disgraced an outdoor rock concert.

4 : Jenny Jones is dead

After the success of *The Whale*, the London Sinfonietta ordered another piece from John, to be performed on the South Bank in the summer of 1969.

His inspiration for this new composition came during a holiday in Ireland, where the beauty of the rugged landscape seemed tinged with a sense of loss. John felt at home in this Catholic country, and resolved to write a requiem, which would include settings of Celtic poetry and a part for children. The first musical idea that came to him was a giant chord of E flat major, but there he became stuck. He stayed stuck for several months, until David Lumsdaine lent him the David Holbrook book on children's games. Manna from heaven. The new composition came to life as a theatre piece for children, built around a central child character, 'Jenny Jones', who is forced by the others to pass through the rite of death. Jenny Jones nearly gave her name to the piece, but in the end John stuck to his original title, *Celtic Requiem*, because it had the right ring to it and because of his debt to Ireland for the genesis of the spirit of the music.

From the broad range of traditional singing games offered by Holbrook he chose only those which took death as their theme. He was affected by what he read about the underlying symbolism of the games, particularly the revelation that hopscotch once represented the path through life to death, or from Purgatory to Paradise. His piece would include a game of hopscotch, played on the concert platform. There would also be a swing. He had learned that swinging games in some societies were lengthy rituals, designed to secure the release of souls from Purgatory.

The final version of *Celtic Requiem* is triple-stranded. In the foreground is the world of children, where death is played out as a game. Beyond are two sets of adult responses to dying: the directness of the Irish balladeer and the ritual of the Catholic Church.

The piece is in three movements, named after sections of the Latin Mass for the Dead: *Requiem in Eternam*, *Dies Irae*, and *Requiescat in Pace*. During the last movement, two new elements creep in. One is 'They are All Gone into the World of Light', the meditation on death by the seventeenth-century metaphysical poet Henry Vaughan. The other is 'Lead Kindly Light', the Victorian hymn by Cardinal Newman, to the tune of C. H. Purday, transposed by John into the key of E flat. This hymn has always been one of his favourites. The decision to include it in *Celtic Requiem* was taken after he attended a service in St Paul's Cathedral, to mark the twenty-first anniversary of the assassination of Mahatma Gandhi. Musicians from Gandhi's homeland performed Indian classical music up at the altar. Then, while the last note from the sitar was still sounding, the Cathedral choir began to sing 'Lead Kindly Light' at the other end of the building. It was a most moving juxtaposition.

★

The London Sinfonietta agreed to accept a piece with the focus on children but left it to John to find the young performers. By a stroke of good fortune, he was in correspondence with just the right lady.

Pat Harrison taught music at the primary school in the village of Little Missenden, in Buckinghamshire. She also ran the Little Missenden Festival of Music and the Arts, which was held each autumn in and around the ancient parish church. This church is famous for a giant thirteenth-century mural of St Christopher, and a play based on the St Christopher legend was a highlight of the Festival in 1962. Pat Harrison planned to put it on again one day, with music. A friend of hers attended the 1968 première of *The Whale* and reported that John Tavener was the most imaginative composer on the British scene. Pat contacted John's publisher, George Rizza, proposing a commission. Word came back that John could not oblige, because he was too busy working on his *Celtic Requiem*. Pat persisted. She sent Rizza the script of the St Christopher play, and spelled out the impressive qualifications of her village and her Festival. It was what she said about her schoolchildren which excited interest at the other end.

On 14 December 1968, John Tavener came to Little Missenden with his mother. They took tea with Pat in her seventeenth-century cottage near the church. St Christopher was not high on John's agenda. He told Pat he was writing something new for children, and wondered if her pupils might like to take part. At this stage, he was toying with the possibility of using village schoolchildren to act out the traditional games on stage, while a choir of more sophisticated children did the singing. Pat invited him to come back to Little Missenden in the New Year and hear what the children at her school could do. The audition was on 28 January 1969. After what he heard, John said he need look no further. Pat Harrison's pupils were to sing in his *Celtic Requiem*, as well as play the games.

Pat Harrison was unusually highly qualified for the position of music teacher in a small village school. She had spent four years in Geneva, studying at the academy of Jacques Dalcroze, the genius of music and movement whose methods helped Nijinsky dance *The Rite of Spring*. As a Dalcroze diploma holder, Pat had confident ideas about choreography and no fear of modern music. John wondered how the children would manage to hit the right note each time they made a vocal entry, when the orchestra might be making outlandish noises. Pat told him not to worry. She was ahead of him. Once he had described the piece to her as 'a gigantic decoration of the chord of E flat', she had been transposing everything sung at school assembly into that key.

John became a regular visitor to Little Missenden, often arriving in a bright yellow Bentley convertible borrowed from Philip Pilkington. Pat says the children loved everything about him: the car, his fancy clothes, his enormous height, his gentle manner, and the zest with which he led the songs and joined in the games. For John, the games were exotic and only to be found in books. For these village children in 1969 they were still part of the playground repertoire. Pat remembers one little girl piping up, 'Oh, Mr Tavener! We don't play it like that!'

After nearly a term of rehearsals, Pat was not best pleased when a professional producer was sent down by the London Sinfonietta, to see how they were getting on.

When he arrived, this grand producer, he said, 'Now then, you children, I know you, you'll be up to all sorts of tricks, well we're not having any of that here.' I couldn't believe it! They adored John and they were very well behaved children, there was NO larking about.

John enjoyed the firm way Pat put this visitor in his place. He has always been drawn to older ladies with sharp minds and sharp tongues. Pat Harrison was in her early sixties, with grown-up children. Like Rhoda Birley, she had social poise, striking looks and a strong personality. She became one of John's friends for life.

★

The first performance of *Celtic Requiem* was to be at the Royal Festival Hall on Wednesday, 16 July 1969. Sixteen of the Little Missenden children, aged between seven and eleven, were chosen to take part. They were needed for rehearsals three days before the performance, so accommodation was provided at a London school. Although their village is only thirty miles from London, many of the children had never been to town before. What excitement there was on the escalators and the tube trains. Pat Harrison remembers the wide eyes and cries of 'That's rude!' which greeted a poster showing 'a girl's bra blowing off in the breeze'. After that, hunt the poster became a favourite London game.

The dress rehearsal was at Sadler's Wells in blistering July heat. Whenever the children were not needed Pat made them lie down on the linoleum, but these rest periods were brief. The hopscotch, the swinging games, the skipping and the jumping were all tightly geared to details in the music. The children took their cues from John. David Atherton conducted the orchestra and the adult singers. Pat remembers a shout going up from Atherton: 'These children are bloody marvellous!'

The rest of the line-up for *Celtic Requiem* was: very high soprano; adult chorus; clarinet, trumpet and trombone; organ; piano; strings; Irish bagpipes; a large percussion section; and an electric guitar.

The packed house for the première paid little attention to the orchestral players and adult singers, who were disposed in three groups at the back of the stage. From the beginning, all eyes at the Festival Hall were on the children. They entered in twos, from the sides of the hall, whispering to each other as they passed through the audience on their way to the platform, where the orchestra was holding an immensely quiet chord of E flat. The little boys carried tambourines. One little girl had a skipping rope tied round her waist. Another was carrying some chalk. A tall girl brought a lace head-scarf and two large safety pins. Already on stage was their large basket of action props. So was their swing – a new one on loan from Hamley's toy shop. They knelt in front of it, still whispering. Gradually, the whispering changed into a chant, which grew louder and louder.

> *Ena mena bora mi*
> *Kisca, lara, mora di*
> Eggs, butter, cheese, bread
> Stick, stock, stone dead.

During this chant they rose up, forming a circle around one little girl. She was 'Jenny Jones', their victim. To the sound of lamentation from the adults, they dressed Jenny in the lace head-scarf. Then they paraded her round the stage.

> We've come to see poor Jenny Jones
> Poor Jenny Jones, Jenny Jones
> We've come to see poor Jenny Jones,
> Is Jenny Jones at home?

At the end of the first movement their chant became a funeral lament, backed by muted trumpet and gentle electric guitar.

> Jenny Jones is dead is dead
> You can't see her now.

At the opening of the second movement, the *Dies Irae*, the girl with the chalk marked out a hopscotch court around Jenny's body. While the adult chorus sang a scat vocal ('dabadaba, dabadaba', representing the trumpets of the Last Judgement), and the orchestra shrieked and banged, the children played a slow-motion game of hopping over the corpse, uncannily synchronized to the shifting accents in the music. Then they moved to the swing, placed the smallest girl on board and pushed her in time to a new rhythm.

> One to earth and one to heaven
> And THIS to carry my soul to heaven.

One swinging game led to another, until

> Die, pussy die
> Shut your little eye
> When you wake
> Find a cake
> Die, pussy die.

This one became enmeshed in a twelve-note series played on the xylophone, dropped to a whisper, then slowed to a stop just as the swing came to rest. The gentle mood was finally broken by the girl with the rope, who started skipping to an urgent new beat:

> Mother, mother, I feel sick
> Send for the doctor, quick, quick, quick.

To ward off evil spirits, the children danced around Jenny's corpse, egged on by the adult chorus, who sang snatches from the *confutatis maledictis* of the *Dies Irae*. When the sound and fury subsided, the children sprinkled earth on the body:

> Ashes to ashes and dust to dust
> If God won't have you, the Devil must.

But Jenny leaped up, and the children scattered, shouting 'THE GHOST!' The boys jumped off the Festival Hall platform into the stalls and raced through the exit doors. The girls stayed on stage and formed a circle round a new victim. Their chant of 'Poor Mary sits a-weeping' brought the second movement to a close.

The last movement, the 'Requiescat in Pace', began with bell-like intoning from the adult choir, ringing changes on the rhythmic pattern 4, 3, 2, 1.

> Come to me, loving Mary
> That I may keen with you your very dear one.

During this Irish lament and prayer to the Virgin Mary, the boys crept back on to the stage. Gradually, the reverent atmosphere was undermined by a corrupt version of 'Mary had a little lamb'.

> Mary had a little lamb
> Her father shot it dead
> And now it goes to school with her
> Between two chunks of bread.

A fluffy toy lamb from the property basket was given a mauling. Pop guns came into play. The soprano clambered above the din, along the high peaks of John's setting of the Henry Vaughan poem, 'They are all gone into the world of light'. Down below, an E flat chord from the Festival Hall organ perverted itself into a series of belches. The children had the last word: 'Her father SHOT it.' Silence. Then the lights went out. Amid the encircling gloom, the adult chorus sang a super-slow, super-quiet version of 'Lead Kindly Light'. The children collected electric tapers from the property basket, 'lit' them, and formed a circle around the lamb, which was held aloft. Two more surprises were in store. First, the sinister reappearance of the ghost of Jenny Jones.

> Mary, I'm on your one step
> Mary, I'm on your two step

Then, the production from the property basket of four giant humming tops in E flat. Humming tops in some societies are harbingers of the risen Christ. Leaving them to work their magic, the children filed from the stage. For a long while, their singing could still be heard in the distance.

> There's red for the soldiers
> And blue for the sailors
> And black for the mourners
> Of poor Jenny Jones.

The tops clattered to a halt. There was a tense silence. Then a huge ovation.

★

Several of the reviewers drew parallels with the music of Benjamin Britten – with the *War Requiem* in particular. These comparisons were intended flatteringly, but John finds them unhelpful. He has always admired Britten's piano playing but has never felt akin to him as a composer. The music of Britten, he says, is 'subjective and emotional', whereas his own music tries to be 'objective and traditional'. Looking back, he sees *Celtic Requiem* as a landmark: the first of his compositions to draw on what he calls 'primordial material'. It also marked the end of his association with David Lumsdaine. Although their musical tastes differed, John has fond memories of the years of friendship. This sentiment is not reciprocated. David Lumsdaine remembers the relationship as 'a very considerable burden'. John was 'too dependent', and he, Lumsdaine, was 'too involved'. In the case of *The Whale*, he was 'definitely *over*-involved!' He needed time for his own compositions. He produced these at the rate of only one a year. Whereas John in 1968 had no fewer than six first performances.

5 : And cause suffocation

Fleet Street knew little and cared less about David Lumsdaine. John Tavener was the photogenic one who made good copy. The August 1969 issue of *Vogue* had a whole Tavener page, divided equally between image and text. On the left, John was pictured on a high stool. The low-angle photograph, taken from down by his Hush-Puppies, emphasized the vast distance between his feet and his waist. On the right, an essay by Marina Warner singled out three of his preoccupations: children, death and the Christian religion. It also noted John Lennon's admiration for his music, and gave him the chance to plug his new opera, *Our Lady of the Flowers*. 'Truly blasphemous,' John told *Vogue* readers. 'It takes the form of a Black Mass, you see.'

Another picture story appeared in the *Daily Mirror* of 5 August. This time the photograph was spread widthways across four columns, above the caption LONG JOHN. It showed him stretched out on a divan, wearing a suit of fashionable cut and a floppy white tie. Once again, a wide-angle lens was used to exaggerate the length of his legs. The text, too, was preoccupied with length. It called on John to stand up:

> Up, up, up, all bone-thin six feet six inches of you. Let's have a long, long look . . .
> Of British composers who are now in their twenties, it seems a fair bet that the Beatles and Long John T. are the ones whose music will echo longest.

The peg for this *Daily Mirror* story was the performance of *The Whale* at a Promenade Concert on 1 August. Reviewing that Prom for *The Times*, William Mann wrote that the Albert Hall and the huge audience were *The Whale*'s natural element. He also noted the contribution made to the performance by the composer himself. As well as playing the Hammond organ, John appeared at the console of the Albert Hall's nineteenth-century monster, 'from which he hauled out sounds of Rheinbergerish tumultuousness'.

*

John's brother Roger remained determined that *The Whale* should be put out on the Apple label. Relations with Ringo Starr were still very good, and at the beginning of January 1970 Roger and his wife Sandra organized a networking party at their home in Barnet Lane, Elstree. It was to start at tea time and end with fireworks. John was to be there with his musician pals, and Ringo was to bring his family. Fancy food and drink were laid on, but the event failed to prosper. Things started to go wrong as soon as Ringo and Maureen arrived in their six-door Pullman Mercedes. After lengthy manoeuvres, which brought traffic chaos to Barnet Lane, it was conceded that the limousine could never enter Roger's drive. He had to negotiate with a neighbour, whose drive was bigger. Although it was a freezing evening, Ringo insisted on leaving his chauffeur to guard the car. Roger and Sandra offered caviar and champagne, but all Ringo wanted was a jam butty and a cup of tea. Fortunately, Roger had learned by now that a butty was a North country sandwich, which must be made with white bread. Butties were served.

The most serious disaster was the firework display itself. Roger had planned for it to be massive, but an early rocket went astray and landed in the box of fireworks, setting the whole lot off.

Progress on the Apple record of *The Whale* remained slow. The drag on proceedings, it seems, was ignorance in the Apple office about how to set up an orchestral recording session. What was needed was someone with the fixing skills of Nicholas Snowman. Eventually, John took his friend Nicholas along to Beatle headquarters in Savile Row. Snowman remembers his first meeting with Ringo, who said enthusiastic things, sent out for chips and tomato sauce, and passed him on to the bunch of smooth young operators who had been put in charge of Apple's corporate affairs. Their drinks cabinet was well stocked and there were some nice touches, like the ice-buckets, shaped and coloured to look like giant apples. But no one here had any grasp at all of the business Snowman was in. He was very happy to take charge. After negotiating a 'colossal' management fee for the London Sinfonietta ('one of the great deals of all time'), he did everything. He booked a church in Islington as the location. He recruited the technical team. He contracted all the artists. He negotiated the royalty deals.

The recording sessions were on July 22, 23 and 24, 1970. John played the organ and the Hammond organ. Alvar Lidell was as immaculate as ever. David Atherton conducted. Roger Tavener stood proudly by. Most of the fun of shouting through loudhailers was shared between Snowman himself, Snowman's father and Snowman's friend Andrew Rosner, but the punchline was given to Ringo Starr. If you are nostalgic for the sixties and listen carefully to the record, it is Ringo's distorted voice you can hear calling out 'and cause suffocation': words salvaged by John from the warning notice on a plastic bag.

PART FOUR

Dark Night

§

1 : Last Rites

In spite of *The Whale* not suiting his Croydon Philharmonic, Myers Foggin was still a Tavener admirer. He had by now left the Royal Academy to become Principal of Trinity College of Music, where one of his tasks was to appoint a new Professor of Composition. He offered the job to John.

So, from the Christmas term of 1968, to his father's delight, John's fees as church organist were boosted by one day of paid employment each week. To begin with, he followed the same timetable as his predecessor: one hour's tuition to each student, in a room at the College, on Fridays. Teaching is of absolutely no interest to him, but he enjoys meeting people, and looked on his students as friends. After all, he was not much older than they were. Several did indeed become friends for life. His favourite, Michael Buckland, has a clear memory of John's arrival at Trinity. Like all the students, Buckland was excited at the prospect of being taught by a real composer – a famous one, who had been on radio and television – but he was quite unprepared for what happened when he arrived for his first lesson. The previous student was still there, talking earnestly to John about his Christian belief. Buckland burst out laughing. John uncoiled himself from his chair and asked what was so funny. He, too, was a committed Christian. Buckland was astounded, both by John's height and by the chronic archaism of a Christian composer in the late twentieth century. During all the years of their subsequent friendship, John has never tried to dislodge Michael from his unbelief.

As Michael Buckland likes to reflect, they became pals simply because he was the last pupil of the day. As he left the College with John at the end of that first lesson, he was asked where he lived. His digs were in Swiss Cottage, conveniently on the way to Wembley Park. John offered him a lift. Michael tried not to look impressed when the car turned out to be an Armstrong Siddeley Sapphire. The lift became a regular event.

Then, after three or four weeks, John announced that he was not going straight home. He would be taking tea in Maida Vale with his friend Philip Pilkington. Would Michael care to join them?

About the actual lessons, Michael is much vaguer. John's memory is of Michael's reluctance to hand over anything he had written. A favourite Buckland evasion was to arrive at his lesson with his manuscript wrapped in brown paper and tied up with string. After picking at the knots for a while, he would assure John 'It isn't worth it, old boy.' John never managed to assess Michael's talents as a composer, but he enjoyed him greatly as a fluent talker. The more conventional of John's friends thought Michael notably eccentric, but he received the usual warm welcome in the Tavener home. He is still a close family friend, although he no longer composes. These days he works as a builder's labourer and writes novels.

Back in 1970, young Michael Buckland was among those roped in by John to stiffen the choir of St John's Presbyterian Church on big occasions. Philip Pilkington was another. Like Buckland, he is not a Christian believer, but he was full of admiration for what John achieved. Wonders were done, he says, with Stravinsky's *Symphony of Psalms* and Tippett's *A Child of our Time*, and there was a 'stunning' performance of Bach's *St Matthew Passion*, augmented by professionals from the London Bach Society, who were persuaded by John to sing for the love of it. A second organ was brought in, which was played by Giles Hewlett-Cooper, another of John's pupils at Trinity. Philip Pilkington played the regular church organ, minus the pedals. John was the conductor.

In Philip Pilkington's view, the choir and congregation of this staid church were immensely lucky to be caught up in the whirlwind of John's musical enthusiasm. Another witness from those days who became a lifelong friend was Penny Turton, the youngest of the regular choir members. She says the choir knew exactly how fortunate it was. The elderly Scots ladies in hats, who formed its nucleus, all adored John. Choir practice on Thursday nights always tingled, and was always followed by a session in the pub, where John beamed and glowed, surrounded by people of all ages, musical abilities and lifestyles. Some of his students were very wild. The Scots ladies were very proper. Young choir members like Penny Turton were starry-eyed.

After *The Whale* John was in great demand, so on some Sundays a deputy organist was needed at St John's. Occasionally John's father stood in, but more often the gap was filled by Giles Hewlett-Cooper, a flamboyant homosexual who insisted the church folk should take him on his own terms. One hot summer Sunday, he reported for duty stripped to the waist and wearing a hat. The Revd Cameron Joyce was unfazed. 'Ah, Giles,' he greeted him, 'I see we are Jewish today,' but even this kindly greeting was not entirely to Giles's liking. He preferred to be addressed as Lord Audley, although he had no conventional claim to such a title. Sometimes he brought a friend to share the organ bench. If the sermon seemed too long, then the two young men would start to take a playful interest in each other. One of these friends of Giles – the one called Roger – liked to come to the church dressed in pink satin hot pants, but there were no complaints. Penny Turton thinks that Giles, as John's apprentice, was protected by the spell his master cast over the church elders. In any case, she says, Giles was a gifted musician and a ruthlessly honest person, with a spiritual ache beneath his outlandish surface.

Unlike Giles, John was entirely non-confrontational, but Penny could see he only ever did exactly what suited him. He listened with an air of grave concern to all the representations made to him about the pace at which he took the hymns. Many in the congregation simply did not have the breath to sing so slowly. John bowed his head. The speed of the hymns altered not at all.

Performing music as an act of worship, rather than for entertainment, meant a great deal to John and the relationship with the minister, Cameron Joyce, was of the highest importance. Cameron Joyce's family background was Northern Ireland Protestant, and he spoke with a hint of an Ulster accent. He was tall and red-faced, with close-cropped white hair and a thin white moustache. According to Philip Pilkington's account there was no charisma, but 'a quiet spirituality'.

Cameron Joyce's wife Jane was also from Ulster. Penny Turton knew the couple well. They had no children of their own, and cared deeply for John. They lived in a cold, sombre mansion flat in Kensington, provided by the church. Tea there on a winter's day was a dismal experience. 'They never put the lights on until you could hardly see anybody. You sat in the gathering gloom, with this heavy, brown Victorian tablecloth.' And yet, Penny says, they were not without a love of beauty.

It was Cameron Joyce who introduced John to the films of Ingmar Bergman. They went together to such grim masterpieces as *Wild Strawberries* and *The Seventh Seal*. Looking back, John sees Cameron Joyce himself as a Bergmanesque figure, racked with doubt, for whom the world was a chilly place. He would often advise John that 'Life is a

creeping tragedy.' When Easter Sunday came round, he had great difficulty in preaching a sermon. He believed Christ was his Saviour, but he
did not believe in the Resurrection. He used to break down in the pulpit,
shaking his head and saying over and over again, 'I don't know.' He
was not unsympathetic when John talked to him of his fascination with
the rites of the Roman Church.

★

John's affair with Catholicism could not be disentangled from the
troubled feelings aroused in him by an extraordinary young woman.
Jean Andersson was the daughter of a member of his choir, Betty
Andersson: a Scotswoman married to a Catholic of Scandinavian
descent. Jean herself was in her early twenties and striking to look at:
six feet tall and big boned. She played the guitar, sang in a high clear
voice and spoke fluent Spanish, which she learned in Mexico when she
was doing Christian work as a prison visitor. Although she was a deeply
committed Catholic, she sometimes visited her mother's church. John
remembers one occasion near Christmas, when she brought her guitar
and sang and played 'Tomorrow Shall Be My Dancing Day', the medieval carol in which Christ on the Cross addresses sinful man as his 'true
love' and calls him to the dance eternal.

John spent every possible moment with Jean, magnetized by the intensity of her religious zeal. She introduced him to the poetry of the
sixteenth-century Spanish mystic, San Juan de la Cruz. He was very
taken with the way San Juan used sexual imagery to suggest the union
of the soul with the Godhead, but he was not ready for the moment
when Jean, sitting on the sofa with him in Wembley Park, told him she
loved him and was going into a convent. He still has the crucifix she
presented to him that day.

He was allowed to visit her during her trial periods at the Convent
of the Sacred Heart in Caterham. There she was among the other
novices, dressed in a white shift. She appeared to be trembling. He
thought she was crying, but when he got to speak to her, it turned out
she had been giggling at the look on his face. He was warned by her
Mother Superior that nuns are in favour of 'opening wounds'.

The relationship with Jean had begun before he started to write *Celtic
Requiem*. The work is dedicated to her. She was allowed out of the
convent to attend the première and the reception afterwards, but was
frankly unimpressed by the music. John's wound took a long time to
heal.

Jean Andersson is seen in retrospect by John as one in the line of what he calls his 'Muses': the inspirational figures who have played major roles in the drama of his emotional life. From the stability of today, he looks back on thirty years of turmoil. During all that time, the women he cared about most were placed on pedestals and left untouched, while he found physical comfort with mortal creatures who lacked the power to inspire. This dichotomy was to bring misery to all concerned.

*

Jean Andersson's monument is all the music John wrote to celebrate the poetry and the life of San Juan de la Cruz.

San Juan was a Carmelite friar at a time when the Carmelites in Spain were deeply divided. In 1577 he was kidnapped by friars from a rival wing of the order, who beat him systematically and kept him for many months in a dungeon, where his wounds became infested with maggots. One hot summer evening, as he lay swooning in his stifling cell, he heard a young man's voice singing a love song in the street outside. The words of the song were 'I am dying of love, my dearest. What shall I do? I shall die.' They sent him into ecstasy, and he composed the mystic poem 'Dark Night', about the soul that rejoices on reaching the height of perfection, which is union with God.

Two verses from 'Dark Night' are included in the first Tavener composition of 1970; an intensely devotional work called *Nomine Jesu*, which dwells on a single chord, and a single word: Jesus. It is written for mezzo-soprano, two choirs, two alto flutes, amplified harpsichord, chamber organ and five male speaking voices, who deliver readings from the Gospels. There are three sections.

The first section has ecstatic sobbing of the Holy Name by the mezzo-soprano, while the choirs keep repeating the name of Jesus in five European languages, using just one chord. An aching sense of unfulfilment comes from this chord (D, C sharp, E, G, B), which is dying to resolve on to the chord of D. As might be expected from John, it bears a meaning beyond the musical. Taking his cue from San Juan's equation of erotic love with love Divine, and referring obliquely to Jean Andersson, he has intensified the chord of A ninth which opens Stephen Foster's romantic ballad 'I dream of Jeannie with the light brown hair'.

The middle section of *Nomine Jesu* introduces the African and Asiatic languages, and comes to a climax with a wild outburst of speaking-in-tongues.

The final section is slow and tender, with a soulful melodic line for the mezzo-soprano, who sings elegiac verses by San Juan de la Cruz, while the choirs quietly maintain their Jesus chord.

*

Nomine Jesu got its first exposure in odd circumstances. BBC Television was running an educational series called *Making Out*, about young people's achievements in various walks of life. To illustrate the composer's lot, they chose John Tavener. *Nomine Jesu* was just finished, so why not see it in rehearsal? Television equipment was installed in Westminster Cathedral. The apse was brightly lit. Musicians were booked to appear in rehearsal clothes. John conducted, wearing a shirt of shimmering silver-blue. An opening announcement described him as 'a deeply religious man, who derives his inspiration from ecclesiastical atmospheres like this'. After which, the rehearsal was relegated to deep background while anchor-man Magnus Magnusson, stationed up in the Cathedral gallery, conducted an enquiry into the music business.

Hauled before the camera and asked how easy it was to 'Make Out' as a composer, Lennox Berkeley said it was a tough profession. Magnus Magnusson submitted that it was less tough for John than for most, because his parents supported him and he had a wealthy patron. That was the cue for film of John arriving at Charleston Manor in his Armstrong Siddeley Sapphire, and engaging in badinage with Lady Birley.

The key witness, John's publisher George Rizza, was grilled about money. Rizza was adamant that, in spite of John's international success, his earnings were tiny, 'because he finds it extremely difficult to compose tailor-made music'. This led to another film clip, of John sitting alone at the grand piano in Charleston Manor, with a prepared statement:

> I go for months and months without composing a note . . . I cannot reconcile the idea of a profession and that of a composer. I have no sympathy with the puritanical concept of work for its own sake . . . I started *Nomine Jesu* after a four-month gap. Then I rang my publisher when it was nearly finished, and he found a commission for it.

Making Out was broadcast on 2 April 1970. Shortly after that, passing a used-car dealership in South London on his way to Charleston, John swapped his Armstrong Siddeley Sapphire for his first Bentley: a 1947 Mark VI, which had lost its front passenger seat.

*

Still within the orbit of Jean Andersson, John wrote a companion piece to *Nomine Jesu*. He called it *Coplas* (Verses), after San Juan's poem 'Coplas hechas sobre un éxtasis' ('Verses written on an ecstasy'), the opening lines of which he used as an hypnotic refrain.

> *Entréme donde no supe,*
> *y quedéme no sapiendo,*
> *todo sciencia transcendiendo.*
>
> I entered where I knew not,
> And stayed uncomprehending,
> All knowledge transcending.

The Spanish text sets the mystical tone, but the musical heart of the piece is the *Crucifixus* from Bach's Mass in B Minor. John remembers how the seed of the composition was planted. It was during a car journey, when he turned on the radio and found himself listening to the very last bars of the *Crucifixus*: the final *sepultus est* (He was buried). Believing all things are meant, he treasured the moment and gradually formulated his response: a composition which treats the Bach as a talisman, or sacred object.

Coplas is written for soprano, alto, tenor and bass soloists, and a chorus of sixteen voices. The lines from San Juan de la Cruz are broken into syllables and divided among the soloists. The text of the *Crucifixus* is similarly fragmented, and delivered by the chorus as a succession of immensely long-held *legato* chords. In the score, John instructs 'Dynamics throughout should be as quiet as humanly possible.'

Both the solo line and the choral harmonies are derived from the music of Bach, whose presence at first is only a distant glow. As *Coplas* draws on, we meet Johann Sebastian face to face, when a tape of four-bar phrases from his *Crucifixus* intervenes seven times. On the seventh occasion, Bach's final *sepultus est*, powerful and quiet, buries the words of San Juan de la Cruz and the music of John Tavener.

The first performance of *Coplas* was at the Cheltenham Festival on 9 July 1970. Six months later it joined *Nomine Jesu* and *Celtic Requiem* on the LP put out by Apple as a follow-up to *The Whale*.

*

Long before the first performance of *Coplas*, John had started to feel that it should form part of a much bigger statement. The way the Bach *Crucifixus* submerged his own music seemed akin to the mystical idea of 'dying to oneself'. In an expanded work, he could offer a meditation on the crucifixion as annihilation of self in favour of something greater.

The scheme that started to emerge was in five movements, with *Coplas* as the last of them. Placed immediately before it would be *Coplas en el Espejo* (Verses in the Mirror), a purely orchestral movement, unfolding the material of *Coplas* in reverse order, with handbells, flutes and oboes marking the *ostinato* of Bach's *Crucifixus*. The central movement would be *Nomine Jesu*, under its Spanish title *El Nomen del Cristo*, and with two additions: brass instruments to expand the Pentecostal climax; and a deep church bell, sounded three times, to signal the centre point and usher in readings of Christ's words at the Last Supper. Movements one and two would be newly written, as pre-echoes of movements four and five.

The architecture of Stravinsky's *Canticum Sacrum* was no doubt at the back of John's mind when he drew up this scheme, but his ambition was for something on a grander scale: an hour-long composition, needing four choirs and large instrumental forces. He was reluctant to give up all his time to it, until he could see there was a chance of a performance. The chance came with Mario di Bonaventura, an American conductor and patron of the arts, who was in London shopping for talent. He contacted George Rizza, who persuaded him that John was the composer he was looking for. A meeting was arranged, and John described to Bonaventura the outline of his new piece, which by now had a title: *Ultimos Ritos*, or *Last Rites*. Bonaventura came up with what seemed to John an enormous commissioning fee. The composition of *Ultimos Ritos* occupied most of the next twelve months.

The first movement is both the mirror and the counterweight of *Coplas*, the last. Whereas at the end of *Coplas* Bach's *Crucifixus* gently puts John's music to sleep, the first movement starts with a savage dissonance, played *fortissimo* by the orchestra, in which all the notes of Bach's choral line for the word 'Crucifixus' are piled on top of one another. This physical shock is John's answer in music to the famous drawing by San Juan de la Cruz of Christ on the cross: a powerful image of brutality, showing the scene from above, in exaggerated perspective, with vicious nails big in foreground. After the chord, two of the four choirs harshly voice the syllables of the *Crucifixus* text, which have been arranged in reverse order and split into groups of increasing size. The effect is like the insistent hammering of nails. Meanwhile, the other two choirs share the first verse of San Juan's poem, 'Canciones a lo divino de Cristo y el alma' ('Lyrics concerning Christ and the soul'). This pastoral allegory tells of a young shepherd who dies, high in a tree, with his arms spread wide, because his heart has been wounded by love. The musical material is based on a sixteenth-century Spanish love song. When the first verse of the poem reaches its end, and the backwards text of the *Crucifixus* has arrived at its beginning, there is another 'crucifixion' chord from the orchestra. Then all four choirs quietly share San Juan's second verse. As in *Coplas*, where Bach's music intervenes, there are here seven interventions. This time they are made by soprano recorders, which pipe a clear account of the Spanish love song previously implied. At the end comes the opening chord again, but now it is quiet and pulsing.

The second movement is spectacular and intensely ritualistic. Essential to it is the space and reverberance of a large building, preferably a cathedral. Like the first movement, it is in two distinct parts. The first is a setting for twelve bass voices and seven high trumpets of San Juan's 'Cantar del alma que se huelga de conoscer a Dios por fe' ('Song of the soul that rejoices in knowing God through faith'). This poem dwells on the mystery of the waters of the eternal spring, which for Christians lie concealed within the bread and wine of Holy Communion. There are twelve short stanzas, each one ending

> *Aunque es de noche*
> Although it is night

John instructs his twelve basses to stand in a circle, facing inwards. They are to chant 'meditatively', but they must 'enunciate meaningfully'. The thrilling confusion this will produce in an echoey building is compounded by having a staggered start: the second bass begins when the first bass reaches his second line, and so on. Seven times during this overlapped chanting, twelve-note fanfares on piccolo trumpets sound from the top gallery.

The second half of the second movement is voiceless, relying for its effect on the geographical spread of instrumental sound. Timpani thunder from the four corners of the building, supported by growling trombones placed in the middle. Six recorders are in a low gallery. Six trumpets are on high. More flutes and trumpets are at ground level. The slow and solemn dialogue that develops between up and down is John's way of representing in music 'the descent of the Eucharist': the real presence of Christ during the service of Holy Communion. The blocks of sound suggest the harmonies of Bach's *Crucifixus*. They close on the chord of E minor and usher in the middle movement, 'El Nomen del Cristo', where Christ's name is celebrated.

Like *In Alium* four years earlier, *Ultimos Ritos* exploits music's spatial dimension, but this time there is a graver spiritual purpose. The work as a whole is intended as a symbol of the crucifixion: the four outer movements are the foot, head and arms of the cross. The central movement is the man. The layout of singers and instrumentalists is cruciform, with timpani to the north, south, east and west. And for the first time, John chooses instruments for their symbolic significance: trumpets for royalty; flutes and recorders for love; timpani and bass trombones for the evil forces of this world.

2 : The little flower

San Juan de la Cruz was not the only enthusiasm of Jean Andersson's to rub off on John. There was also her devotion to the example of the French Carmelite nun, St Thérèse of Lisieux: a devotion shared by Father Malachy Lynch, head of the Carmelite order in England, who had a framed photograph of Thérèse hanging on the wall of his cell. This photograph was always dressed with white roses, the saint's favourite flower. Thérèse became a big talking point during John's visits to Allington Castle.

★

Thérèse Martin was born in Normandy in 1873, the ninth and last child of pious Catholic parents. When she was four years old, her mother died. She clung instead to her seventeen-year-old sister Pauline, and when this surrogate mother entered the Carmelite convent at Lisieux, Thérèse became extremely ill. She suffered from uncontrollable fits of shaking, known as St Vitus' Dance, which no medicine could cure but which went away miraculously when she had a vision of the Virgin Mary smiling at her. After that, she dedicated her life to loving God.

When she was fourteen she insisted she was ready to enter the Carmelite convent. Her local bishop refused permission because she was under age, so she went with her father to Rome and put her case before the Pope. Acknowledged to be an exception, she was allowed to enter the convent in April 1888, when she was just fifteen years old. She dreamed of herself as a priest and as a glorious martyr, but knew these were impossible dreams and settled instead for a doctrine of her own devising: the 'Little Way', in which the most trivial things she did were offered to God as acts of love, and prayers went up to Jesus for 'a whole multitude of souls who share my littleness'. She referred to herself as 'the little flower'.

Her sister Pauline eventually became her Mother Superior, and
ordered her to write her autobiography. This she did, while suffering
agony from the ravages of tuberculosis. On her death-bed, after a
desperate crisis of faith, she resolved to spend her eternity doing good
on earth. She died in 1897, aged twenty-four, and her autobiography
was published a year later, as *The Story of a Soul*. Millions of copies
were sold around the world, and sightings of her were reported in many
countries. During the First World War, she made miraculous appear-
ances in the trenches. By 1918 five hundred letters a day were arriving
at the convent, attesting to her holiness. By 1923 the daily number of
letters had risen to one thousand.

She was canonized in 1925. St Peter's Cathedral in Rome was
garlanded with roses for the occasion, which was attended by thirty-four
cardinals, two hundred bishops and a congregation of sixty thousand.
During the proceedings, rose petals fell mysteriously from on high.

★

John identified strongly with Thérèse's physical suffering, her short life,
her spiritual intensity and her agony of doubt. She would be an ideal
subject for an opera, and it seemed Covent Garden was about to invite
him to write one.

The Production Director Peter Hall, the Music Director Colin Davis
and the General Administrator, Sir John Tooley, had drawn up a list of
composers who might be commissioned by the Royal Opera House.
John Tavener's name was high on that list, endorsed by Benjamin
Britten, who had heard *Celtic Requiem* and advised Tooley that here
was a composer of significance. In the summer of 1971, Davis, Hall and
Tooley came to Wembley Park for dinner.

Peter Hall had a good conversational opener: he had recently invited
the firm of Tavener to make proposals for the improvement of his
country cottage. Then John did his best to sell them his Black Mass
opera, based on Genet's *Our Lady of the Flowers*. Peter Hall was not
keen. He dismissed Genet as 'adolescent'. The three men from Covent
Garden wondered what else John might have in his locker. John
launched into the story of St Thérèse of Lisieux. He spoke with
missionary zeal, but the reception was lukewarm. Peter Hall wondered
how one conjured operatic excitement from the life of a girl who did
nothing and went nowhere. John quoted Father Malachy's paradox:
that on a deeper level Thérèse had done everything and been everywhere.
The visitors still felt this interior drama would be hard to render theatri-

cally. Nevertheless, at the end of the evening St Thérèse looked a better bet than Jean Genet.

Not long after that dinner, John's publisher, George Rizza, discovered that Genet was unlikely ever to agree to his book being turned into John's opera. Eventually, after a conference in Tooley's office, St Thérèse of Lisieux became the official subject of the Covent Garden commission. The hunt was on for the right librettist. Once it became known that John was intending an opera about Thérèse, Catholics of the most depressing sort started beating a path to his door. They seemed to gloat over the prospect of making the audience suffer. One fanatic in particular was convinced it was his mission to turn Covent Garden into a vale of tears. He said John was sure to become ill while composing the music, and announced that his own daughter had already contracted meningitis. John's parents feared this dismal creature might become a Wembley Park regular.

Meanwhile, demand was growing for Tavener the media personality. BBC Television at the time was running a documentary series called *One Man's Week*. In each programme, someone famous was followed by a film crew for seven days. One of the chosen celebrities was Ariana Stassinopoulos, undergraduate at Girton College, Cambridge, darling of the Young Tories and President of the Cambridge Union. The centrepiece of her *One Woman's Week* was to be a Union debate, chaired by her, on the motion 'Criticism is killing art'. The star speaker was to be André Previn, but at the last minute he withdrew and John received an urgent invitation from the BBC. He drove up to Cambridge with his friend Philip Pilkington, who helped him cobble together a speech in defence of the critics. It turned on the comic paradox that a bad review of a piece by Stockhausen could give more pleasure than the music itself. The Cambridge Union enjoyed the joke and the evening brought John a double dividend. First, he became a regular at the Belgravia home of the Stassinopoulos family and constant companion to Ariana's sister, Agape. Secondly, BBC Television gave him a *One Man's Week* of his own.

*

One Man's Week: John Tavener was broadcast on 17 October 1971. It provides a handy snapshot of the public John Tavener at that date: naïve, provoking and engagingly frank. His first words, delivered while he sprawls on the sun-lounger on his lawn, are 'A great deal of my summer is spent lying on my back in the garden.' In the next scene, he

is at the wheel of his Bentley. 'There's something about the largesse of
this car which allows my mind to expand,' he explains, as he cruises to
Little Missenden for a rehearsal of the piece he has written for Pat
Harrison's Festival.

His three-minute canon, for flutes, chamber organ and handbells is
called *In Memoriam Igor Stravinsky*. The musical material is from a
Spanish folk song. The rehearsal takes place in Little Missenden's bijou
parish church, with John conducting. He tells the viewers that this is
the first time he has heard the piece, except in his head, and he rather
likes 'the grey and colourless sounds that emerge'.

Next stop is Aylesford, and the evening atmosphere of the outdoor
shrine. This is the place where music should be performed, John says.
Here or in cathedrals. Or in caves. Anywhere except in concert halls.
Then he becomes confidential about his opera *Our Lady of the Flowers*,
which 'is incredibly blasphemous and deals with homosexual mastur-
bation'. He goes on to talk about the opera Covent Garden has
commissioned from him, on the subject of St Thérèse of Lisieux, 'who
lived a life dominated by physical suffering, and died in excruciating
agony at the age of twenty-four'. He announces his intention of turning
those twenty-four years into twenty-four scenes, or games, with Thérèse
singing throughout. He also reveals that he has found a librettist, and
he takes the TV crew to meet her.

She is Ann Prior, a successful young novelist, who lives on a houseboat
on the Thames near Oxford. On this lovely summer day in 1971 John
sees no clouds ahead. He tells Ann Prior that Scene 1 of the opera should
be a mirror image of Scene 24. At the beginning, Thérèse should be in
the grip of St Vitus' Dance, which is the dance of the Devil. At the end,
freed by death from the tuberculosis gnawing her hip, she should dance
in the Court of Heaven, to the medieval carol 'Tomorrow Shall Be My
Dancing Day'.

One Man's Week moves on to Allington Castle, where John has
brought Ann Prior to meet Father Malachy Lynch. This bright-eyed,
rosy-cheeked priest once visited the convent at Lisieux and had the
privilege of gazing through a grille at Thérèse's surviving sister, Céline.
In a strong Irish brogue he warns that 'a great deal of sentimentality
has been wasted on St Thérèse. She was in reality very serious. A mystic,
and a very simple one.' The camera lingers on a corner of Father
Malachy's cell, where white roses decorate Thérèse's photograph.

The final event in *One Man's Week* is dinner with his old friend Philip
Pilkington, who by now is married and living in a palatial home in

London's Little Venice. John explains to viewers that he dines here 'three or four times a week'. Other friends from student days are also here tonight, and there is much giggling. John's commentary explains that 'although we all know a considerable amount about music, we never talk about it. We're usually far too drunk.' After dinner, drunk or not, he performs a scene from Mozart's *Così fan tutte*, playing all the parts.

★

John has always said it would be impossible for him to make the compromises that go with writing film music, but he did once agree to try: when he was invited to compose a song for Elizabeth Taylor. She was to star in a screen version of the Dylan Thomas radio play *Under Milk Wood*, and the producers thought a score by Tavener would be a trendy touch of class. The test piece was to be the song that Miss Taylor would sing in the character of Rosie Probert: 'What seas did you see, Tom Cat, Tom Cat?'

John did his best to obey the formula 'easy on the ear and easy on the voice'. It was a miserable experience, and he remembers drinking a lot of whisky while he was about it. He describes the resulting music as 'rather cool, tonal, near to the more tender moments of Stravinsky's *Perséphone*, or *The Rake's Progress*'. He sent his demonstration tape to the *Milk Wood* production office. Word came back that the song was very nice, but Miss Taylor could not sing it.

A happier experience with the world of bespoke music began when he was approached by the stage director Braham Murray. So impressed had Murray been by *The Whale* that he wrote John one of those 'You don't know me but . . .' fan letters. He says he had no idea that he and John would ever work together. 'I simply thought I have to get in touch with the person who wrote this. Because it's thrilling!' He was with the 69 Theatre Company, based in Manchester, but he often came to London. A meeting with John was arranged, and the two became friends. Braham Murray has hazy but warm memories of life on the town with John. There was fun. There were girls. John drove him everywhere in his Bentley. 'He was normally extremely inebriated and it was very alarming!'

They developed an idea for a piece of music theatre based on the quest for the Holy Grail, but the project never got off the ground. Then Braham was approached by Mia Farrow's agent, asking if he would be interested in directing her in a stage play. He was extremely interested. Mia Farrow had become a household name in Britain through the

American TV serial *Peyton Place*, and scored another hit when she played the lead in Roman Polanski's horror film *Rosemary's Baby*. Formerly married to Frank Sinatra, she was now living in England with her second husband André Previn, conductor of the London Symphony Orchestra, and she wanted to make a low-key return to the stage. When she was eighteen she had played Cecily in the Broadway production of *The Importance of Being Earnest*. Braham Murray was asked to suggest plays which might suit her. He strongly recommended *Mary Rose*, by J. M. Barrie: a three-act ghost story in which the eponymous heroine hovers between this world and the spirit world of a magic Scottish island. It seemed to him perfect for her. She agreed. The play calls for some music, both frightening and beautiful, to represent the island's seductive power. Braham wanted something just like *The Whale*, and John was happy to oblige.

Mary Rose opened at the University Theatre in Manchester, home of the 69 Theatre Company, on 2 May 1972. Rehearsals were in London, at a disused ballroom in Victoria. John attended the first read-through, and it was on this occasion that he and Mia Farrow met. It has not been forgotten by either of them. Mia Farrow can still see John coming through the door: 'eccentric-looking, taller than he is now, very thin, and elaborately clad'. John recalls 'an instant connection'.

When the cast moved up to Manchester, John went too. Braham Murray had arranged for him to pre-record the music, using choristers from Manchester Cathedral. John and Mia Farrow spent their evenings exploring what they had in common, including a shared enthusiasm for wine. On the eve of the dress rehearsal, John remembers, they stayed out all night. They found a restaurant in the seedy part of town which let them drink until 3 a.m., with the unlikely bonus of Tchaikovsky's *Nutcracker Suite* as background music. When it closed, Mia said the time had come for her to hear John play the organ. Since she was a Catholic and John was a fellow traveller, the setting should be a Catholic church. They drove around until they found one, but it was locked. Mia spotted the doorbell to the priest's quarters, and kept ringing it until the holy man appeared. He was in his pyjamas. She gave her name, repeating it several times. She said she hoped he knew who she was. Then she explained her urgent need to hear her friend play the organ. The priest was neither impressed nor amused. He told her he didn't care who she was, and slammed the door. After some further exploration of Manchester's darkened and locked buildings, and an abortive attempt to drive to Liverpool, the two friends sat down to continue their heart-to-heart on the kerb outside their hotel at six o'clock in the morning. John remembers there was romantic talk of following the example of Mary Rose, the heroine of the play, and vanishing to an island in the Outer Hebrides. What they decided to do in the end was go into the hotel and have breakfast.

Mia Farrow fitted exactly into John's category of Muse, and the two stayed good friends. When *Mary Rose* transferred to Brighton, he introduced her to the draughty delights of the Seaford Head Hotel. She pronounced it lovely. He took her to Charleston Manor, where she was drawn to Lady Birley and even more fascinated by the intensity of John's feelings for this ravaged 72-year-old beauty, described by someone as 'like a Picasso whore'. When *Mary Rose* came to the Shaw Theatre in London, in July 1972, John and Mia met regularly in town, often with Braham Murray making up a threesome. Braham had plans to cast Mia as Joan of Arc, in a new play he would be directing in York Minster.

John by now had traded his Bentley for a Rolls Royce. Mia remembers the day the Rolls got stuck in traffic. John became so frustrated that he leaped out, escorted her to the pavement, and led her away, insisting, 'It doesn't matter.' John remembers the day Mia made a snap decision that he should drive her to Westminster Cathedral, so she could confess her sins. When she emerged from the confessional the priest came out too, and stared after her, thunderstruck. John succumbed to what he now calls 'an absolutely bonkers idea'. His friend Clive Wearing, conductor of the London Sinfonietta Chorus, held a senior position in Westminster Cathedral Choir School. John took Mia into the school to see him and asked, 'Is there any possibility she could develop the voice to sing the part of Thérèse in my opera, when it goes on at Covent Garden?' He remembers Clive making Mia go up and down the scales, and saying, politely, 'Aha, I think there *is* a possibility there.' On sober reflection, the idea was dropped but Mia continued to feel part of the Tavener family. She still does. Interviewed for this book, she said that, although they can't see each other much these days, John and she are still of one mind: 'Joined at the hip or something. There's no one on this planet more like me than John . . . This kindredness, that is unexplainable and undeniable, has been an extremely powerful influence on my life. It's just a pity he's so far away . . . I'd like to see him all the time. I wish he was round the corner.'

★

On 8 June 1972, while *Mary Rose* was playing in Brighton, a new piece by John was premièred at the Queen Elizabeth Hall, as part of a concert by the London Sinfonietta. *Canciones Españolas* are settings of six Spanish folk songs about love and death, for two high voices, two flutes, organ, harpsichord and percussion. Acting as both prelude and postlude is the instrumental canon previously published as *In Memoriam Igor Stravinsky*. The première of this modest and charming piece was conducted by John. It was the last music he wrote for the London Sinfonietta under the original management. In the autumn of 1972 the special relationship ended, when Nicholas Snowman took a job in Paris as director of music projects at the Pompidou Centre. Even before Snowman left, a gap had opened up between John and the orchestra. At the same time, a new haven for his music had appeared.

Martin Neary had been appointed organist and choirmaster of Winchester Cathedral in 1971. He also took charge of the annual Southern Cathedrals Festival, which involved the choirs of Winchester, Salisbury and Chichester. What the 1972 festival needed, he decided, was sacred music from new composers, and the first one he approached was John Tavener. Among the options he put to John was a setting of the Mass.

In the spring of 1972, when his thoughts were turning to the Neary commission, John heard of the death of Father Malachy Lynch. He would badly miss this unusual priest, who had counselled against haste whenever John threatened to fling himself into the arms of the Catholic Church. Father Malachy had been a great promoter of the ecumenical spirit. John remembers seminars at Allington Castle attended by all types of believer, from Methodist to Sufi. It was here, as a teenager, that he first heard the term 'Russian Orthodox' and caught sight of the head of the Russian Church in England, Archbishop Anthony Bloom.

Father Malachy's funeral was held on 10 May 1972 at the outdoor shrine at Aylesford. John remembers the service was very dramatic. 'When they got to the *Dies Irae* in the *Requiem Mass*, there was lightning and a gigantic clap of thunder, and everybody had to run for shelter. And there was his body in the open coffin, with rain pouring in. I think he would have enjoyed the irony of that.'

As so often with John, death triggered music. The seven-note theme he heard in his head when he was leaving the funeral service became the kernel of the *Little Requiem for Father Malachy Lynch*. This short work, in three movements, uses fragments from the Latin Mass for the Dead. It is written for choir, two flutes, trumpet, organ and string orchestra. When it was finished, he sent it to Martin Neary, hoping it would do for the Southern Cathedrals Festival. Although it was not Anglican, Martin Neary found it exceeded all expectations. He still talks about the piece with huge enthusiasm. What thrilled him was the way John exploited 'the daunting musical discipline of serialism', to produce something which worked magnificently in the reverberance of Winchester Cathedral. For Neary, the *Little Requiem* marks a watershed in John's career, and a new high in modern church music. He loves to point out that the melody, which came into John's head at the funeral, 'is actually a serial theme, of seven notes. And they work most beautifully in retrograde and inversion.' All the harmony, too, arises from those same notes. 'Which other composer', asks Neary, 'would have been able to use serial technique so beautifully, in terms of melody and harmony? John was quite capable of writing in a modern way, but he showed in this work that he could write in a way that communicated instantly!'

This did not mean that the *Little Requiem* was immediately easy to sing. It was quite unlike anything normally found in the library of Anglican anthems, and the Cathedral choir struggled when Martin Neary first took them through it. He was grateful for John's inspiring presence at the later rehearsals.

The first performance was given in Winchester Cathedral on 29 July 1972, by the Choirs of the Southern Cathedrals and the Bournemouth Sinfonietta. Among the enthusiastic audience was Martin Cooper, music critic for the *Daily Telegraph*, who wrote that this short piece had a 'deeply touching character, worked out with a wholly contemporary sensibility'.

Martin Neary determined to have music by Tavener again the following year. Since John would be too busy with *Thérèse* to fulfil a new commission, it was decided to stage the *Celtic Requiem* in Winchester Cathedral: a decision encouraged by the success of that work in the Albert Hall, as part of the 1972 season of Promenade Concerts.

Another fan of *Celtic Requiem* was film director Ken Russell, who had heard the Apple recording and detected cinema potential. Indeed, he had written John an enthusiastic letter, saying that the character of Jenny Jones was perfect for a film he was dreaming up: 'a modern *Fantasia*'. John remembers going round to Russell's house in Ladbroke Square and sitting on the swing in the garden while Ken outlined his plans. As explained in the letter, one of the plot lines for the film concerned 'the dilemma of a commercials director, trying to go straight, in an industry where integrity is a dirty word'. It sounded intriguing, until Ken announced his vision of the spectacular opening sequence. As John understood it, this would be a crucifixion scene, with chirpy blonde Mandy Rice-Davies, who had figured in a Tory sex scandal, on the cross.

By October, rumours that the village children might star in a Ken Russell film had reached Little Missenden. The local paper said Ken would be at the Festival. He did not appear, and the project fizzled out. But the paper got another story, just as good, when the performance of the *Little Requiem for Father Malachy Lynch* in the parish church was attended by Mia Farrow.

3 : The hell of life

Although she would not be singing in it, Mia Farrow continued to take an encouraging interest in John's opera, *Thérèse*. As a child she had been a victim of polio, and it was believed in her family that the prayers offered to St Thérèse of Lisieux were the reason for her miraculous recovery. Nevertheless, progress on the writing of the opera was slow. The collaboration with Ann Prior was not delivering results, and John confided his worries to Braham Murray. Braham assured him there was only one person to tackle a libretto about the interior life of a saint, and that person was Gerard McLarnon.

For years to come, Gerry McLarnon would be of critical importance to John's creative and spiritual life. Yet the backgrounds of the two men could hardly have been more different. McLarnon grew up in Catholic Belfast during the 1920s. All he ever wanted to be was an actor, and as soon as he left school he joined the Irish touring company of Anew MacMaster, the best Shakespearian actor he had ever seen, 'far above your Oliviers and Gielguds', who had been forced to flee London 'because of some incident in Chelsea baths'. MacMaster 'comprehended completely the hell of life, so that when he went into the dark parts of Oedipus, Othello or Macbeth, he was infallible'.

During the war, Gerry McLarnon came to England and toured with ENSA in a morale-boosting farce called *Why Not Tonight?* After the war, he acted for several years with the Bristol Old Vic. He wrote his first play in 1953, as a result of what he describes as 'a strange accident'. He was out of work, in London, and took a summer evening stroll in Kensington Gardens. 'I saw, walking towards me, a girl whom I knew was dead.' Once she had passed, he realized it could not have been his friend from beyond the grave, but he went home and wrote a play nevertheless. It was about a priest whose sister's body is invaded by another girl. He called it *Unhallowed*. It won an Arts Council prize, and was staged in Scotland. More plays followed. The most notorious was *The Bonefire*, which had its première in Belfast in 1958, produced by Tyrone Guthrie.

The Bonefire is set in contemporary Belfast, during the annual celebration of the Battle of the Boyne, where Protestant William of Orange defeated Catholic King James. The play is strong on background action. Bonfires are lit, effigies of King James and the present Pope are hurled into the flames. The throb of Lambeg drums and the shrieks of Protestant hatred are incessant. In the foreground, a Catholic boy seduces a Protestant girl, for which offence he is blinded and beaten to a pulp by a mob of drunken Orangemen.

Unionists flooded the newspapers with complaints about what one of them called 'a most offensive slur on the Orange Order'. The Mayor of Belfast was petitioned to close the play down. The City Fathers were appalled when Tyrone Guthrie transferred the production to the Edinburgh Festival.

In Edinburgh, Harold Hobson, theatre critic for *The Sunday Times*, watched *The Bonefire* 'first with disgust, then with incredulity, then with horror, and finally with a kind of battered admiration'. He thought the scene in which the mob falls on the Catholic boy 'as awful as anything devised for the theatre since Shakespeare decided that Gloucester's eyes must be put out upon the stage'. When the curtain came down, Hobson stayed in his seat, stunned. He and a clergyman were the last two people to leave the stalls. The clergyman's face was white with distress. 'As we went through the door together, he could not help saying to me, a total stranger, "I have never been so upset in a theatre in my life." I could well understand his emotion.'

Gerard McLarnon likes Catholics no better than Protestants, but he needs the comfort of organized religion. Through his love of Russian literature and his friendship with a family of Russian émigrés, he was drawn to the little world of Russian Orthodoxy in London. This was in the early 1950s, before the London Russians had their own Cathedral. When Gerry met him, the future Metropolitan Anthony of Sourozh was plain Father Anthony Bloom, living in West London with his mother, in a house known as 'the little church', because there was a room where the Orthodox faithful could worship. Gerry's digs were not far from 'the little church'. Once he had been introduced, he became so fascinated by Anthony Bloom and Orthodox Christianity that he went there every day.

Bloom was a cultured individual, nephew of the Russian composer Scriabin. His family had fled Russia after the revolution, and he was educated in Paris. He qualified as a doctor of medicine, fought with the French Resistance during the Second World War, then entered the priesthood. He did not come to England until 1949, but he spoke excellent English, which was just as well for Gerry McLarnon, who spoke no Russian or French. The two used to sit quoting poetry at one other.

Gerry McLarnon was received into the Orthodox faith in 1958. By the time he met Braham Murray, the Anglicans had provided the Russian Orthodox with a surplus church building in South Kensington. This became the Cathedral, where Gerry stood at Bishop Anthony's side during services, wearing a gold coat and performing the office of server.

Plays written by Gerry for the 69 Theatre Company included *The Trial of Joan of Arc*. Braham Murray's plan for it to star Mia Farrow came to nought, but his production, in York Minster, was a big success. He thought Gerry would be ideal as John's collaborator, 'because they both have very pure souls'. When he telephoned Gerry to say a friend needed a libretto for an opera about St Thérèse, Gerry's immediate question was 'Which one?' He was hoping for St Teresa of Avila, the charismatic Spanish nun who inspired San Juan de la Cruz. Gerry still remembers Braham Murray's answer: 'It's the French one, I'm afraid. I don't think she'll give you much help.'

Gerard McLarnon had not heard of John Tavener. When they first met, he discovered that other candidates were still queueing up to write *Thérèse*. 'The most idiotic people possible – fervent Catholics who knew nothing about the theatre, and probably never put pen to paper.' He made his position on Catholics plain. John took him to Oxford to see Ann Prior. All Gerry can remember about her is that she had plans for a musical number on the stage of the Royal Opera House, featuring St Thérèse tapping on her teeth. He was taken to meet John's parents in Wembley Park. They seemed not to mind that he swore like a trooper. He was presented to John Tooley, who said to him, 'You know, Thérèse is a terribly, terribly difficult subject,' before offering him the job of librettist. Gerry took it. He had no idea he would be slogging away at it for the next three years, and waiting for a performance for three more years after that. He has since done a sum which shows his fee worked out at two pounds per week.

He studied Thérèse's autobiography and the vast literature surrounding it. What could he do with this 'little flower' and her short life? He found one incident, at least, which suited his dramatic sense. Thérèse records in her autobiography that when she was a child she heard about 'a poor abandoned wretch who had just been condemned to death for his appalling crimes'. This was Pranzini, a Sicilian who wormed his way into French society and cut the throats of two women and a child in pursuit of his ambition. Thérèse became desperate at the thought that Pranzini might die unrepentant. She prayed and prayed that he might be saved from an eternity in hell, and she asked for a sign. The day after the execution, she secretly defied her father's ban on children reading newspapers and scoured his copy of *La Croix*. She read that when Pranzini was on the scaffold 'he suddenly availed himself of the crucifix which the priest was holding out to him and kissed the sacred wounds three times'. It was a miracle. She adopted Pranzini as 'the first child of my prayers', so Gerry felt entitled to stage a confrontation between the 'little flower' and the forces of darkness.

John and Gerry visited Lisieux. They found there was a nun at the convent, Marie-Lucille, who had been close to Thérèse's sister Céline. Céline had nursed Thérèse when she was dying and it was Céline who had received a visit from Father Malachy Lynch. She died in 1959. John and Gerry were allowed to speak to Marie-Lucille through a grille which, Gerry remembers, was made of plastic. They explained their ambition for the opera. She listened in silence. When they had finished, she called for a piece of paper and wrote one word, in French: *athéiste*. At first they thought the word referred to them. But it turned out to mean that Thérèse lost her faith for periods throughout her life, right up to the close. A startling paradox, but the opera still refused to take shape.

Hoping the muse would descend, John and Gerry used to start their days in Lisieux on the piece of waste ground opposite their hotel, where they waited silently, leaning against trees, with their eyes closed. Gerry remembers the time John fell asleep in this attitude. When he woke up, he called out hopefully, 'Any ideas, Gerry?' The full answer is unprintable.

Back in London, at the end of their working day, John sometimes took Gerry for a relaxing evening with the Pilkingtons, or to the Stassinopoulos family residence. John was still partnering Agape Stassinopoulos at the start of 1973, but something momentous was about to happen.

*

One of John's students at Trinity was an American boy called Martin Kessler. Knowing of John's friendship with Agape, he enthused about his own Greek girlfriend, Vicky, a dancer who had come to London to train at the Royal Ballet School. Victoria Maragopoulou had been at school with Agape in Athens. Why not have a night out as a foursome?

THE HELL OF LIFE

John liked the idea. In March 1973 a trip to the theatre was planned, to see Mia Farrow in Chekhov's *Three Sisters*. But first there would be drinks at the Stassinopoulos place.

As soon as he arrived with Vicky and introduced her to John, Kessler saw danger. Vicky was dark and intense, with good features and huge lustrous eyes. John's first words to her were, 'You look just like Stravinsky's wife.' Then he asked if she had ever done any choreography. She said yes, she had choreographed Messiaen's *Quartet for the End of Time*. John announced he no longer wanted to go to the play. The theatre trip was cancelled and conversation went on until very late. Afterwards, Martin Kessler warned Vicky that being compared to Vera Stravinsky by John was like receiving a proposal. She remembers answering that whoever married him would have a very difficult time. However, when John rang her the next day she immediately agreed to see him again.

Vicky Maragopoulou was twenty-two. She had a lively mind and secular outlook. Her family belonged to the left-wing intelligentsia in Greece, who equated the Church with superstition and corruption. John's religiosity shocked her at first, but she fell in love with him nevertheless. She enjoyed sitting beside him on the organ bench when he played for services at St John's, and she was touched by the painful honesty of Cameron Joyce. John was anxious she should recognize the merits he saw in Catholicism. He took her to services in Westminster Cathedral. He read her poetry by T. S. Eliot. He argued that St Thomas Aquinas had a claim on her because he derived his doctrine from Aristotle.

So far, the Orthodox Church which had claimed Gerry had not captured John's imagination. Although he had never been there, he was for Spain against Gerry's Russia and Vicky's Greece. Then he became side-tracked by a spell of enthusiasm for the charismatic Methodist Donald Soper, who challenged the world from a soap-box in Hyde Park on Sunday afternoons. John took Vicky to hear him. She was strongly attracted by Soper's caring Christianity, which confronted the day-to-day evils of this world. But this was not John's interest. Soper welcomed hecklers, so John tested him. Why, he shouted, did Soper refer so often to God the Father and so rarely to the Mother of God? Philip Pilkington was there. He remembers that Soper looked intrigued by this unusual line of questioning and provided a perfectly rational answer, which acknowledged the importance of the feminine principle. John had been hoping for something more arcane. He pursued Soper to his headquarters in Kingsway, to extend the dialogue. In the end, Soper's Christianity with a social conscience failed to satisfy John's hunger for the transcendental.

★

The writing of the opera, meanwhile, was in the doldrums. It seemed John and Gerry were not the winning combination that Braham Murray had forecast. As a change from Thérèse, John read a new play Gerry had written about the miseries of Job. He became excited by the musical possibilities. There were conferences in Manchester, but no immediate results. And there was still no meeting of minds on how to handle 'the little flower'. Gerry started referring to her as the lamp-post, from which nothing could sprout. Like John, he hated theory. He wrote instinctively and seemed to be stimulated by the smell of hellfire. John had not imagined Thérèse as an opera of unrelieved darkness and despair, but he did not know how to contradict Gerry, who was much older than he was.

What was needed was a mediator, and fortunately John found one. He was Clive Wearing, whose intellect and scholarship came to fill the gap left by David Lumsdaine. John introduced Clive to Gerry, who liked him too, and welcomed his advice.

Conducting the London Sinfonietta Chorus and singing in West-minster Cathedral were just two of Clive Wearing's jobs. He also wrote authoritative articles on early music, particularly the works of Orlandus Lassus, and directed the Lassus Ensemble. John took to telephoning Clive at all hours, and summoning him to Wembley Park several times a week. Luckily for John, Clive Wearing was a workaholic.

★

In July 1973, Granada Television made a TV adaptation of the Celtic Requiem. The whole operation lasted eleven days, and John was there for most of them. First, a complete performance of the music was recorded. Then the children's games were filmed at Little Missenden in the graveyard, the school playground and the woods. Finally, scenes to represent Ireland were filmed on the Pembrokeshire coast. As tokens of their gratitude for the wonders she performed, the Granada team presented Pat Harrison with a humming top and the clapper board.

Celtic Requiem was shown on ITV on Palm Sunday, 7 April 1974, with an introduction spoken to camera by John, looking cool and confi-dent. Other big occasions in 1974 were to be more fraught.

4 : Forgive me

Although the American Mario di Bonaventura had paid good money to commission *Ultimos Ritos*, he never managed to stage it. The opportunity to mount the première was seized instead by Jo Elsendoorn, who ran the Holland Festival. He set up a performance in the Great Church of St Bavo in Haarlem, and persuaded the Dutch and British broadcasters to act as co-producers. They would relay the *magnum opus* to both countries, on both radio and television.

The première was to be on 22 June 1974. Elsewhere in the Holland Festival were church performances of *In Alium* and *Celtic Requiem*. A large contingent of Tavener supporters crossed the Channel, including John's parents, Pat Harrison, Gerry McLarnon, Martin Neary, Penny Turton and Clive Wearing. Vicky was now engaged to John and attended the rehearsals with him. Representing John's publishers were Robin Boyle, who had taken over from George Rizza as managing director, and Sheila MacCrindle, appointed by Chester's to cosset their composers. Robin Boyle had been a choral scholar at King's College, Cambridge. He was hugely enthusiastic about *Ultimos Ritos*, and still is. 'It's a young man's piece, it's "theatre of music" as opposed to "music theatre". It's reckless. It's got four lots of timps, in a church. Trumpeters in the dome. Nobody in their right mind would write a piece like that. But John loves these bold gestures.'

The performers in Holland were the BBC Singers, with mezzo soloist Patricia Fowden-Price; the augmented Dutch Radio Orchestra; and five Dutch actors to read the biblical texts. The conductor was John Poole. An eye-catching set, of cruciform design, was constructed in St Bavo's Great Church. The television coverage was directed by Barrie Gavin, whose wide experience included nothing on this scale. To illuminate the vast spaces of St Bavo's and to capture in sound and image all the far-flung performers, ironmongery was needed in awesome quantities.

John sat among the invited audience. The first four of the five

movements sounded sensational in St Bavo's, but during the last movement, 'Coplas', a disaster occurred which, for John, destroyed the whole
purpose of the piece. The tape of Bach's *Crucifixus*, which was due to enter
seven times, gradually burying his own music, failed to make itself heard. By
the time the third of its seven entries had been missed, he forced himself to
act. Robin Boyle describes what happened. 'John leapt out of his chair and
said "Stop!", stretching out his fingers and pointing like Struwwelpeter. So
they stopped and went back to the beginning of that section, and did it a
second time. And the second time, the tape again failed. "Stop!" John leapt
up. We never had the definitive performance in Haarlem.' 'Coplas' was
played yet again, all the way through this time, still without the Bach. John
made a silent gesture of despair. Pat Harrison remembers 'People were
beginning to leave, so he never got his applause. It was tragic.'

The pandemonium in the cathedral was a mystery to Barrie Gavin.
The tape of the Bach was heard perfectly in the TV control room. It
seems someone had trodden on the cable feeding the cathedral loudspeakers. Fortunately, it was not a live broadcast and there was time
between recording and transmission to edit out the commotion.

The cock-ups were what dominated the press coverage, however.
Hugo Cole in the *Guardian* complained that the whole performance
was geared to the needs of television. Stephen Walsh's piece for the
Observer was headlined TAVENER AND THE TAPE THAT FAILED. John
vowed he would never use tape again.

Martin Neary was shocked by the lack of respect shown for the Great
Church by the Dutch television technicians. 'The nearest thing we got
to incense was the smoke from their cigarettes.' Nevertheless, he went
home convinced by *Ultimos Ritos* and, the following summer, conducted
the British première in Winchester Cathedral. It was a flawless performance, glowingly reviewed, and John wrote him a deeply felt letter of
thanks. Two months later came the London première: a special BBC
Promenade Concert from Westminster Cathedral.

★

By way of relaxation after the horrors of Holland, John went with Vicky
to stay at Charleston Manor. On 13 July 1974, as part of Lady Birley's
Festival, he gave a recital of piano music and songs with the soprano
Kathleen Moss: everything from traditional Spanish airs to the works
of Stravinsky, Cage and Berio, leavened with show tunes by George
Gershwin and Noël Coward. Kathleen Moss was a member of the
London Sinfonietta Chorus and the girlfriend of Clive Wearing. She

sometimes came with Clive to Wembley Park, where she helped by testing the vocal lines John was sketching for *Thérèse*. The opera was proceeding very slowly and John had no financial prospects, but he and Vicky were still heading for marriage. Michael Buckland remembers that John took exhaustive soundings. 'He asked everybody, including waitresses in restaurants and people who served him drinks in bars: "I'm thinking of getting married – not at all sure about it." Everybody said, "Perhaps you had better not." It was deeply unanimous. But he was determined to go for it.'

Vicky took John on an introductory tour of Greece. She remembers he hated it, and insisted to her that Spain was superior in every way. She did not think the Orthodox Church worth defending, but she was proud of her classical inheritance. She took John to sites she imagined would inspire him: Epidaurus, Nafplion, Delphi. 'But everywhere we went there were catastrophes!' She asked him to concede, at least, that the countryside was beautiful. He refused to find anything special. All he could see was 'Ireland with sun'. Byzantium meant nothing to him. He dismissed the chanting coming from the churches as 'terrible' and 'naïve'. In Vicky's recollection, the only thing John liked immediately about Greece was her father.

Costas Maragopoulos had a musical training, but was prevented by illness from taking up a career as a violinist. He qualified instead as a doctor of medicine. Vicky describes him as 'certainly a spiritual man, but not in a churchy way'. To show his left-wing sympathies he drove a Russian car.

Since John and Vicky could not be deflected from marriage, a joint family holiday was arranged on the island of Skiathos. The two sets of parents and the young lovers sat down for a serious talk. John remembers a speech by his father, 'blackening my character'. Kenneth's version is that he was frank about the difficulties Vicky would have to face, given John's self-obsession, lack of income and unconcern with practicalities. John's mother said little, but left no doubt that she would be distressed to lose him. It was to no avail. The wedding was arranged for 17 November 1974. At John's insistence, it was to be an Orthodox ceremony, performed by Metropolitan Anthony in the Russian Cathedral.

John was still a long way from conversion to Orthodoxy, but something was stirring. Gerry McLarnon had never preached the virtues of the Orthodox way, but his stories about Metropolitan Anthony never failed to intrigue. When John met Anthony Bloom for himself, he was not disappointed. The man he had glimpsed from afar at Allington

Castle turned out to have a powerful presence, a rich, mellifluous voice, and a pair of piercing eyes.

Vicky had no wish for the Orthodox ceremony which was her birthright. She would have preferred to be married by Cameron Joyce, who by now was extremely ill with cancer. However, she went with John for instruction in the ways of matrimony from Metropolitan Anthony, whose theatricality was not to her taste. She remembers the Metropolitan was fond of using capital letters for emphasis. She and John were told, for example, 'If you want to live Life, with a capital L, then you must learn to Love, with a capital L.' She found this mildly amusing, but was less entertained when Anthony told her, 'From now on, Victoria, when you say to John "I love you", it will be like saying "I am ready to die."' This seemed a bit one-sided, to say the least.

Vicky's parents came to London for the ceremony, where they were vastly outnumbered by John's family and friends, none of whom were Orthodox apart from Gerry McLarnon. Penny Turton acted as Vicky's bridesmaid. John was greatly taken with the elaborate ritual, which involved the placing of crowns on the heads of bride and groom: crowns, he was told, of both joy and martyrdom, signifying the happiness of marriage and the need for self-sacrifice.

Kenneth Tavener laid on an extravagant reception in the Canaletto restaurant, by the canal in Little Venice. Gerry McLarnon remembers staggering to a friend's house nearby when it was over, and sobering up before he could tackle the journey home.

For Pat Harrison, the reception seemed filled with portent. She has a vivid recollection of an awful moment, just before John cut the cake, when he held the long, sharp knife with its point towards his bride. And then there was the speech by the best man, in which she thought she heard John described as a musical undertaker.

The best man was Philip Pilkington and he has kept his notes for that speech. It included what he hoped was an entertaining *jeu d'esprit*, which turned on the fact that John, whose music was regularly concerned with death, had ancestors who were funeral directors. Another subject for humour was John the British sunworshipper. And then there was the true story of the young girl who spotted this irregular-looking fellow at the wheel of his very large car and climbed on board hoping something irregular would happen, only to find she was on her way to church with a regular organist.

★

Whatever his misgivings about the marriage, Kenneth Tavener had bought a house for the couple in Wembley Park, just two minutes away from John's family home. It was painted, decorated and furnished by the Tavener firm, ready for occupation by John and Vicky on their wedding night. At the last moment, John refused to go there. His explanation was, and is, that he could not leave his mother. With a heavy heart, Vicky embarked on married life under the roof of her in-laws. There was no honeymoon. The morning after the wedding, John took up his usual station at his composing table in the dining room.

A few weeks later, he took his friend Michael Buckland for a walk around the neighbourhood. He wanted to show him what he called 'my house'. Michael remembers they peered through the windows and admired the wedding presents. John could not find his key.

Vicky was fond of Muriel Tavener and did not blame her for what had happened, although the relationship between John and his mother was extremely intense. Kenneth was the one dedicated to John's career: always attentive and seeking the right opportunities. But Vicky felt this keenness was resented by John, who could not bear to think of music as a job. His mother's silent, intuitive sympathy was what really mattered to him: 'to do with the soul, not with the profession'.

By the time of the marriage, John had deserted the institutional atmosphere of Trinity College. He preferred to meet his pupils in a pub or, better still, invite them to Wembley Park. Vicky watched them hungering for musical know-how, while John talked about everything except music. For Kenneth, John's aversion to a structured career was deeply disappointing.

When his services as organist at St John's were no longer required, John was as sad as his father. He saw the position not as a job of work but as an opportunity to serve God. It was lost because the successor to Cameron Joyce was a minister of a different stamp: not prepared to accept hymns at a snail's pace, or put up with the antics of Giles when John was away.

Before she met John, Vicky's plan had been to take her Royal Ballet School qualifications back to Greece. She had not planned to dance in England, which was just as well, because John was opposed to her having a career in the performing arts. To retain a shred of independence, she took a job as a sales assistant in Foyle's bookshop in the Charing Cross Road, commuting each day by tube from Wembley Park. She had been a keen theatre and cinema-goer, but John railed against what he called her 'artiness', and advised her that art meant nothing unless it was in the service of God.

The marriage was of course received coldly in the Stassinopoulos household, but there were other parties to go to, in the land of Lady Birley. Vicky watched John behaving badly at these gatherings: getting drunk, arguing, breaking things. It seemed to her he despised himself for being there. Then there was his drinking to unwind at the end of the day. His drinking as a cure for insomnia. His drinking to fortify himself when he had to make a public appearance or meet the press. She came to see their marriage as the victim of extremely bad timing. John was terrified that no progress on *Thérèse* meant his inspiration had dried up for ever.

Plans were laid for a family visit to Lisieux. John wanted to show the convent to Vicky and his parents. But when Kenneth found there were no top-notch hotels in the little pilgrimage town he booked accommodation in the fashionable seaside resort of Deauville, where the Taveners ate in all the best restaurants. They also visited the casino, and who should they find playing the tables but eighty-year-old George Smart, retired headmaster of Arnold House, John's preparatory school. The visit to the Carmelite convent was a very brief one.

Back home, the creative breakthrough refused to come, but John maintained a superstitious reverence for the family hearth, the garden, the piano in the window, and the round dining table in the front room that had become his composing table. Here was where the Muse had descended in the past. He told Vicky he could not allow the spell to be broken. If he moved out, he would never be able to compose again.

Holidays were permitted, so John and Vicky took another trip to Greece, in June 1975. This time she introduced him to the mountainous island of Hydra, hoping he would be pleased with this favourite location of film-makers, artists and intellectuals. Here at last he began to respond to the beauty of the scenery, and he particularly liked the company of the drifters and odd-balls who hung around the tavernas. But he deplored the primitive sanitation and suffered terrible migraines. The attacks were so bad that Vicky sent for her father, who arrived by helicopter and treated the pain with shots of morphine.

In this distressed condition, John and Vicky were visited by Penny Turton and her husband, who were on their way home to England overland, after seven months in India. Penny was deeply shocked by what she found. She thought Vicky was lovely, but she could see the marriage was over.

Back in Wembley Park, Vicky was lonely and isolated. When she tried to talk to John's friends about the difficulties of the marriage, most of them gave her that look which said 'I told you so.' Just eight months after the wedding day, she packed her bags and said goodbye. She was going back to Greece to pick up her career as a dancer. John could not accept that the marriage was finished, however, and Vicky agreed they should continue to meet, whenever she was in London or he was in Greece. John hoped her father would forgive him. Vicky was sure he would.

As his closest friends were aware, John's marriage had not put an end to the mundane relationships with other women. He was tormented by his inability to form a perfect union, and confessed the ghastliness of his life to Metropolitan Anthony. There were many meetings, but the Metropolitan did not find John's sex life very interesting. He certainly did not call on him to renounce sin and cling to the bosom of the Church, preferring to deal in what seemed to John at first to be trivial anecdotes. The efficacy of this casual approach became apparent later.

Meanwhile, Clive Wearing's input to *Thérèse* was becoming crucial. John took him to Lisieux, more than once, to peer through the grille. Clive stressed the importance of soaking up the atmosphere. The writing began to make progress.

One of Gerry McLarnon's early ideas had been to create a part in the opera for the French poet of sacrilege Arthur Rimbaud, who spent his short life exploring mysticism from a heathen perspective. Thérèse and Rimbaud had probably never heard of one another, but they were contemporaries and they came from the same part of France. Gerry remembers arguing for licence to include the precocious poet, on the grounds that he would provide 'the astringency needed after all the soppiness of Thérèse'. John accepted Rimbaud's dramatic *raison d'être*, but felt the opera still lacked the element of beauty which would allow his music to flower. Clive Wearing recommended the inclusion of quotations from the *Song of Songs*: the anthology of Hebrew love poetry in the Old Testament. Early Christian writers, including San Juan de la Cruz, had interpreted these erotic verses as descriptions of the love between the soul and God. They could provide the vocabulary for a dialogue between Thérèse and her heavenly Bridegroom. Gerry agreed. Now John had a love theme, he was able to move forward.

The opera's form is palindromic. A long opening section deals with the descent of Thérèse and her faith into divine darkness. The central section is divided into three 'journeys': versions of the road to self-abnegation taught by San Juan de la Cruz. The final section is an elaborate mirror of the first, rising from dark despair into the light, triumphantly singing a love song to God.

The whole drama is set during the Easter weekend of 1896, when Thérèse, coughing blood on her bed of pain, passed through her 'dark night of the soul'. Although her struggle is an interior one, and the cast of principal characters is small, John wrote to exploit the entire space of the Opera House. Heavenly voices emanate from the dome. Brass fanfares sound from the four corners of the building, to signal the Last Judgement. Tam-tams toll from beneath the stage, as from the pit of Hell.

As usual with John, the orchestra is an unconventional one, geared to the expressive needs of the occasion. A band of recorders is preferred to oboes or bassoons, and the range of percussion is extraordinary and vast, requiring twelve players.

The chorus has a churchy sound to it – only basses and children are used – and much is demanded of the solo singers. Thérèse is a soprano part, full of contrasts: by turns hysterical, sombre, calm and ecstatic. Her vocal range embraces the extremes of high and low, and she is always on stage. Christ is a high lyric tenor. The vocal acrobatics of Rimbaud were first assigned to a counter-tenor, but then dropped an octave when Robert Tear convinced John that the power of a straight tenor could bring more ferocity to the part. Pranzini is a deep bass.

Gerry provided comprehensive stage directions, which John wrote into his score. What follows is a synopsis of their vision of how the drama should unfold.

The first sounds come from on high. They are Slavonic Alleluias, chanted by basses, who are joined in the heavens by the amplified voice of Christ, calling tenderly to Thérèse in Latin, quoting from the *Song of Songs*. From her bed in the centre of the stage, Thérèse answers her bridegroom. She too quotes from the *Song of Songs*, this time in English: 'I rose to open to my beloved.'

She is surrounded by threatening black figures, yelping 'Night of nothing', like a pack of dogs. Christ appears, arms outstretched, crying in Aramaic, 'My God, my God, why hast Thou forsaken me?' Figures in white insist shrilly 'Christ is Risen!', but Thérèse cannot respond and retreats into childish babbling. The black and the white figures join forces to hiss like vipers, 'Atheist, Atheist, Atheis-s-tttt.' Thérèse, at her lowest ebb, slowly sings, 'I do not know how to die.'

Christ comes to the bedside and serenades her in English: 'Behold, thou art fair, beloved.' He takes off his crown, mask and robe and now appears as an upright elderly man: Thérèse's father. He kisses her, raises her from the bed and draws her on her first journey, while boys' voices off-stage sing, in Spanish, verses by San Juan de la Cruz:

> One dark night I went out unseen
> Leaving my home silent and still.

The journey leads to Thérèse's childhood, where little girls in white communion frocks chant the French nursery song 'Oh que j'aime la souvenance', which Thérèse used to love. Also there, waiting for her, is Arthur Rimbaud with some deeply offensive opening lines.

> Once I had a delightful childhood
> To be written about on sheets of gold.
> You too had a delightful childhood
> To be written about on sheets of SHIT!

Rimbaud's music is a corruption of the children's song. He makes Thérèse read from her childish writings, and attacks their arrogance. Her quiet answer is 'I saw as a child.' He forces her to look at herself at the age of ten, afflicted by St Vitus' Dance, then miraculously cured. He accuses her of spiritual pride in boasting about the miracle.

> At the tickle of flattery
> You vomited out eternal life.

Real humility seems to wither Thérèse's body as she sings

> All is true. I shall sit with sinners now
> And with dark souls for whom God is dead.

The second journey leads to the dark world of the murderer Pranzini: Thérèse's spiritual child. Each of his murders is re-enacted ritually. The third and most awful, the murder of a child, is accompanied by a girls' chorus, chanting lines from the *Song of Songs*:

> We have a little sister
> And she hath no breasts
> What shall we do for our sister?

Rimbaud calls on Thérèse to choose between murderer and innocent victim. Instead, she cries the name of Jesus with all her might.

The third journey brings Thérèse to the battle field of Flanders, where Rimbaud takes his leave with the admiring lines

>Saints are the strong ones
>Artists are no longer needed.

Thérèse vows to spend her eternity doing good on earth. The horrors of battle and of a concentration camp pass before her eyes. She cries out triumphantly

>My God, Thou has not forsaken them.

A blinding white light and a series of orchestral clusters, like tolling bells, represent the nuclear holocaust. In the long silence which follows, Thérèse prostrates herself and kisses the earth. Then she rises and begins her song of love to God, which becomes a duet when the voice of Christ answers her from on high, quoting from *Song of Songs*. Her dark night has passed. The chanting of Alleluias by the basses is heard again.

★

Looking back at it now, John can see that the completion of *Thérèse* closed the book entitled 'Catholicism and Jean Andersson'. Hidden away inside the opera is a final tribute to Jean. No one would know it, but all the music, apart from the children's and Rimbaud's, is serially derived from her favourite carol, 'Tomorrow Shall Be My Dancing Day'.

6 : Time to come in

Thérèse had been five years in the making. Three more years would go by before the Royal Opera House was ready to accommodate it. During those years, John's distaste for Catholicism became absolute. Even before the opera was finished, Metropolitan Anthony was in the saddle as his spiritual mentor. The next composition, the *Canticle of the Mother of God*, is headed 'To the most Rev. Metropolitan Anthony of Sourozh, His Grace Archbishop Anthony Bloom.' The score is dated 'Athens–London July 29th 1976'; a reminder that John was now commuting to Greece, where he stayed with Vicky, with whom he got on well now the conjugal pressure had been lifted.

The fourteen-minute *Canticle* is music like none John had written before: a setting of the Magnificat for soprano soloist, singing in Hebrew, and choir, singing in Greek. Although serial technique is used, the florid soprano line, with its 'breaks' in the voice, has a distinctly Eastern flavour, which is enhanced by a drone from the choir.

When the choral part takes over and moves forwards, it does so in block chords of unremitting dissonance and powerful beauty. John had in mind the idea of the ancient Greek chorus, which delivers its commentary without emotion. There are no bar lines. The instruction at the head of the score is *hesychia*, and a footnote explains that this Greek word refers to 'a process to let the mind go back into the heart . . . a feeling of an inner warmth and physical perception of a *divine light*'.

John found the perfect soprano for the *Canticle*. She was Elise Ross, a young American who had made a name for herself in Europe with her interpretations of the music of Luciano Berio. John liked the unaffected nature of her voice. She was also a very attractive girl. The première was in Rye Parish Church in the spring of 1977, and later the same year Martin Neary mounted a performance in Winchester Cathedral, which was broadcast live by the BBC.

In the score of the *Canticle*, John stipulates that 'the soprano soloist must be separated by a considerable distance from the choir'. At Winchester, Martin Neary suggested that Elise Ross be placed on the screen overlooking the vast nave. The suggestion appealed to John's dramatic sense, and he went shopping with Elise to choose the right dress. Neary remembers she sang superbly and looked divine.

*

During the long wait for the performance of *Thérèse*, John and Gerry McLarnon kept up the momentum of their collaboration by creating a chamber opera. The subject was Gerry's idea: a short story by Dostoyevsky about a pawnbroker's wife who commits suicide by jumping from a high window, clutching an ikon to her heart.

The libretto of *A Gentle Spirit* sticks close to Dostoyevsky's gloomy tale, and employs the same narrative device: the tragedy unfolds as a series of flashbacks, seen by the husband while he sits alone beside his wife's corpse.

First, he sees again their peculiar courtship. The wretched young girl who was to become his wife visited his shop, bringing shabby items to pawn. He was stern with her. The third time she came, she brought an ikon. He refused to allow her to pawn it, and offered to marry her instead. She accepted.

Next, the disastrous progress of their married life passes before the husband's eyes. He was cold towards her from the start, but after she heard gossip that he was forced to resign from the army because he refused to fight a duel, things got worse. From then on, they slept in separate rooms. One night, while he pretended to be asleep, she crept to his bedside and held his pistol to his head. Then she could not bring herself to pull the trigger. She fell ill. There followed a winter of silence. When spring came, he was ready for a fresh start, but it was too late: she threw herself to her death.

The relentlessly savage music of *A Gentle Spirit* is for two voices and small orchestra, with heavy percussion. The part of the man requires an exceptionally high tenor, capable of enormous leaps. The role of the young wife includes hysterical outbursts, similar to those of Thérèse, and a despairing Slavonic chant of 'Gospodi pomilui' ('Lord have mercy').

Punctuating the opera are six 'suicide falls': the husband's visions of his wife plunging through the air. At each of these sickening moments, a tape loop of the girl's voice is heard calling from on high. Her four-note plea, 'Let my soul live', rises plaintively, while orchestral sounds cascade downwards.

John felt very close to *A Gentle Spirit*. It chimed in with the disastrous condition of his own marriage. The music was written extremely quickly, and an outlet was soon found for it: a commission from Sir William Glock, who was now running the Bath Festival. The première would be at the Theatre Royal, Bath, on 6 June 1977. The performers would be the Nash Ensemble, conducted by Mark Elder, with soloists Elise Ross and Kenneth Woollam.

Still to be found was a producer. Gerry McLarnon wanted Braham Murray to produce it. He was also keen that Braham should be the producer of *Thérèse*, but John had set his sights on Ingmar Bergman. In 1974, on the occasion of the Swedish première of *In Alium*, he had spent time in Stockholm with Bergman, who came to the concert and enthused about the Tavener brand of music. John Tooley wrote to Bergman, and it looked promising for a while, but by the end of 1975 Bergman was pleading an epic commitment in Italy: a TV series about the last days of the life of Christ. He wrote to John, 'As you perhaps understand, this task touches me strongly.' He would not be available to produce *Thérèse*. John was deeply disappointed. Other candidates, including Ken Russell, were discussed with the Royal Opera House, but nothing was agreed.

For *A Gentle Spirit*, John put the Bath Festival in touch with David William, a theatre director recommended to him by his friend the actress Jane Wymark. The Bath Festival and David William agreed terms, but unfortunately John had not taken the precaution of consulting Gerry McLarnon. When Gerry found out, he was beside himself with rage. He announced to everyone, including John's publishers, that his libretto for *Thérèse* was withdrawn. For months he could not be budged, not even by pleading phone calls from Mia Farrow and desperate letters from John's mother. Rehearsals for *A Gentle Spirit* went on without him, and so did the performance, for which there was a big gathering of the Tavener clan in Bath, including Vicky and her father, who came over from Greece.

John was the Festival's 'featured composer'. As well as *A Gentle Spirit* at the Theatre Royal, there was a performance of the *Canticle of the Mother of God* at Bath Abbey, and a big concert in Bristol Cathedral conducted by Martin Neary, which included both the *Little Requiem for Father Malachy Lynch* and *Ultimos Ritos*. In the *Sunday Times*, Desmond Shawe-Taylor described Martin Neary's direction of *Ultimos Ritos* as 'a stunning account of the most characteristic expression of Tavener's evident genius'. He also had praise for *A Gentle Spirit*, and in particular for the 'brilliant assurance' with which Elise Ross carried off her role. His only complaint was against 'the deafening thumps on assorted percussion'.

Straight after the Bath Festival, *A Gentle Spirit* came to London, where it played for three nights at the Collegiate Theatre. There was still no sign of Gerry McLarnon, but backstage was crowded with White Russians, mostly elderly ladies, reduced to tears by the tragic character played by Elise Ross. John remembers, 'they all found Ellie so terribly Russian'.

There was praise from the musical *cognoscenti* for what was achieved in the tenor role by Kenneth Woollam, who had little previous experience of modern music. He thinks he was chosen because 'I'd always had a very strong and secure top, and this of course was an incredibly high tenor part'. Now a Professor at the Royal College of Music, he still admires *A Gentle Spirit* as 'a fantastic piece of writing, structurally and musically', and is surprised it is not performed more. Getting to know it, and to know its composer, was an amazing experience. He remembers John coming to his house to explain how the piece should sound. His way of doing this was to sing both the tenor and the soprano parts, 'including the high notes, in a sort of falsetto', while thumping out the orchestral part on Kenneth's piano. By the time he had finished, two strings had snapped and two hammers were broken. Kenneth easily forgave him the damage. He is only sorry John doesn't write music like that any more. 'It's a great loss to opera. He had an incredible sense of theatre.'

A month after the London production of *A Gentle Spirit*, John took Elise Ross and Kenneth Woollam down to the Charleston Festival, to give a semi-staged performance in the Tithe Barn, with himself at the piano. Kenneth Woollam remembers the journey back to London in John's limousine:

> I think he was driving a Bentley in those days. And we had to give a little performance in the car, with Ellie and I singing, and John putting in the orchestral cues, thumping the steering wheel, doing all the percussion. We'd had quite a lot of drink, and I thought, as we kept hitting the kerb and going on the hard shoulder of the motorway, I thought, 'Well, I don't know, I think God's on his side and looking after him.' I was terrified.

Gerry McLarnon finally relented, and caught up with *A Gentle Spirit* when the David William production was mounted in Cheltenham. He complained that the décor was rubbish ('rags hanging down to try to suggest a broken life'), but he was back in the Tavener fold.

*

All this time, John's conversations with Metropolitan Anthony were continuing. One day, in the late spring of 1977, the Metropolitan announced he was ready to talk about something really important. He said it was time for John 'to come into the Church'. John assumed that at last the conversation was going to take a deeply religious turn. Instead, he was presented with a request. The Metropolitan wanted him to make a musical setting of the Orthodox Liturgy, in the English language.

The liturgy in the Orthodox Church is a fixed system of dialogues between priest and choir, together with prayers, hymns and processions, lasting about one hour. There are three versions of the text, the most popular of which is the Liturgy of St John Chrysostom. This was the one John was asked to set.

*

Orthodox Christianity was embraced by the Slav people in AD 988. With it from Constantinople came the manner of singing known as Byzantine chant, in which an elaborate melodic line is accompanied by a drone, or *ison*. The Greek Orthodox Church still maintains that style, but Russian choral singing has been tempted by the juicy harmonies of the Victorian hymn book, and it is this nineteenth-century sound that is heard in London's Russian Orthodox Cathedral. Between the hymns are long stretches of recitative, led by the priest and shared by the choir. Everything happens in accordance with a system of tones, or melodic patterns. There is a cycle of eight of these tones, and each one is used for a week at a time. Metropolitan Anthony insisted that John should not trouble himself with the intricacies of the tone system. Over-ruling the diehards among his parishioners, he announced, 'English Orthodoxy must find its own texts and melodies: it may take decades, but it will happen.' John was hugely grateful for the opportunity. He saw his task as a privilege and a mission.

For his setting of the Liturgy, he rejected what he called 'the senti- mental nineteenth-century harmonizations of Russian chant', and followed instead a path of austerity which was distinctly his own, using a rising and falling five-note phrase as the musical basis of the entire work. And unlike Tchaikovsky and the other great Russian composers who had entered the field, he provided music for every single moment of the service, including entrances, prayers, processions and readings. Although his *Liturgy of St John Chrysostom* has rarely been performed, it was immensely important as a test-bed. Here, for the first time, he contemplated the beauties of the 'Trisagion' or thrice-holy hymn (Holy God, Holy Mighty, Holy Immortal), and the 'Hymn to the Mother of God': texts he has returned to again and again. And here he practised the Byzantine method of setting a melodic line against a drone.

In September 1977, while he was still working on his *Liturgy*, he was formally received into the Orthodox Church. Metropolitan Anthony took the service, which included the ceremony of chrismation, or anointing with oil. Gerry McLarnon and the Russian ballerina Svetlana Beriosova were appointed as John's Orthodox godparents.

The première of his *Liturgy of St John Chrysostom* was set for the evening of Wednesday, 30 November 1977. It was to be in the Russian Cathedral, but it would not be a service. Metropolitan Anthony advertised it as a musical performance and an experiment.

Although John had been asked to produce something 'immediately realizable by amateur voices', the Cathedral choirmaster, Father Michael Fortounatto, declared the music to be beyond the scope of his singers. The vocal range was modest enough, but the sparseness was upsetting to a choir fed on lush harmonies, and the progressions were not what their ears were used to. The occasion was rescued by Clive Wearing's Europa Singers, renowned for their performances of both early and contemporary music. Clive Wearing conducted. John himself took the part of the priest. Several hundred attended, including a hostile faction from the Cathedral congregation. These snipers were not Russians but English converts to Orthodoxy, now behaving with proprietorial zeal. They told John to go away for several centuries and steep himself in the tone system. Metropolitan Anthony urged him not to be discouraged.

This was John's Russian period. He drank vodka in Russian restaurants and became passionate about the music of Mussorgsky. The elderly Russian ladies at the Cathedral were touched by his interest and gave him tapes of their favourite songs. He set half a dozen of these for soprano and small ensemble, including the *domra*, a traditional Russian instrument similar to the balalaika. The *Six Russian Folk Songs* were premièred at the Queen Elizabeth Hall on 15 January 1978. John conducted the Nash Ensemble. The soloist was Elise Ross.

★

The next Tavener composition was in response to a commission from
the London Sinfonietta: the first from that quarter for five years. John
called it *Kyklike Kinesis*, which was the term used by the Desert Fathers
of the Early Christian Church to describe the circuit of the soul, leaving
and returning to God. To convey this concept, he started and ended the
piece with presentations of his *Canticle of the Mother of God*. At the
beginning, the *Canticle* is heard as originally written, for soprano and
chorus. At the end, the soprano voice is replaced by a solo cello. The
three middle movements of *Kyklike Kinesis* are instrumental, and use
material abstracted from the *Canticle*. All five movements carry Greek
names, taken from the vocabulary used by the Desert Fathers to describe
spiritual states.

Looking back on it now, John sees *Kyklike Kinesis* as important only
because it indicates that he had started to read the Desert Fathers. Back
in 1978, he did not have the musical equipment to tackle the big theo-
logical themes, and the rather grand use of Greek terminology is
embarrassing. He still loves the stillness and simplicity of the *Canticle*,
in which a Middle Eastern atmosphere is created by pure instinct, but
the middle movements of *Kyklike Kinesis* are remembered ruefully:

> Because I was using the serial idiom, I couldn't get anywhere near the
> concept of the Desert. Those middle movements sound to me like – me,
> writing serial music. In the East, the serial technique means nothing at
> all. It's a man-made thing, not coming from tradition.

The première was in the Queen Elizabeth Hall on 8 March 1978.
Elise Ross and Christopher Van Kampen took the solo parts, and the
London Sinfonietta Orchestra and Chorus were conducted by Simon
Rattle.

★

Against expectations, John's next important piece was purely instrumental. He has a detailed recollection of its genesis. It happened during
a holiday with Vicky on the island of Patmos, where St John the Divine
wrote the Apocalypse. They stayed close to the Monastery of St John,
which perches high above the town and has a panoramic view of the
surrounding islands. On their first evening they went to the nearest
taverna, where John particularly enjoyed the local retsina. As they were
leaving, he fell down the steep stone steps and broke his leg. Other
tourists helped Vicky carry him back to his lodgings, the island doctor
was called and the leg was set in plaster. He was not now mobile enough

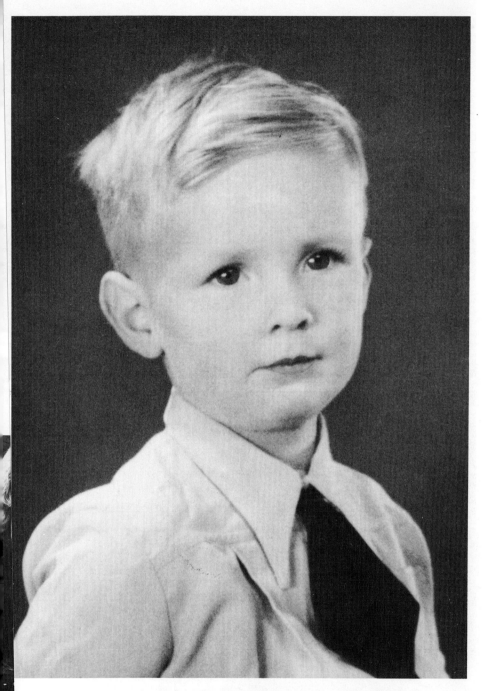

John aged five

John at Paleochora on the island of Aegina, 1993

to clamber down to the grotto where St John received his Revelation, and visits to the monastery terrace were by taxi. He remembers one magical day spent up there, talking with Vicky and one of the Orthodox monks. As the hours passed, he watched the spectacular changes of light and colour across land and sea. On his mind was a fragment for solo piano he had written just before leaving England. The transformations taking place in the landscape and the seascape triggered responses in this little piece, which expanded into a soundscape for piano and orchestra. The experience was enhanced by the Orthodoxy of the environment – bells and Byzantine chant could be heard in the background – but what grew in John's head was not 'Orthodox' music. He likes to describe it as 'my only impressionistic serial piece'.

When he got back to England, he wrote it down very quickly. He called it *Palintropos*, and added a note explaining that 'the title means literally "A Turning-Back Structure", and the idea of turning back is essential to the piece'.

The qualities of light he saw on Patmos were harsh as well as soft, and there is a hard edge to some of *Palintropos*, and a rhythmic ferocity. The four contrasting movements are not separated by silence, but divided by columns of music, which rise up from the strings to be topped by pulsating brass. Much use is made of the piano's sustaining pedal, to produce hazy resonances like the rich colours of the Greek islands, but this is not a 'concerto' in the normal sense. Sometimes the piano decorates, sometimes it anticipates. It never dominates the orchestra, even in the last movement, where it shows off brilliantly amongst the brass chords, handbells and throbbing strings. After all the excitement, *Palintropos* subsides and ends as it began: on the note of C, held by a single double bass.

The score is inscribed 'For Stephen Bishop-Kovacevich', who was an old friend of Vicky's. It was he who gave the first performance, in Birmingham Town Hall on 1 March 1979, with the City of Birmingham Symphony Orchestra conducted by Lawrence Foster. The next evening it was performed again, in London's Festival Hall, by the same orchestra and soloist.

The seed from which *Palintropos* grew – the little piece for solo piano called *Palin* – was performed a year later in a Wigmore Hall recital given by Annette Servadei.

★

After the success of *A Gentle Spirit* at his Bath Festival, Sir William Glock came up with a further commission. This time he wanted an orchestral piece, for the series of Friday Concerts he was running at the Festival Hall. The orchestra would be the Royal Philharmonic.

As always, John eschewed the conventionally orchestral. This time he thought a Greek theme would be appropriate, since Sir William and his wife had become extremely fond of Vicky, who took good care of them when they visited Athens.

Canvassed for ideas, Gerry McLarnon proposed a monodrama for soprano and orchestra on the subject of Antigone, daughter of Oedipus, the king who married his mother. Antigone's fate was to be walled up alive, because she disobeyed the law in order to bury her dead brother. This was one of Gerry's favourite stories from the classics. To create a text for her to sing, he imagined Antigone's state of mind as the wall went up around her: first up to her loins; then up to her heart; then up to her head.

John and Gerry wanted an extremely sparse staging: just a podium for the singer, who would be dressed in black, with a veil which she would drop over her face at the end. In a note at the front of the score, John explains how he approached his musical task:

> I conceived the vocal line of the entire work 'complete', as a somewhat anguished continuous melodic line. All the orchestral material derives from this, and the constant pulse of the whole work, marked out by the timpani, helps to build the inevitability of the tragedy.
>
> The vocal line is constantly entwined and mirrored by the instruments . . . This emphasises the deeply incestuous nature of Antigone's birth and the appallingly claustrophobic manner of her death. As the tragedy proceeds, the accompaniment to Antigone's death song thickens by degrees until she is almost 'covered up' by the orchestra.

The Immurement of Antigone is dedicated to John's parents. The first performance was broadcast from the Festival Hall on 30 March 1979. The Royal Philharmonic Orchestra was conducted by Wolfgang Rennert, and the soprano soloist was Vivien Townley. Her powerful voice was exactly the right one to be heard through the orchestral 'wall', but neither the audience nor the critics could summon up much enthusiasm for this insistently unhappy piece. It has not been performed again.

Covent Garden finally scheduled *Thérèse* for a five-day run, starting on 1 October 1979: a time when Colin Davis and the Opera House's own orchestra and chorus would be in Japan. The search for a prestigious producer had been abandoned, and the job given to David William, who was thought by everybody, except Gerry McLarnon, to have made a decent job of *A Gentle Spirit*. John argued that Simon Rattle should conduct, but Rattle was rejected by Covent Garden as too young. Their choice was Edward Downes: hardly a star name, but know to be sympathetic to contemporary music, and an old hand at the Opera House.

Ever since John first heard her sing, he knew Elise Ross was Thérèse. And so he had told Covent Garden. She was a frequent visitor to Wembley Park, and she joined John and David William on a final visit to Lisieux, when the party was allowed into the room where Thérèse died. The management team at Covent Garden was uneasy. Sir John Tooley remembers they warned John that 'much as we admired the artistry of Elise Ross, we were doubtful that her voice was of sufficient size to fill the opera house. John was unmoved. He said, "No, I want Elise and I am writing this role around her."'

Vivien Townley was appointed Elise Ross's understudy. The part of Rimbaud went to Robert Tear. Christ was to be sung by Keith Lewis, a young tenor from Glyndebourne with spectacular top notes.

The orchestra would be made up of freelances, and there was good news for John about the chorus: he could have the London Sinfonietta, which meant his confederate Clive Wearing would be on board.

Showtime drew near, but Robin Boyle at Chester Music could get no sense out of Covent Garden. As John's publisher, he was responsible for providing the orchestral parts, but he needed a dialogue. He remembers that, although he was entirely without authority, he took it upon himself to convene a meeting at the Royal Opera House, where he eventually got answers to his most urgent questions. Covent Garden's lack of commitment still rankles with him fourteen years later. As he saw it, they felt stuck with an obligation they had incurred during the days of Peter Hall, and were hoping to discharge it with the minimum of fuss and expense. 'I am sure some accountant somewhere was saying, "My God, this is a modern opera! Do you realize we're going lose on this? And there's no interval, so we're not going to have any bar takings! This is a bloody disaster! Let's get this over and get back to Bizet as quickly as possible."'

By the beginning of September, *Thérèse* was in rehearsal. Gerry McLarnon was away for most of the rehearsal schedule, acting in a Braham Murray production up in Manchester. John went to all the rehearsals. To his horror, he became convinced that Elise Ross did not have the vocal strength to sing the part of Thérèse at full throttle from beginning to end. He became afflicted with terrible migraines. He remembers Ted Downes told him he must report the Elise problem to John Tooley. Asked to talk about *Thérèse* for this book, Sir Edward Downes insisted he could recall nothing whatsoever about John Tavener or his music.

The certain fact is that John Tavener phoned John Tooley to say he could not continue with Elise Ross. As our John remembers it, Tooley was staying with Sir William Walton on the island of Ischia. Tooley is not sure about that, but he clearly remembers that 'It was quite close to the opening, and I had the unhappy task of telling Elise that she was no longer wanted.' Vivien Townley was engaged in her place, although she too was without experience of singing large roles in a major opera house.

The Covent Garden press release stated, 'In the light of recent changes in the concept of the role of Thérèse by the composer, Elise Ross has asked to withdraw from the title role.' The 14 September edition of *Private Eye* carried an item of 'Opera News', signed by 'Sparafucile', which challenged the official version. In Sparafucile's view, the 'change of concept' on Mr Tavener's part was 'of a Ugandan rather than an artistic nature'. In other words, the 'eccentric composer' had simply transferred his affections from one lady to another. The allegation was wounding and John's drinking became heavier. The cause of Elise Ross was fiercely championed by Simon Rattle, who later married her.

Vicky came over from Greece to lend John moral support. She went with him to visit Gerry McLarnon at home, and witnessed a degrading spectacle. Gerry mocked the chances of *Thérèse* getting a decent performance. He said the producer didn't know what he was doing, and neither did anybody else. The première was now very close, and John was unbearably tense. In a rare explosion of rage, he overturned Gerry's table. The two men came to blows. They both remember the incident, although with different details: John thinks he finished up on the floor, and Gerry's teenage son had to plead with his dad to stop it. Gerry says his assault on John was frustrated because 'Me being short and he being long, I could only hit him at bollocks level, though I was aiming for the head.'

In spite of all that, Gerry attended the first night. He says the ham actor in him could not resist taking a bow on the Covent Garden stage. Relish was added to his evening by the presence in the upper stalls, alongside the punk hairdos, of a contingent of nuns. Most piquant of all was the moment when these runs threw themselves to their knees.

Before the event, the press ran two kinds of trailer. For *Now!* magazine, Richard Baker described Tavener as 'a tall figure with flowing hair, deeply tanned from long periods on the Greek islands and wearing an open shirt and many dangling silver objects, including a large crucifix'. To readers of the *Musical Times*, the analyst Paul Griffiths promised an opera like no other. '*Thérèse* will be awesome or it will fail.'

After the event, the consensus was that it had failed. Derwent May in the *Listener* thought it 'a powerful and elegant Catholic sermon', but Arthur Jacobs, for *Opera Magazine*, found it 'repetitive to the point of tedium'. Andrew Clements, for *Music and Musicians*, thought the tedium 'as much the fault of the music as of the libretto'. Winton Dean, for the *Musical Times*, put his finger on a fundamental problem. 'If we are invited to take part in some mystical ceremony or ritual – do we need an opera house?'

Even John's staunchest supporters found it hard to raise a cheer. The *Observer*'s Stephen Walsh said Tavener's 'typically unhelpful recourse to a variety of languages' made the plot almost impossible to follow. Edward Greenfield in the *Guardian* concluded that 'believers may well find more to move them than I did'.

John and Gerry McLarnon did not collaborate again, although they saw one another frequently at the Russian Cathedral. Some of John's friends blamed Gerry for the shortcomings of *Thérèse*, believing John was led astray, but that is not the view John takes. Looking back on it, he can see that the Royal Opera House at Covent Garden was not the proper context, and he blames himself for raising the wrong expectations by writing music that sounded 'contemporary'. Moreover, what should have been a simple story was expressed in a complex way. Worst of all, he had used *Thérèse* as a vehicle for his own *angst*. 'I did what I've accused other composers of doing: I hung out my dirty washing in public.'

More kind is the verdict of Robert Tear, who was unanimously praised by the critics for his performance as Rimbaud. Interviewed for this book, he described *Thérèse* as an opera ahead of its time, in which the composer was on a search for spiritual truth. 'It was a crossroads for John. I really do think he's a great composer, responsible for a trend which is going to go right through art, where the spiritual quality will reassert itself.'

★

After *Thérèse* came another grand and sombre work, inspired by quite a different kind of heroine.

By 1966, when she died, Anna Akhmatova had been acclaimed in the West as Russia's greatest modern poet. In her homeland she was banned from publishing poetry in 1925, rehabilitated during the Second World War, then denounced again in 1946. Stalin's cultural henchman Andrei Zhdanov described her as 'half-nun, half-whore', and the official line on her poems was that they were full of 'mists of loneliness and hopelessness alien to Soviet literature'. These attacks were on the poetry she had been allowed to publish. Stalin's *apparatchiks* were unaware of the works she dared not write down, but stored in her mind and recited in whispers to her friends. Although she was persecuted, she survived the Stalinist terror. Others close to her fared worse. A poet friend died in a labour camp. Another committed suicide. Her first husband was shot for alleged involvement in a political plot. Her only son spent years in prison.

After the death of Stalin, the unpublished poetry of Anna Akhmatova's 'silent' years surfaced in the West. Among it was the cycle of poems called *Requiem*, in which she commemorated all of Stalin's victims. John was introduced to a translation of *Requiem* in 1979. He was so moved by it he felt he must set it to music in its entirety, in its original language. For his guide, he needed a bilingual Orthodox believer with a literary background. Such a person was found. He was Oxford-educated Father Sergei Hackel, who had served as a priest at the Russian Cathedral before taking up a teaching post at Sussex University. He travelled regularly to London to present programmes for the Russian service of the BBC. What was needed was a central location where he could meet John after the broadcasts. John's friend Philip Pilkington had the very thing: a vacant Belgravia penthouse. It was here that the foundations for John's *Akhmatova: Requiem* were painstakingly laid. Three versions of the text were cross-referenced: original Russian, transliterated Russian, and Father Sergei's English translation. John found Russian a much more difficult language than Greek. He went through the text with Father Sergei one word at a time, mapping every detail of pronunciation, stress and meaning.

Anna Akhmatova's *Requiem* is made up of fourteen poetic meditations on suffering and death, set in a bleak landscape corrupted by tyranny. John's response is one hour of continuous music, symmetrical in design, mostly derived from a twelve-note row. All the poetry is sung by a soprano soloist, whose melodic line recalls the contours of the *Canticum Sacrum*. The poetry is sometimes savage, but the music never becomes overwrought. Instead, it generates an atmosphere of icy despair. Strings, brass and percussion create a dark undertow with glinting highlights. There is no woodwind. From time to time handbells and fragments from the Russian Orthodox funeral service, chanted by a bass, interrupt the soprano and reinforce the sense of solemn ritual. Just once, for the poem called 'Crucifixion', the bass steps out of his priestly role and joins the soprano in a duet. He is Christ and she is his grieving Mother.

This was the first time John had introduced Orthodox Church music into a concert piece. He regards *Akhmatova: Requiem* as a key work. As well as giving a clear indication of his music to come, it harks back to the manner of his favourite *Donne Sonnets*, written sixteen years earlier. He dated the score in accordance with the Orthodox Church calendar: 'Great Monday: March 31st 1980'.

*

Within weeks of the completion of *Akhmatova: Requiem*, John's brother Roger underwent major heart surgery. He was thirty-three. This time-bomb had been ticking away since 1977, when he went for a routine life insurance medical and was told he was a classic case of Marfan's syndrome, a hereditary disease found in people who are exceptionally tall and long-limbed. A common symptom is weakness of the tissue in the aorta: the main vessel coming out of the heart. Surgery for Marfan's syndrome was still new in 1980, but Roger's condition was deteriorating badly and there was no alternative. He was admitted to the Ealing clinic of heart specialist Professor Magdi Yacoub.

John brought him an ikon, but Roger's main comfort came from music. He took his favourite tapes into hospital and listened to them constantly. The most played was 'All Flesh Is Grass', from Brahms' *German Requiem*, which he had on at full volume as he was wheeled down to the operating theatre. The operation involved the replacement of his aortic valve with a pig's valve. It lasted eight hours, and there was a post-operative crisis with internal bleeding, but Roger pulled through.

★

Two months after Roger's operation, in June 1980, John went to Aldeburgh, where Sir Peter Pears was giving the first performance of a song cycle John had written for him.

John had known Peter Pears since the summer of 1963, when the singer accepted an invitation to take tea in Wembley Park after a rehearsal of music by Lennox Berkeley in Wembley Town Hall. John's mother served refreshments in the garden, and Pears dazzled the family with his charm. After that, John kept in touch with him. He tried to persuade Pears to lend his artistry to *Thérèse*, but the great tenor found the part of Christ was pitched too high. To ease John's disappointment, he commissioned a song cycle, suggesting the texts might be culled from the writings of the Greek poet Cavafy. John found Cavafy's poetry too blatantly homoerotic. Instead, he chose six lyrics about love and death from an anthology of poetry written in Baghdad during the Abbasid dynasty.

The *Six Abbasid Songs* are for tenor voice, alto flutes, bells and gongs. Serial technique is used and there is no premeditated borrowing from Eastern tradition, yet they sound distinctly oriental. The flavour comes partly from the timbre and the sparseness of the instrumental accompaniment, partly from the ornamentation of the vocal line. There are few tonal references. Pears found them fairly difficult, but sang them beautifully.

The première was in the Maltings at Snape on the evening of 18 June 1980. After the recital, John decided to drive back to London. He was on his own. Along the way, his Rolls Royce seemed to be tugging persistently to the left. Not far from home, he crashed into a parked car on the nearside of the road. It was not a drink-related accident. John had suffered a stroke. He was thirty-six years old.

PART FIVE

Ikon of Light

§

When John was brought home after the accident it was not clear at first what had happened to him. His blood pressure was sky high, but several doctors made the wrong diagnosis, taking the stiffness down his left side to be the result of the collision.

After a week of feeling desperately strange, he collapsed in the lounge and was unable to get up from the floor when his father told him to pull himself together. Finally, he was admitted into the care of Dr David Thomas, consultant neurologist at St Mary's, Paddington.

Dr Thomas' finding was that John had suffered a mild stroke, not unconnected to the Marfan's syndrome he shared with his brother. Marfan's predisposes to problems with the arteries which, in unlucky cases, can lead to a blockage or a bleed which damages an area of the brain. In John's case, the damage was to the area behind the right temple, called the right temporal lobe. Its main manifestations were paralysis down the left side and malfunction of the vocal cords. He was severely hoarse for some days. Also, his vision on the left side was temporarily abnormal.

While Dr Thomas was conducting tests, Vicky arrived from Greece. As soon as she saw John, she burst into tears. During the desperate days before he was admitted to hospital he had made a phone call to Vicky's father, describing his symptoms. From what he was told, Dr Costas Maragopoulos feared the car crash might have caused a brain injury, or that John might have a tumour. Vicky flew to London at once. She remembers her dismay when she found Dr Thomas testing John's memory with questions about British prime ministers. She protested that such a quiz would be beyond him at the best of times.

John's father could not bring himself to accept the term 'stroke', so many people, including John's publishers, were never told about it. Kenneth tried to cheer the bedside with a choice selection of

Greek wines, but Dr Thomas insisted the alcohol must leave immediately.

★

With John's permission, Dr David Thomas was interviewed for this book. He explained that a stroke like the one John had, which damages a small part of the temporal lobe, is quite commonly followed by intermittent episodes of abnormal experience called 'temporal lobe attacks'. These are electrical discharges at the point where the damaged area of the brain meets the rest. Among neurologists, there has long been curiosity about the relationship between these temporal discharges and creativity, so when John began to describe strange happenings Dr Thomas took more than the normal clinical interest. Without detracting in any way from John's 'basic brilliance', he ventures the thought that John's creative mode may have been shifted by what happened to him:

> In neurological circles, it has been put forward that St Paul had some sort of a temporal lobe event on the road to Damascus, when he had that amazing visionary experience. And that some of his behaviour subsequently was attributable to this event. A number of features are common to temporal lobe attacks. They can produce hyper-religiosity, and people often write a lot. They write diaries and letters . . . to the Corinthians and all the rest of it. A schizophrenic will get auditory hallucinations: voices telling him or her what to do. Whereas in a temporal lobe attack, the hallucination will be more commonly of a visual nature. And it can be musical, of course: music is thought to be from the right temporal lobe, and that's where we think John had his problem.

Dr Thomas was not surprised that the music John heard during his attacks often ran through his head too fast for him to 'get it'. Patients often describe things as 'speeded up' or 'slowed down', and often 'familiar things appear distorted'. Sometimes, and it was so in John's case, patients have *déjà vu* and *jamais vu* experiences. During an attack of *jamais vu*, familiar things appear strange and common occurrences seem to be unique.

The point to be insisted upon, says Dr Thomas, is that no amount of temporal lobe attacks could produce a composer, 'without a pre-existent matrix of compositional creativity'.

★

To Vicky, John seemed very ill. She was amazed when he insisted he must get on with his composing. He said her presence at the hospital was extremely fortunate: he was making settings of poetry by Sappho, which would be sung in Greek. She could sit beside him and make sure he did not betray the Greek language. And, since his left hand was numb, she could manage his papers for him. As with the *Akhmatova: Requiem*, John was anxious to capture the niceties of the original verses. He made his selection from Sappho using a standard translation, but then had to have parallel texts in Greek and transliterated Greek.

Strictly speaking, there is nothing Greek about the music he wrote. There is no reference to ancient Doric hymns, nor any reliance on Byzantine chant. The music – loosely serial, but strongly suggestive of tonality – is a purely personal response to the lyrics of the legendary poetess from Lesbos.

Characters from Sappho's verses chosen by John include Aphrodite, goddess of love; Cleis, Sappho's darling daughter; and Atthis, the woman from Sappho's past she never ceased to love. To convey the charged atmosphere of Sappho's feminine world, *Sappho: Lyrical Fragments* is scored for string orchestra and two intertwined sopranos. Sometimes one voice provides a drone for the other, while the strings offer a version of the *Akhmatova* sound in which bleakness has given way to softness.

The John Tavener of today looks back on his *Sappho: Lyrical Fragments* as a transitional piece, leading towards the unopened door marked Tradition.

★

After he was released from hospital and Vicky had gone back to Greece, John had to face the tedium of physiotherapy, to bring relief to his left side and restore the use of his left hand. Attendance at the treatment centre depressed him enormously. All the other patients wading in the pool looked wrinkled and ancient. Life slowly returned to his left arm and he was able to play the piano again, but never so brilliantly as before. The injury to his vocal cords was permanent. For a long time he could not sing at all, and even now his voice quickly tires and becomes croaky.

During the early stages of his convalescence, while he was still in a state of demoralization and shock, he sent for Father Sergei Hackel and, seated in front of an ikon in the Wembley Park lounge, made a three-hour confession of his sinful life. By now the lounge, where the piano was, had started to fill with ikons. Many were printed reproductions, pasted on to wood, but some were originals: a Mother of God from

Russia, bought for John by his father at considerable expense; and a striking head of Christ, in the Greek peasant style, which Roger rescued from Paul McCartney's dustbin.

In the autumn of 1980 the Little Missenden Festival came round again. Until John suffered his stroke, Pat Harrison had been hoping he would provide a new piece of music for them. Now, she expected nothing. But John had a surprise for everyone: an arrangement for piano duet of an Ivor Novello-like tune composed at the keyboard years ago by grandfather Ernest Brown. On 10 October 1980, in Little Missenden Parish Church, John and Pat Harrison were warmly applauded for their performance, four hands at one piano, of *My Grandfather's Waltz*, in which Pat took the more difficult of the two easy parts.

2 : Where shall I make my beginning?

As he moved into 1981 and the season of Lent approached, John continued to review what seemed a misspent life. He became fascinated by a booklet on the theme of repentance, which contained two classic Orthodox texts: *The Great Canon of St Andrew of Crete* and *The Life of St Mary of Egypt*. The editors and translators were Sister Katherine and Sister Thekla of the Greek Orthodox Monastery of the Assumption, in Buckinghamshire.

The Great Canon of St Andrew of Crete is an eighth-century liturgical poem consisting of nine odes: an epic statement of penitence. John decided to set it to music. Martin Neary had commissioned a new choral work for the Festival in Winchester in July. This would be it. John's publishers warned that he would need permission from the translators, so he made enquiries among his Orthodox friends about the two nuns in their Buckinghamshire retreat. It turned out they had moved to the Yorkshire moors. Their abbess had died, and they were now to be addressed as Mother Thekla and Mother Katherine. John was given their telephone number and urged to dial it. With friends standing over him, he made his first call to the Greek Orthodox Monastery of the Assumption, North Yorkshire, in February 1981. He looks back on it as the most momentous call of his life.

The phone was answered by Mother Katherine. John explained that he was an Orthodox composer, interested in making a setting of *The Great Canon of St Andrew*. Mother Katherine was keen on music, but she had never heard of John Tavener. She asked him to hold on, and ran to fetch Mother Thekla from the garden. Mother Thekla was less musical, and equally ignorant of John Tavener, but she was the Abbess now, and it was she who had annotated the booklet about St Andrew of Crete and St Mary of Egypt. John repeated his request to set *The Great Canon of St Andrew*, and added that he hoped one day to make an opera from the life of St Mary. Mother Thekla wished him well with his opera, but begged to be spared any involvement. About his setting of *The Great Canon of St Andrew*, she saw no problem. John mentioned the possibility of a copyright payment. Mother Thekla said there could be no commercial transaction. Would he simply mention somewhere that his text came from the translation of the Canon by the Monastery of the Assumption? She had just written a short history of the Monastery. She would send him a copy.

★

Five years passed before the Orthodox Monastery of the Assumption became John's lodestar, but here is a convenient place to set down its story.

Three nuns founded the Monastery. One was born in Switzerland, one in England and one in Russia. The Swiss girl grew up in Paris, where she met exiled Russians and converted to the Orthodox faith. She studied theology at Basle University, then came to England to finish her doctoral thesis on the Cambridge Platonists. She joined the Russian Orthodox community here. In 1951 Father Anthony Bloom, as he then was, professed her as a nun.

The girl born in England studied science at London University, then entered the Anglican Benedictine Abbey at West Malling, where she became Dame Mary Thomas, Novice Mistress and Bursar.

The girl born in Russia and baptized Orthodox was brought to England to escape the Revolution. She grew up here, read Russian and English at Girton College, Cambridge, and served in RAF Intelligence during the war. Afterwards she became a teacher, finishing up as Head of English at Kettering High School.

In 1951 there was no Orthodox Monastery in England for the novice nun from Switzerland. The Anglican Benedictine Abbey at West Malling agreed to make room for one Orthodox inmate, and appointed Dame Mary Thomas as her Novice Mistress. She became Mother Maria, and she was still there fourteen years later, in 1965, when the Russian-born teacher came in search of spiritual refreshment during her school holidays. Three months after their first meeting, Mother Maria and the Russian-born teacher knew they must found an Orthodox Monastery. They found a suitable building near Newport Pagnell, and the Benedictine Abbess generously provided them with the money to buy it.

In December 1965 Metropolitan Anthony received the Russian-born teacher as an Orthodox novice, and in July 1966 she and Mother Maria moved into their monastery. Five years later, Dame Mary Thomas

announced to her Abbess that she wished to join them. Her request was
furiously opposed by the Archbishop of Canterbury, who insisted Dame
Mary should wait a year, during which there should be no communication with the other two. At the precise termination of the stipulated
twelve months, Dame Mary Thomas joined the Orthodox Monastery
which, after sharp differences with Metropolitan Anthony, was in the
process of transferring itself from the Russian to the Greek orbit. In
November 1971 the Greek Archbishop received Dame Mary Thomas
into the Orthodox Church. He named her Sister Katherine and at the
same time he gave the ex-teacher the unexpected name of Sister Thekla,
after a follower of St Paul.

Mother Maria was consecrated Abbess and the three strong-willed
ladies began publishing religious pamphlets. They called their output
the Library of Orthodox Thinking, and they delivered it by hand to
bookshops in London, Oxford and Cambridge. Word spread, and letters
started to arrive from readers as far away as Finland and Zimbabwe.
Their Monastery became a place of pilgrimage, particularly popular
with Cypriot Greeks from London, who came in coachloads. By the
summer of 1974 Mother Maria was seriously ill with cancer and all this
was too much. They decided they should move to somewhere quiet,
before Mother Maria became too frail to travel. Sister Katherine and
Sister Thekla went ahead and explored the moorlands of Yorkshire.
They found a small farmhouse near the coast, with twelve acres of land.
It was safe from coaches, down a narrow, muddy lane. And there was
a stone-floored stable attached, which they saw immediately as a church.

The removal northwards, complete with monastery cat, is relived in
Mother Thekla's History:

> It could be called our last madness and Nimmy howled dismally all the
> way. We appeared to choose to leave a completed house, a reasonable
> climate, friends, priests, and the three of us – a dying Abbess and two
> elderly nuns – to betake ourselves to the bleakest strip of the coast in
> north-east Yorkshire, a strip so windblown that it is always three
> weeks behind in any harvesting, not behind the rest of England, but
> the rest of Yorkshire! Of course it was not our choice; we simply
> knew that we must go.

They moved into their new Monastery just before Christmas 1975
and just ahead of a snowstorm. For the next two years, Mother Maria
fought cancer in this austere but peaceful setting. She died in November
1977, and was buried in a field behind the Monastery. Mother Thekla

and Mother Katherine, as they now called themselves, channelled their grief into creating and publishing a memorial – *Mother Maria: her life in letters*. Then they returned to the daily round: writing, translating, adapting Orthodox melodies to English words for their services, and growing vegetables. They also became experts at rearing goats. They learned the symptoms of mastitis and magnesium deficiency, and achieved self-sufficiency in milk.

★

From Mother Thekla's translation of the immensely long *Great Canon of St Andrew of Crete*, John elected to set the first Ode. It divides conveniently into twenty-three *troparia*, or verses, preceded by an *irmos*, or chorus, which is repeated at the end. This allows the music to take the form, fitting for Lent, of a long, slow prostration: a chromatic descent through all the scales, major and minor. At the top of the score, John quotes from St Andrew's prologue to his confession:

> Where shall I make my beginning
> to mourn the deeds of my wretched life?

The music for the *irmos* is a traditional Russian chant, sung in unison by the basses. The twenty-three *troparia* are chanted by a single male voice, borrowing note patterns from the *irmos*. Each *troparion* brings the response from the choir 'Have mercy upon me, O God, have mercy upon me', which is sung by turns in English, Greek and Church Slavonic. Its melodic line is each time a different permutation of the seven notes of the scale, harmonized alternately in major and minor triads. The overall effect is solemn and intensely ritualistic. The score is dated 'March 1st 1981, Sunday of the Last Judgement'.

The *Great Canon* is improbable fare for an Anglican cathedral, but Martin Neary loved the beauty John produced by moving triads around with complete indifference to Western musical grammar.

In his note for the Festival booklet, John quoted some words of Mother Thekla:

> We must repent from minute to minute, person by person, because the day of judgment is at hand, and there we can only be alone, face to face, alone with the judge.

So the Festival audience had been warned. What was coming was not a concert piece, or even a church anthem. *The Great Canon of St Andrew of Crete* is an act of prayer, closely connected to the most penitential days of the Orthodox Church year. However, a choir of the calibre of Martin Neary's is needed to sing it.

*

Trisagion, the piece John composed after the *Great Canon*, is both solemn and festive, taking its tone from the season which follows Lent in the Orthodox calendar. And it is a Tavener rarity: a purely instrumental composition. The choice of instruments — two trumpets, French horn, trombone and tuba — was to suit the brass ensemble which had been formed by his friend the trumpeter Philip Jones.

The *Trisagion*, or thrice-holy hymn, had already been set by John for four-part chorus, as part of his *Liturgy of St John Chrysostom*. The new piece for brass quintet is more than another setting: it is a study in contrasts. It opens with a sequence of brilliant flourishes. These fanfares, dominated by the trumpets, are almost Venetian in character: Monteverdi through a filter of Stravinsky. Then comes a sonorous statement in Orthodox style of the thrice-holy hymn. The fanfares and the traditional chant continue to alternate, before a final, triumphant statement of the Russian-based chorale.

The score is headed 'For Philip Jones', but that master of brass declared it unplayable by a quintet of mere mortals. It was shelved.

*

The saddest event for John in 1981 was the death of Lady Birley: a major blow, but not unexpected. She was as old as the century, and had been confined to a nursing home for some time. The funeral service was held on 26 June, in the tiny parish church of West Dean, near Charleston Manor. The Bishop of Lewes officiated, and John provided the music. There was no organ in the church, but he was quite prepared to play the harmonium, which he thought could provide a fitting atmosphere. Unfortunately, the church wardens did not consider the ailing wheeze-box worthy of him, and brought in a brand-new small upright piano. Out of politeness, he used this soulless instrument to accompany Kathleen Moss as she sang the traditional Russian Orthodox *Kontakion* for the departed. Those who were present can still remember the intensity he brought to the occasion.

Charleston Manor passed to Lady Birley's son Mark, who sold it. In Rhoda Birley's will, John was left a trio of elegant Regency music stands, which he placed near the piano in Wembley Park, loaded with ikons.

*

Meanwhile, Sheila MacCrindle, from John's publishers, had taken
Akhmatova: Requiem to John Drummond, who was now director of
the Edinburgh Festival. Drummond's passion for things Russian was
well known. The *Requiem* interested him immediately. The score was
also taken to Gennady Rozhdestvensky, who was in his last season as
chief conductor of the BBC Symphony Orchestra.

Rozhdestvensky not only knew Anna Akhmatova's *Requiem*: he had
grown up in the Soviet Union during the Stalin era of which it spoke.
After glancing through the sketchy manuscript, which John took to him
in person, he declared he must conduct this piece. It was arranged that
he should do so twice; first in Edinburgh on 20 August 1981, then again
at the Albert Hall in London seven days later, as the climax to his
farewell BBC Promenade Concert. The orchestra would be the BBC
Symphony and the soloists would be the baritone John Shirley-Quirk
and the American soprano Phyllis Bryn-Julson.

John remembers the first rehearsal in Edinburgh:

> Phyllis Bryn-Julson had the most fantastic voice, perfect for it, but
> although she was *note* perfect, no way was she *Russian* perfect. I don't
> think she'd ever looked to find out what the text was about. The first
> word in the piece is 'nyet', the Russian for 'no'. She pronounced it
> 'net'. Rozhdestvensky pulled me towards him and said, 'Darling, you
> must spend all night telling her how to speak Russian!'

What in fact was arranged was some intensive coaching for Bryn-
Julson from a Russian actress, after which the soprano's singing of the
gruelling solo won her some glowing notices.

Rozhdestvensky admits now that when he first said he must do the
piece, he was responding impulsively to the sight of a text in Russian
by his favourite poet. But when he came to examine the score, he was
astonished to find that the music partnered the words perfectly. It was
not just a good mechanical fit: it was an exact spiritual match. Nevertheless, the performance was a flop with the Edinburgh public. It was
the largest work John Drummond had ever commissioned, and he
describes it as a commercial disaster: 'the most unsuccessful concert I
put on in my five Edinburgh Festivals. It played to an audience of about
240, in the Usher Hall, which holds 3,000.'

When *Akhmatova: Requiem* came to London's Albert Hall, John and
Father Sergei Hackel found the experience even more miserable than
the première. For the first half of his farewell Promenade programme,
Rozhdestvensky chose to conduct Beethoven's Pastoral Symphony. This

had evidently brought out the Beethoven crowd, because after the interval quite a few seats stayed empty. Worse, once *Akhmatova: Requiem* got under way and those left behind came to realize they were faced with a gloomy modern epic, there began a steady trickle towards the exits. John and Father Sergei had been given aisle seats, for their convenience when it came to taking bows. John remembers tactless folk tripping over his legs while making their escape.

If anything, the situation of Gennady Rozhdestvensky was worse. During the interval, between the Beethoven and the Tavener, his dressing room had been visited by two quiet men from the Soviet Embassy. A reminder that Akhmatova's *Requiem* was still banned in the Soviet Union. His response was to sit down straight after the concert and write John a note, in Russian. It translates as follows:

> Dear John,
> Permit me to thank you from the bottom of my heart for entrusting me with the first performance of your *Akhmatova: Requiem*. This composition is a glorious page in the history of twentieth century music.
> Thank you.
> Long life!
> Gennady Rozhdestvensky. 27.8.81

John had it framed and keeps it on his piano.

The story was not over. When Rozhdestvensky flew back to Moscow, he was stopped at the airport by a customs man who searched his bag, seeming to know what he was looking for. The officer pulled out the programme for the farewell Promenade concert, turned to the text of Akhmatova's *Requiem*, and accused the conductor of trying to bring forbidden literature into the Soviet Union. Rozhdestvensky denied that a concert programme could be categorized as literature and insisted it was part of his musical archive. The official called his boss, who read the verses of the *Requiem* with intense interest, then declared, 'He is right! It is not a book.' He gave the programme back, but called after Rozhdestvensky, 'You will have a lot of trouble, I warn you!' These were the days of the Brezhnev regime.

The story of *Akhmatova: Requiem* was still not over, but it had to wait eight years for its happy ending.

★

After his stroke, composing did not come easily to John, and he was frequently distressed by temporal lobe attacks. Sometimes he felt a strong compulsion to become a monk. In the shop at the Russian Cathedral he found two books which made a deep impression: *His Life Is Mine* and *We Shall See Him As He Is*, both written by a Father Sophrony, whose address was given as Tolleshunt Knights, in Essex. John wrote to Father Sophrony and was granted permission to pay a visit. He had been advised not to drive a car during his convalescence, so his mother took him there.

Father Sophrony was born in Tsarist Russia in 1896. As a young man, he had some success in Paris as a painter, but then his enthusiasm for the religions of the East crystallized into a passion for Orthodox Christianity. He made the pilgrimage to Mount Athos, the Holy Mountain in Greece which is Mecca for the Orthodox, and there he lived for twenty-two years: first as a monk in the Russian monastery, then as a hermit in a cave. He came back to Paris to write a book about his experiences, which was published in 1952. Then he came to England and took up residence in the Old Rectory at Tolleshunt Knights. His writings and the power of his personality attracted followers from far and wide, and the Old Rectory became home to a self-styled Orthodox community of monks and nuns. The heads of the Orthodox Church in England were scandalized by the mingling of the sexes, but tourists came flocking. A frequent visitor was the Estonian composer Arvo Pärt, who took a house nearby.

John was enormously impressed by his first meeting with Father Sophrony, who encouraged him to talk about his temporal lobe attacks and explained that these were not uncommon among spiritual folk. When John said he despaired of living in this world and wanted to renounce composing and become a monk, Father Sophrony reached out, took John's face in his hands, and declared, 'I am optimistic.' The cause for optimism was a mystery, but John felt encouraged and positive. Perhaps he could channel his yearning for the religious life into acts of composition. He was impressed when he noticed, on Father Sophrony's desk, a copy of T. S. Eliot's *The Cocktail Party*.

Assemblies for prayer in the Old Rectory were most unusual by Orthodox standards. Monks and nuns of many nationalities would congregate and then, one by one, as the spirit moved them, they would recite the Jesus Prayer, 'Lord Jesus Christ, Son of God, have mercy upon us,' each in the language of his birth and always adding the tag favoured by Father Sophrony: 'and upon Thy world.'

John learned that the origin of this prayer is in the Gospel story of the blind man Bartimaeus, who sat begging at the side of the road. When he heard that Jesus was passing, Bartimaeus cried out, 'Jesus, thou Son of David, have mercy upon me,' to which Christ replied, 'Go thy way, thy faith hath made thee whole,' and Bartimaeus was cured. The plea of blind Bartimaeus became the basis of a prayer of the early Church, which today plays a central role in the spiritual life of Orthodox believers. Often it is repeated silently, when it takes on the rhythm of breathing. Inhale: 'Lord Jesus Christ, Son of God'. Exhale: 'Have mercy on me a sinner.' John set about making a musical composition from it, with Father Sophrony's 'and upon Thy world' tagged on to the end.

By the autumn of 1981 he seemed in reasonable health and spirits, and his parents felt able to leave him while they took a short holiday in Paris. The lounge was to be decorated during their absence, so the furniture was draped in dust sheets. Shortly before they came back, John suffered his worst-ever temporal lobe attack: an episode of *jamais vu* which robbed him of any memory of who he was or where he was. The shrouded furniture became strangely terrifying, and when his parents walked in the door he did not recognize them. They called a nurse who lived nearby. She calmed everybody down, and John's memory slowly returned. What came back first was the name and the face of Father Sophrony. Then he heard music, which at first he could not identify. It turned out to be the piece he had been composing: *Prayer for the World*, for sixteen solo voices. He sat down to write it out in detail. As can be seen from the diagram overleaf, *Prayer for the World* is architecturally a perfect palindrome. Atmospherically it is a chant, akin to an Indian mantra.

Its most important feature is its circularity. During its thirty minutes it goes nowhere, preferring to sustain a single spiritual state. A note by John at the front of the score warns 'This is essentially a meditative piece, and therefore sudden changes of time and dynamic should be avoided.' The sixteen singers spend most of their time confined to single droned notes, which can last for several minutes. Intensity is brought to the stillness when the drones are interrupted by decorated melismas, which include microtonal 'breaks' in the voice, as in Byzantine chant. Although the melismas have an improvisatory air, they are in fact strictly controlled: designed to enhance key words in the prayer.

John looks back on *Prayer for the World* as the most radical piece he has ever written, and on its performance as one of the most awkward evenings of his life. His publishers had found a commission for it: it was to be the only new work in a concert at the Round House on 11 October 1981, to celebrate the tenth anniversary of the Contemporary Music Network. Also billed were motets by William Byrd and Arnold Schoenberg's *De Profundis*.

PRAYER FOR THE WORLD
John Tavener

Logos 1 to 12
Each logos is set three times:
first in Church Slavonic, then in Greek, then in English.

1–3   Lord

4–6   Lord Jesus Christ

7–9   Lord Jesus Christ, Son of God
                          have mercy upon us

10–12   Lord Jesus Christ, Son of God
                have mercy upon us and upon Thy world

Logos 13 to 24
Each logos is set three times:
first in English, then in Greek, then in Church Slavonic.

13–15   Lord Jesus Christ, Son of God
                have mercy upon us and upon Thy world

16–18   Lord Jesus Christ, Son of God
                          have mercy upon us

19–21   Lord Jesus Christ

22–24   Lord

The performers were the John Alldis Choir, and our John knew there
was trouble ahead when Alldis complained, as soon as he saw the score,
that there was nothing in it for his singers. They liked to make a noise
and be extrovert. They would not appreciate being asked to keep on
chanting the same old prayer. After the first rehearsal, John wrote a
despairing note to Clive Wearing.

> My Dear Clive,
>   I never seem to be able to *reach* you by *phone*.
>   I would *love* you to hear Prayer for the World on Sunday evening
> – Round House. 7.30.
>   I feel you might be in greater sympathy with it than anyone else –
> and I feel somewhat isolated.
>   With love,
>   John.

Clive was not able to be there, and John spent a very lonely evening indeed. It seemed to him that the atmosphere during the performance of his piece was worse than indifferent: it was downright hostile. Unlike *The Great Canon of St Andrew of Crete*, *Prayer for the World* employs a twelve-note row as its building material. The dissonant and atonal consequences roused but failed to satisfy the expectations of the Round House audience. As always with John, the mathematics are subordinate to the imperatives of his ear, and the musical 'argument' serves only to reinforce the condition of *stasis*.

Prayer for the World was unwillingly applauded, and at the party after the concert no one wanted to catch John's eye. He escaped as quickly as he could, not even speaking to the deputation from his publishers.

Next morning, he could hardly wait until the time when he knew Robin Boyle would be at his desk in Chester Music. Boyle had been very pleased when *Prayer for the World* was commissioned for such an important concert, and had ordered that the score should be printed expensively. His phone was ringing when he walked into his office. It was John, hoping he didn't feel too let down last night. Boyle had to say that he was very disappointed.

John reacted positively: he sat down and put the finishing touches to his next composition, *Mandelion*, which is dated that very day, 12 October 1981.

*

Mandelion was originally scored for orchestra, but it ended up as John's only major composition for the organ.

The word *mandelion*, in Orthodox terminology, refers to 'the ikon not made by hands': that is to say, the imprint which was made on a cloth by Christ's face. John intended his orchestral piece to be 'a meditation upon ikons, and upon the changing and distorting images of the face of Christ'. Like *Trisagion*, it makes dramatic use of traditional Russian chant, which seems here to be doing combat with the forces of serialism.

When his scoring for orchestra did not work, John had the idea of taking the score to St Andrew's Church and trying it on the organ. As soon as he began to play he knew this was the instrument for which *Mandelion* was intended, so he spent several days at St Andrew's, working out the registration and the exact pitches. All the original material survived the transformation.

Robin Boyle found a commission for *Mandelion*. It would be played by Peter Sweeney, in St Patrick's Cathedral, Dublin, as part of the 1982 International Organ Festival. John went to Dublin for the occasion. He thought his music sounded splendid on the big, romantic organ. But looking back on *Mandelion* today, he blames it for 'compromising with modernism' and for lack of clarity. 'It's not clear when one moves from one image to another. Nowadays I would tend to make this extremely clear, by the use of modes.' The delicate closing passage, which represents the Dormition of the Mother of God, still pleases him, but he regrets the overall failure to be simple. And he deplores the traces of Messiaen. The best he can say of *Mandelion* is that it is a transitional piece, still on the road to Tradition.

★

The winter of 1981/2 continued to be a hard one for John, and the weather was bitterly cold. Now that *Mandelion* had been translated into a work for organ, he was without the orchestral piece he needed to fulfil a commission from the City of London Sinfonia. Seeking to redefine the commission in his own terms, he remembered the bowed psalteries he had heard at the Purcell School of Music: an exquisite sound, delicate and very ancient. According to legend, the psaltery was the instrument King David used to accompany his Psalms.

Having settled on his sound, John became stuck again. He can remember feeling empty and depressed as he stared through the French windows at the snow-clad garden in Wembley Park, and at the sky of unmodulated grey which shut out the sun. When inspiration finally came it was from the words of the British saint, Gildas the Wise, who lived as a hermit on the banks of the River Severn around AD500. Welcoming the warmth of Christianity to his chilly landscape, St Gildas wrote:

> These islands, stiff with cold and frost, and in a distant region of the world, remote from the visible sun, receive the beams of light, that is the Holy precepts of Christ, the true sun.

John gave his new piece the punning title *Towards the Son*. It would take the form of a ritual procession. The orchestra, without violins but with prominent handbells, would have to climb twelve steps of wintry serial music, before it could at last come into the light and warmth of the bowed psalteries, generators of pure Byzantine chant. At the end, to celebrate the orchestra's enlightenment, three treble voices would be heard from on high, singing a Byzantine setting of the *Trisagion*.

Now that he had his structure, John wrote the music down quickly. The score is dated 11 February 1982. He was pleased with what he achieved. Looking back on it today he feels no inclination to change it. However, it was far from popular with the management of the City of London Sinfonia. Their policy of commissioning new works to be performed alongside the popular classics was a recent one. They had already commissioned a flute concerto from Nigel Osborne, who had exactly followed the stipulation that he should write for Mozartean forces. This had been a great joy to the orchestra's manager, Ian Ritchie. When John's score arrived, it was a great irritation. Ritchie did not mind the boy trebles: he could get those free. But he wanted to throw *Towards the Son* back at its composer because of the infuriating expense of the bowed psalteries. The conductor, Richard Hickox, persuaded him to live with it. It was Hickox who had persuaded the City of London Sinfonia to go for a Tavener commission in the first place. He remembers, 'What I asked for was a chamber orchestra piece which would go well in a programme with some Mozart. I didn't know John very well.'

3 : The sound of their voices

The unhappy night at the Round House had not deterred John from writing choral music, but the search was on for more willing performers. One of his pupils, Martin Stebbing, shared a flat with Peter Phillips, the founder of an up-and-coming choral group called the Tallis Scholars. Their field was the sacred music of the Renaissance. John went to hear them sing music by the Tudor John Taverner. He was bowled over by the sound of their voices. There was none of that wobbliness and preciousness which affects so many English choral groups. The women, in particular, sang with an exceptional purity of tone.

Peter Phillips remembers that he and John got on well immediately. He told John he had founded his group as a protest against the awfulness of the BBC Singers. John grumbled about the resistance at the Round House to his *Prayer for the World*, then showed Phillips another piece he had written, of a different character. This was *Funeral Ikos*, which has nothing to do with serialism. It began life as a melody derived from Russian chant, which John applied to a translation of verses from the Orthodox Burial Service for Priests. Elise Ross had sung it, to great effect and entirely without accompaniment, at the funeral of the Revd Cameron Joyce in June 1978.

By the time of the memorial service for Rhoda Birley, at St James's Church, Piccadilly, in November 1981, John had turned *Funeral Ikos* into a choral piece. The words meditate calmly on death and the eternal yonder. The melody is strong and the harmonization is simple. The choir of St James's sang it well, and John got a measure of its effectiveness when he was cornered after the service by Sir James Goldsmith, hard man of high finance, who said this was exactly what he wanted sung when his own funeral came along.

Peter Phillips found *Funeral Ikos* a lovely, restful piece – ten minutes of uncomplicated, highly singable music. He was also enthusiastic about the *Great Canon of St Andrew of Crete*, and knew his choir could do it justice. This meant there was already more than half an hour of Tavener music which the Tallis Scholars could perform. The idea evolved of presenting a balanced programme of music old and new. The old music would come from the unexplored tradition of choral polyphony in medieval Russia. John had just stumbled on this tradition, in a book belonging to Father Michael Fortounatto, the choirmaster at the Russian Cathedral. It fascinated Philip Pilkington, who declared this early Russian repertoire to be a sound world of its own: dissonant, seemingly illogical, a challenge to the contemporary ear. Pilkington said if it could be sung, he would find the funds to make a commercial recording of it. Peter Phillips and John went for study sessions with Father Michael. Although they had to take some arbitrary decisions about Russian performance practice, Phillips and his singers arrived at believable interpretations of half a dozen eight-part motets.

The Tallis Scholars got the chance to try out their mixed programme when they were invited to give a concert of Orthodox music in the chapel of Keble College, Oxford. The singing was to be prefaced by an explanatory talk from the Oxford don Timothy Ware, the first Englishman to be made a bishop in the Orthodox Church. Bishop Kallistos was his Orthodox title, and he already knew John Tavener quite well, having answered all sorts of queries from him about Orthodox theory and practice. The concert took place on 1 December 1981, and although it was an intimate occasion it had landmark significance: the first public performance of Tavener by the Tallis Scholars, and the official world première of *Funeral Ikos*.

Soon afterwards came the recording of the LP. As well as the examples of Russian medieval polyphony, it included a chant by Tsar Ivan the Terrible, a setting of the Lord's Prayer by Stravinsky and another by Rachmaninov. John was represented by his *Great Canon of St Andrew of Crete*.

★

By now the sound of the Tallis Scholars had inspired a new Tavener choral work, called *Doxa*, which is Greek for 'glory'. *Doxa* is much shorter than *Prayer for the World*, but with similar mystical attributes.

Peter Phillips got an inkling of what was coming when he was woken at six o'clock one morning by a Tavener telephone call. 'He asked me, "Can your sopranos sing top C for five pages?" So I said, "No. Course not!" Grumpy, you see. So he said, "Oh, all right. Then I'll score it for the basses."'

After he put down the phone and woke up properly, Peter Phillips savoured this insight into the workings of the Tavener musical mind. When the score arrived, it lived up to expectations. The only text is the single word *doxa*. The music is for double choir. It is cast in five movements: five sonorous blocks, each resting on a bass pedal note, or drone.

The first movement has the tenors of Choir 1 singing the word *doxa* to a twenty-note melody. They sing it in minims, and are followed at different speeds by the altos (in semibreves) and the sopranos, who sing in breves and so only cover the melody's first five notes. The bass drone is on the first note. Choir 2 follows Choir 1 in strict canon.

During the other four movements the bass drone progresses through the next four notes of the melody, while the other voices sing its permutations, always at three different speeds, and always with Choir 2 shadowing Choir 1.

At the end of each movement, John imposes a five-second silence. He added an explanatory note to the score.

> The whole of *Doxa* must be sung as quietly as humanly possible –
> indeed at the threshold of audibility. In order to create this 'unearthly'
> sound, it may be necessary to place the choir in a very remote place,
> with the doors open or half open. During each of the five second
> silences, the choir should move nearer the audience – not singing
> louder but becoming nearer and yet not seen.

★

The Tallis Scholars gave the first performance of *Doxa* at the Wigmore Hall on Sunday, 12 September 1982, as part of their programme of Orthodox music old and new. From John's point of view, the acoustic of the Wigmore Hall was less than adequate, and it was disappointing that his proposal for the disposition of the choir was ignored. Nevertheless, the concert was warmly received.

Reviewing it for *The Times*, Nicholas Kenyon described *Doxa* as 'perfect liturgical music, un-self-advertising, drawing attention only to its text'.

For the *Guardian*, Meirion Bowen marvelled at the depth of the Tavener suntan, which belonged, he was sure, in the *Guinness Book of Records*. About *Doxa*, he said, 'Its five sections seem to circle slowly round the text, shedding light, as it were, from all directions.' He also referred to the other new Tavener work of the evening: a setting of the

Lord's Prayer, which he thought even more restrained and ritualistic than the one by Stravinsky in the same programme.

*

John's *Lord's Prayer*, for four-part choir, makes compelling use of the simplest means. It starts in unison, with all four parts singing the note of F. The altos and tenors then stay on F for the whole of the recitation, while the sopranos climb the rungs of a minor scale, more properly described as Byzantine tone II, and the basses make a matching journey in the opposite direction. The magic is in the timing of the moves from step to step.

John can remember exactly how this Lord's Prayer came to him. His mother was driving him back to London from their country cottage in Devon. 'Her greatest earthly wish was to drive as fast as she possibly could down a motorway with no cars on it. She hated people passing her. By the time we'd got back, I'd composed the piece.'

*

John has always been diligent about providing occasional pieces for family and friends: musical *bonbons* to celebrate birthdays and weddings. Several of these have been published. One has become a classic. It began as a present for John's nephew Simon, when he was three. John remembers how it came into his head, fully grown. 'I looked through the poems of William Blake and I found "The Lamb". I read the words, and immediately I heard the notes.'

Those notes – one short phrase and its interlocking permutations – form a simple and unforgettable melodic line: the perfect match for Blake's vision of God's gentlest creature. Instinct rarely tells John he has written a hit, but this time he had that feeling. He rushed *The Lamb* to his publishers, urging them not to bother about a commissioning fee but to get it to King's College, Cambridge, as fast as possible: in time to be included in their Christmas Service of Nine Lessons and Carols. He also sent a copy to Martin Neary down in Winchester.

The Lamb was first performed, as part of the Carol Service in Winchester Cathedral, on 22 December 1982. Then, on Christmas Eve, it was broadcast from King's College, Cambridge. Audience response was overwhelming, and *The Lamb* has since become a staple of church choirs and choral societies all over the country. John's publishers have licensed a company in America to print copies for that market. They are pleased to announce that *The Lamb* is 'the biggest selling choral title in our catalogue, by any composer, living or dead'.

One musical feature of *The Lamb* never before remarked upon is the chord which goes with the word 'lamb'. It deserves our notice. It has a bitter-sweet quality which John finds particularly expressive. The notes are B (sopranos), G (altos), C (tenors) and A (basses). He calls it the 'joy-sorrow' chord. He used it first as the penultimate chord in *Funeral Ikos*, then found it perfect for the little lamb, because of its suggestions of both innocence and sacrifice. In the years to come, we shall find him exploiting its symbolic potential over and over again.

4 : The magic square

Once *The Lamb* had been despatched, John started to consider the commission from Pat Harrison for next year's Little Missenden Festival. Pat was expecting something about fifteen minutes long, to share a programme with Debussy's Sonata for flute, viola and harp.

While he was waiting for inspiration, John got a phone call from Greece. It was Vicky, wanting to share her discovery of the Yeats poem 'To a Child Dancing in the Wind'. It seemed to speak to her very directly.

> Dance there upon the shore;
> What need have you to care
> For wind or water's roar . . .

Coincidentally, John had just made friends with a new set of people who preached the importance of Yeats, because of his allegiance to Sacred Tradition. Vicky's phone call triggered the creative process and a major composition was under way: settings for soprano, flute, viola and harp of eight poems by W. B. Yeats, with 'To a Child Dancing in the Wind' as the centrepiece.

Although the music sounds Celtic, its well-springs lie not in Ireland but far to the East. Yeats' image of 'Old Men Admiring Themselves in the Water', for example, is set to a Byzantine chant. Even 'The Fiddler of Dooney', with its toe-tapping rhythms and its drone on the viola, was inspired not by the Emerald Isle but by a concert of Indian music John attended with his mother. The setting of the last poem, 'All the Heavy Days Are Over', sounds like an Irish lament, but the musical material is from medieval Russia.

The songs are joined one to another by an instrumental bridge, played on the harp. Its twenty-five notes read exactly the same forwards and backwards, and it has to give us pause, because this device was to

become a Tavener stock-in-trade. John calls it his 'Byzantine palindrome'. He says a Traditionalist told him there is an arrangement of
twenty-five Greek letters which, when read either forwards or backwards, spells out the same message. And that this message can be found
on Byzantine gravestones.

Research for this book failed to turn up that Greek message, so John
was asked again to rack his brains. He remembered he first saw the
palindrome in a book about Webern: a heavy volume, lent to him by
Philip Pilkington. When this was put to Philip, he identified the tome
without difficulty. It was the chronicle of Webern's life and work by
Hans Moldenhauer.

Lo and behold, on page 431 of Moldenhauer, the ancient palindrome appears. Apparently it was familiar to the early Christians,
but it is in Latin, not Greek, and forms a word square rich in
possibilities.

```
S A T O R
A R E P O
T E N E T
O P E R A
R O T A S
```

An English translation might be 'Arepo the sower holds the wheels for
his work', but the meaning is not the point. What matters is that the
words can be read four ways: both horizontally and vertically, starting
either from top left or from bottom right.

Webern sought analogies between the 'magic square' and the dodeca-
phonic system. John has always been content to use it more plainly. He
reads it horizontally – SATOR AREPO TENET OPERA ROTAS – and he finds
it highly convenient that it is made up of only eight different letters.
Once he dumped modernism, his music came to inhabit a world made
up largely of traditional modes: scales of seven notes, discounting their
microtonal sub-divisions. To create a 25-note palindrome using the
magic square he begins with a five-note phrase from such a scale. This
phrase is defined as SATOR. In other words, S = note 1, A = note 2, and
so on. When he comes to AREPO, he already knows that A = 2, R = 5
and O = 4. The new letters, E and P, are assigned to the next two notes
of the scale. So E = 6 and P = 7. The eighth and last letter is the N in
TENET. That one becomes the octave or duplicate of the root note, and
gets the number 8. The magic square drawn up as numbered notes
therefore looks like this:

```
1 2 3 4 5
2 5 6 7 4
3 6 8 6 3
4 7 6 5 2
5 4 3 2 1
```

John's 'Byzantine palindrome' is explained here because of its recurring importance, but the impression must not be left that *To a Child Dancing in the Wind* is coldly mathematical. The opposite is true. This is music of exceptional warmth and lyrical beauty. The score is headed 'For Victoria . . . but these are private songs addressed to you in public', which, oddly enough, is a quotation from T. S. Eliot.

When Pat Harrison was eventually told that the fifteen-minute piece she was expecting for harp trio had turned into a forty-minute song cycle, she acted with her usual decisiveness. A lecture on Yeats was set up in the village hall, as an introduction to the concert. *To a Child Dancing in the Wind* was performed in Little Missenden Parish Church on 16 October 1983, by the Nimrod Trio, with soprano Alison Gough from the Tallis Scholars. The critics responded coolly, but Vicky was thrilled to receive a tape of it.

*

Reference has been made to John's new circle of friends. At its centre was the painter Cecil Collins, who had written to say how much he had enjoyed *Thérèse*. John had been extremely grateful for Collins' enthusiasm. He was invited to take tea in the Bohemian quarters at the top of a house in Paultons Square, Chelsea, where Collins lived with his wife, Elizabeth, who was also a painter. Although the Collinses were both in their seventies, they still loved to entertain kindred spirits. John became a regular. He counts his years of friendship with Cecil and Elizabeth as some of the most important and happiest of his life.

Tea at Paultons Square would be brewed by Elizabeth on the tiny top floor landing, which accommodated a gas stove, pots and pans, paintings and provisions. The refreshments were served in the low-ceilinged attic sitting room, among stacks of books, a collection of *objets trouvés*, and statuettes Elizabeth had made from painted paper. Before tea was taken, in accordance with ritual, visitors would spend some time with Cecil in his tiny studio one floor below. Also on this floor was a good-sized bathroom, largely irrelevant to Cecil since he had a horror of water. His studio was heavily double-glazed, and intensely expressive of his character. Most of the limited space was taken up with unsold canvases. Then there was a divan, which meant his nights need not be spent up on the top floor, where Elizabeth had her own studio/bedroom. What space was left was given over to a fancy hi-fi system and a large record collection: everything from Bruckner to the music of the Sufis, with a prominent place for the neo-classical works of Stravinsky. Spare surfaces where things might be put down, including the floor, had long since been piled high with the notes Cecil was always writing to himself.

The principal subjects of Cecil Collins' visionary paintings were fools and angels. In his view, Art was Sacred and it was the duty of the artist to grapple with primordial Truths. He quietly subscribed to the Bahai religion, but in argument he steered clear of sectarian terms. Instead, he offered a personal cosmology, encompassing 'the Eye of the Heart' and the quest for 'the Great Happiness'. There were those who compared him to William Blake.

A central tenet of the Collins philosophy, which chimed in precisely with how John felt, was that the secret desire of every heart is for the Paradise lost, and that all art is a striving towards that Paradise. John and Cecil grew very close. They talked on the phone two or three times a day. And John was fascinated by the other visitors to the Collins studio. Keith Critchlow, for example, the great authority on sacred architecture, who could talk equally well on the symbolism of Chartres Cathedral and the meaning of mosques. And Marco Pallis, an old Etonian of Greek extraction, who combined a commitment to Buddhism with a love of mountain climbing, and wrote a spiritual autobiography called 'Peaks and Lamas'.

The ground and first floors of the house in Paultons Square were occupied by the poetess and Blake scholar Kathleen Raine and one would have expected a joyful mingling between upstairs and down. Kathleen Raine was the founder of *Temenos*, a magazine devoted to the Sacred Arts of the Imagination. Once upon a time she and the Collinses had been very close, but a quarrel whose origins became lost in the mists of time meant that upper and lower floors were not in communication. The difficulty for visitors was that those coming to see Cecil were just as likely to have something to share with Kathleen, but the separate front doorbells were clearly marked and could never be rung in tandem. John was advised of the tricky situation by third parties, so when Kathleen Raine let it be known that she would be happy to receive him, he took tea with her then left the house for a few minutes, before returning to ring the doorbell marked Collins.

The network of Collins fellow-thinkers was international. One day John got a call from Elizabeth, to say there was a Greek lady in London, whose home was near the hotel where he liked to stay when he was on the island of Aegina. She was Anastasia Morosinis, wife of the aristocratic poet and scholar Petros Morosinis. John went to meet her in Paultons Square. Anastasia explained that her husband's fragile temperament kept him confined to their island home. Next time he was on Aegina, John promised, he would pay them a visit.

★

The Nafsika Hotel on the island of Aegina, twenty miles south of Athens, had once been recommended by Vicky for a Tavener family holiday. John liked it a lot, and took to going there by himself.

The proprietor, Dimitri Poulakos, does not care for the general run of tourist, so the Nafsika is hardly advertised. It shares the promontory above the port with what's left of a temple to Apollo. The hotel's forty cabins are arranged on a curve, west-facing at its centre, to enjoy the sunset over Epidaurus fifteen miles away in the Peloponnese. Embraced by the curve of the buildings is a garden of flowering shrubs.

Mr Poulakos was pleased to receive a visit from Mr Tavener's biographer. He likes to point out that his hotel is a favourite of artists. Painters from the Greek Academy come here, and it has attracted two of Greece's most distinguished poets: Mr George Seferis and Mr Odysseus Elytis. The Poulakos tour pauses outside a pair of cabins at the north end of the arc. Number 5 is synonymous with Mr Elytis. Number 3 is where Mr Tavener stays. Mr Tavener is a sun-worshipper, so his terrace faces south, towards the ruined temple of Apollo and the sea beyond. Just below the terrace is a mass of bougainvillaea, which flowers in early June. According to Mr Poulakos, it 'blazes like fireworks' and can be seen as far away as Epidaurus.

On his own admission, Mr Poulakos is not musical. Nevertheless, he has arrived at a view of Mr Tavener the artist. He describes him as 'an alien in his own land', who first identified with the Celts, then turned to Orthodoxy because it is a religion under siege, squeezed by Rome from the West and Islam from the East. The hotel proprietor is an authority on the Balkans. He publishes a magazine, the *Eurobalkans and East European Quarterly*, which he says is read in Washington. In his office he keeps a copy of the full score of John's *Akhmatova: Requiem*. He cannot read the music, but he appreciates the words Mr

Tavener has chosen, and sometimes he listens to the tape he was given. In his judgement, Mr Tavener's understanding of Anna Akhmatova is profound. He foresees a time when music by Tavener will be the battle hymn of Orthodoxy militant.

Mr Poulakos used to enjoy the evenings spent pouring *ouzo* for Mr Tavener, but there have been fewer of these since his guest composer found a new friend further up the hill. Mr Poulakos has never set eyes on Mr Petros Morosinis, and he hints there is something odd about a person who never shows his face in public.

*

John describes Petros Morosinis as 'a reclusive hypochondriac, but immensely impressive'. The Morosinis mansion, which Petros shares with his wife, his mother and other members of his extended family, is the most splendid on the island. After an expensive education, Petros locked himself inside with the writings of the Desert Fathers, founders of the Orthodox Church. John has been making the short pilgrimage from his hotel to this mansion since 1983. Here, he is granted insight into the wisdom of the East, and he counts the foibles of Petros a small price to pay. He looks away tactfully when the thermometer under his host's arm is checked during meals. And no offence is taken when Petros rushes to fetch his hoover after John has dropped bits of food on the floor.

It was Petros Morosinis who introduced John to the verses of George Seferis, poet and member of the Greek diplomatic corps, who died in 1971. Although Seferis was a prized guest at the Nafsika, Petros never met him. His recommendation was based solely on the poetry, which he described to John as profoundly Greek.

Between August and November 1983 – his longest stay on the island so far – John responded to the poetry of Seferis with musical settings reminiscent of his *Sappho: Lyrical Fragments*.

Sixteen Haiku of Seferis are written for soprano, tenor, timpani, hand-bells, gongs and strings. They are sung in Greek. The music matches the moodiness of the epigrams and their evocative nouns: coral and pomegranate and statue and sea and sun and wine.

Just as the harp palindrome unifies *To a Child Dancing in the Wind*, a canon for the strings binds the *haiku* together. To add a touch of hierarchy and ritual, there is also a four-note phrase on the gongs, which rings the changes on the familiar rhythmic pattern 4, 3, 2, 1. The vocal lines often sound like Orthodox chant, and once, when the soprano oscillates between three pitches above an instrumental drone, her ululations seem to come from still further east.

Asked to comment on the *Sixteen Haiku* for this book, John looked at the score and noticed that here, for the first time, he quotes from his favourite moment in the Orthodox Lenten Services: the fragment of chant which goes with the words 'Behold the Bridegroom comes at midnight . . .' The connotations of the musical fragment have only the slightest bearing on the pagan world of the *haiku*, but musical allusions to the Bridegroom will become much more important and frequent in the big Orthodox pieces which are to come.

*

Back in England, John hurried to share his enthusiasm for the poetry of Seferis with his friends Cecil and Elizabeth Collins. To his surprise, they already knew all about the man and his work. They met him during the sixties, when he was Greek Ambassador to London. Not only that: it was Seferis who had arranged the Collins exhibition in Athens which led to four of Cecil's pictures being purchased for the Greek National Gallery.

Cecil spoke highly of Seferis, but could not help adding that something about the fellow's appearance called to mind an untrustworthy dealer in olives. It was also revealed to John that when Cecil was in Athens he hardly left his hotel room. He refused to ride on public transport with the natives, and brooded about what might be lurking in his hotel washbasin.

*

One of John's favourite hunting grounds in London during the early eighties was the bookshop of the Society of St Alban and St Sergius, in Ladbroke Grove. Browsing here one day, he found a text which affected him as powerfully as the poetry of San Juan de la Cruz. It was the *Invocation to the Holy Spirit* by St Symeon the New Theologian, who has been described by Bishop Kallistos as 'one of the greatest mystical writers in the history of the Orthodox Church'.

St Symeon was born in Asia Manor in AD 949 and became a monk in Constantinople. Throughout his life he received visions of the Divine Light, and all his writings are dominated by the theme of God as Light. His was a world of paranormal states not unfamiliar to John, who responded with his most ambitious sacred choral work since *Ultimos Ritos*. He called it *Ikon of Light*.

Cecil Collins had once done a painting called *The Icon of Divine*

Light, and this may have been at the back of John's mind when he chose his title. The important reference, though, is to the glories of traditional ikon painting. John wanted to do as the ikon painter does: to work strictly within the confines of a Sacred Tradition, creating compositions free of novelty but filled with serenity. He loved the Orthodox definition of ikons as 'windows into heaven'.

Ikon of Light, for double choir and string trio, is in seven movements. The central movement is a setting of St Symeon's *Invocation to the Holy Spirit*. The outer movements are like pairs of mirrors. The first and second are reflected in the sixth and seventh. Number three comes back as number five. John's earlier piece for the Tallis Scholars, *Doxa*, is part of the musical scheme. In its original form, it serves as the second movement. Transformed, it becomes movement number seven.

The score is prefaced with a clear manifesto:

> I hope that this work will be performed with restraint and majesty. It should unfold as a ritual, attempting to express the inexpressible, i.e. 'uncreated light'. The Greek words FOS and DOXA mean 'light' and 'glory'. The Greeks had a natural inclination towards the luminous, hence the central role of the Transfiguration in the mysticism of the Orthodox Church. The music calls for a building with a large acoustic in order to accommodate the long 'silences'. The string trio may be thought of as 'the soul yearning for God', and is best placed in a gallery, or somewhere similarly distant from the singers.

Appended to this preface is a quotation from St Symeon: 'He was wholly in the presence of immaterial light, and seemed himself to have turned into light.' The first movement, called 'Fos (I)', is an intensely dramatic setting of the one Greek word, meaning 'light'. The choirs, pre-echoed *pianissimo* by the string trio, project this word *Fos* six times. The duration doubles each time, but the notes in the chord are always the same, and this *Fos* chord turns out to be none other than the joy-sorrow chord which epitomized *The Lamb*. John's explanation is that a chord containing joy and sorrow can also express the duality of light and dark.

The last of the *Fos* chords dissolves into the second movement, 'Doxa', which we already know.

The third movement is 'Trisagion (I)': a setting of the thrice-holy hymn. The traditional Byzantine melody is given first to a single baritone voice, then to the tenors and basses, then to the string trio. John asks that it should *not* be sung or played 'in a westernized manner'.

The central movement is St Symeon's 'Invocation to the Holy Spirit',

From manuscript sketchbook

sung in Greek. A translation is provided at the front of the score. 'Come, true light; come, life eternal; come, hidden mystery;' is how it begins, and there follows a long recitation of the qualities of the Holy Spirit, with each quality prefaced by the invitation 'Come'.

To provide music for this catalogue, John turned to the magic square. A page from his manuscript sketchbook (reproduced above) shows how

he used it. He began by choosing a five-note phrase for the Greek word
Elthe ('Come'). His chosen notes descend from the fifth to the first of
the scale. These form the top line of the square, or SATOR, and the rest
of the 25-note palindrome is produced in the usual way. To extend
his range, he drew up a second magic square, this time based on the
inversion of his phrase: five notes ascending, from the same starting
point.

The movement is divided into five sections. In the first section, the
form of the music follows the form of the text. Just as St Symeon begins
each new thought with *Elthe* ('Come'), each musical statement begins
with SATOR. The pattern is SATOR ROTAS; SATOR AREPO; SATOR OPERA;
SATOR TENET, but this is not always obvious, because the elaborations,
extensions and microtonal decorations introduced at the beckoning of
the words.

During the second section, the string trio sets out the palindrome
straightforwardly: SATOR AREPO TENET OPERA ROTAS, with some octave
displacement, and a prolonged silence between each five-note phrase.

The third section brings back the choirs, who continue with
St Symeon's *Invocation*, this time using the magic square based on the
inversion.

The fourth section is a canonic statement by the trio of the inverted
palindrome.

For the fifth and final section, the string trio and the choirs join forces
to produce repeated, overlapping statements of magic square number
one: glittering cascades of notes ending with a radiant re-statement of
St Symeon's opening words, 'Come, true light'.

The 'Invocation to the Holy Spirit' is as long as all the other movements together. It is followed by a repeat of the 'Trisagion', this time
bringing in the sopranos. Then comes 'Fos (II)', with the joy-sorrow
chord again, but now with a pendant of downward notes, like pealing
bells. 'Fos (II)' dissolves into the last movement, 'Epiphania'. The Greek
word *epiphania* means literally 'a shining forth'. The choirs sing it five
times. Their music is the inversion of 'Doxa', plus a halo of fiercely
bright sound from the strings. To introduce 'Epiphania', John has
written another quotation into the score, this time from the Russian
Saint Seraphim of Sarov:

> I can't look at you, Father, because the light flashing from your eyes
> and face is brighter than the sun and I'm dazzled.

★

When Peter Phillips saw the score of *Ikon of Light*, he recognized a great work, with major but not insuperable difficulties for the performers. A première was arranged: it would be performed by the Tallis Scholars at Tewkesbury Abbey in the summer of 1984, as part of the Cheltenham Festival. With help from Philip Pilkington, it would also be issued as an LP. John suggested that Peter Phillips join him on his winter holiday in Greece, so they could talk about it some more. They went to Aegina together straight after Christmas 1983, and Peter Phillips has tales to tell.

The Nafsika Hotel was closed, so they stayed in a modest little place on the sea shore. 'Herculean amounts of retsina were drunk. One day we drank two and a half litres at lunch, then we went back for dinner and the bloke in the restaurant said, "You can't be here!" John said, "Yes. Here we are again. More, please."'

Just when Peter Phillips began to think that *Ikon of Light* had been forgotten, John produced the score one breakfast time. 'We sat enjoying the view and discussing the business of recording it.' That same evening, while John sat at the water's edge soaking up the last of the sun, Peter Phillips took the snap that was used on the record cover.

New Year's Eve, John decided, should be spent in Athens, so they took the hydrofoil to the mainland. 'He insisted on staying at the Grande Bretagne Hotel in Syntagma Square,' says Phillips. 'It was a hundred pounds a night, even in those days. I said, "John, I just can't afford this. You stay here and I'll find somewhere cheaper." He said, "Oh no! It's New Year's Eve. I'll pay for you." So he hired two rooms, then we had a night on the town. He had all his favourite drinking haunts, and his churches. When they shut we went back to the hotel and made some telephone calls from my room. We rang up his ex-wife, Vicky, and then we rang a girl I'd met on Aegina. We rang her at midnight. She was obviously horrified. Then we fell asleep! Sitting in my room, with the television on in the background. We woke up at 7 o'clock in the morning, with the television going z-z-z-z-z, and he'd never been in the room he'd paid so much money for.'

Back in London, Peter Phillips threw a party in his Maida Vale flat to celebrate John's fortieth birthday: 28 January 1984. He can recall every detail of the evening:

Some of the Tallis Scholars came round and we sang to John, at midnight. We sang some of the old Russian stuff, then we sang his own music to him. People were in tears. One girl was blubbing her heart out. To add tone to the occasion, John had brought some

Russian nobility with him, and a Russian professor, and various extra-ordinary people I have never seen since. After the singing, John got very drunk. He slumped in his chair and he said, 'I am an old man, and sinking fast.' So we said, 'Come on, John, cheer up, it's not that bad.' He just went on and on and on, repeating the same phrase like a mantra: 'I am an old man, and sinking fast.' He was terrifically good company, though.

5 : The Sacred Tradition

John's forty-first year was an outstanding one for first performances. In May there was the première of *Sixteen Haiku of Seferis* in St David's Cathedral. In July both *Towards the Son* and *Ikon of Light* were unveiled at the Cheltenham Festival.

Towards the Son is dedicated to Richard Hickox, who admits that when he came to conduct it he could make little of it. He found it arid and contrived, and unredeemed by the bowed psalteries. As a matter of fact, these were an infernal nuisance. The administrator of the City of London Sinfonia, Heather Baxter, was the one deputed to hire them from the Early Music Shop. She remembers that at the first rehearsal the players tried tucking them under their chins. Luckily, she says, John Tavener was there to point out that psalteries go between your legs! There was no time to achieve mastery, because *Towards the Son* was squeezed into a heavy Mozart programme. On the night, the psalteries sounded weedy rather than delicate: no match for the orchestra. The critics were polite but puzzled. John hopes that one day *Towards the Son* will be revived, with more commitment, and in an ambience more spiritual than Cheltenham Town Hall.

The première of *Ikon of Light* was quite a different matter. It was given in the sublime surroundings and generous acoustic of Tewkesbury Abbey, and the performance, by the Tallis Scholars with the Leda Trio, was thoroughly rehearsed and deeply committed. The triumphant evening prefigured the success of the *Ikon of Light* LP. When the recording was issued in France, the critic Didier Louis described *Ikon of Light* as 'one of the great religious works of the late twentieth century'.

*

The acclaim for *Ikon of Light* did little to relieve the pressure John felt himself under on the subject of Tradition. The spiteful clique at the

Russian Cathedral rubbed his nose in the fact that Arvo Pärt was Orthodox by birth, and he began to doubt the value of everything he had written before his conversion.

In his anxiety, he turned to a member of the Orthodox congregation who was a Jungian psycho-analyst: an American called Bani Shorter. For a fee, she advised him to make a major Orthodox musical statement, and then to drive off in his Rolls Royce, leaving his detractors choking on his exhaust.

'A major Orthodox musical statement' was something John had been considering for some time: ever since his *Liturgy of St John Chrysostom* came under fire. What he planned was a complete setting of the two-hour Orthodox Vigil Service, which would show proper regard for the Orthodox rule book. Rachmaninov had set parts of the Vigil Service, but no one before had provided music for every second of it: entrances, exits, prayers, processions and readings from the Gospels.

As a rule, the music for Orthodox services is drawn from the fund of material, mostly anonymous, that has been handed down from choirmaster to choirmaster. In the Russian Church, material can be chosen from the ancient settings known as *Znamenny* chant, as well as from the more popular nineteenth-century harmonizations. But the choice must be informed by an appreciation of the Russian Orthodox tone system. There are eight Russian Orthodox 'tones', or sets of characteristic melodies, and each is used for one week at a time. In other words, there is an eight-week cycle, at the end of which Tone I comes round again. Russian choirs know these tones by heart. John was determined to avoid basic error. There were long and intense sessions with Father Michael Fortounatto, who found himself in the role which was once David Lumsdaine's.

Although extremely grateful to Father Michael, John did not intend to confine his Vigil Service to Russian musical vocabulary. He was equally stimulated by the tone system of Byzantium. Here again there are eight tones, but they work in a different way. Unlike the Russian tones, they are essentially modal (see Appendix D). John's source book – a rare volume, in Greek, but showing Byzantine chant in Western notation – had been unearthed in an Athens junk shop. Once found, it never left John's composing table. It sits there alongside his much-thumbed copy of the standard guide to Russian chant, the *Sputnik*.

The text for his *Orthodox Vigil Service* would be partly in Greek, partly in Church Slavonic, but mostly in English. His ambition was for no less than 'a huge but musically connected tapestry, from Byzantium,

Znamenny chant and my own musical heritage'. But who would commission such a colossus? And who could perform it?

The eventual source of patronage, both surprising and apt, was Christ Church College, Oxford, where the Tudor John Taverner had once been in charge of music. The present choirmaster, Francis Grier, happened to mention to Clive Wearing that he would love to commission something from the present John Tavener, but had never met him and wondered how he would react. Clive Wearing moved fast, as Francis Grier recalls:

> Clive organized a meeting, and got John to come to Oxford. We went out to supper. It must have been a very good supper. The idea of the commission at the start of the meal was just another anthem. By the end of the meal, it had turned into the Vigil Service. I said to John, 'I don't know if the Dean and Chapter will buy this one, but I'm keen.'

A fortunate combination of people and circumstances then helped the *Orthodox Vigil Service* through the commissioning process. First, Francis Grier was a most unusual Anglican choirmaster, with leanings towards mysticism and the East. Secondly, a canon of Christ Church, Oliver O'Donovan, was a member of a working party of Anglican and Orthodox clergy, set up to find common ground. Thirdly, the unique Bishop Kallistos was a major influence in the theology faculty.

*

The Vigil Service in the Orthodox Church can be held on any Saturday evening. Its underlying purpose is the watching through the night for the Resurrection of Christ. Certain parts never change, but others vary with the seasons. John's version is designed for use between Easter and Ascension Day. He was emphatic that it should be an authentic act of Orthodox worship. He wanted the complete choreography, with all the ceremonial details, although Christ Church is, of course, an Anglican cathedral. Bishop Kallistos arranged for a full complement of English-speaking Orthodox clergy. He himself would be the Celebrant.

Musical instruments are not allowed in either the Greek or Russian Orthodox Churches, but it seemed imprudent to carry authenticity quite so far. Christ Church Cathedral has a fine choir, but two hours of unaccompanied music by Tavener was a daunting prospect. The compromise was handbells. Their ancient sound had always been a favourite of John's, and Bishop Kallistos was able to give them his blessing on various grounds: church bells are sometimes rung during

Orthodox services; there are little bells attached to the censers, which sound when they are swung; bells and cymbals feature in the Orthodox Churches of Egypt and Ethiopia.

When he finally sat down at his composing table, with two hours of music to write, John compared himself to Richard Wagner, pen poised at the start of *Parsifal*. The purpose of the *Vigil Service* was entirely different, but the need for pacing was just the same.

A full analysis of the 200 pages of the *Orthodox Vigil Service* is outside the scope of this book, but we cannot pass by without a broad survey of its musical world, because this will be the world of Tavener for years to come.

The hallmark of the mature Tavener style – the free combination of Russian, Byzantine and subjective elements – is displayed at the very beginning, when the choir sings

> Christ is risen from the dead,
> Trampling down Death by death,
> And upon those in the tomb bestowing life.

The melodic contour of the setting belongs in Russian Tone VIII, but the melody is John's own, and the underlying drone is characteristic not of Russia but of Byzantium.

The Psalms which follow start in Byzantine Tone II, then there is a switch to *Znamenny* chant, freely used. While some voices ornament the Russian melody, others are confined to long-held notes. The effect is of clusters around a drone: less Russian than Indian.

When we reach the first text in Greek, we hear the sopranos and the handbells for the first time: a synchronicity dictated not by Tradition but by John's instincts as a composer. The text is a famous one, 'Fos Ilaron' ('O Gentle Light'), and its melody can still be heard at Vespers in parish churches all over Greece. John's version is elaborate. While the chant is carried plainly by some voices, others move it forward at a different speed. On top of that, a twenty-five-note palindrome derived from it is given to the handbells and a second choir.

'The Song of Simeon' ('Lord now lettest Thou Thy servant depart in peace') sounds strangely modern. John explains why: 'That setting is entirely my own. Nothing to do with Tradition. It is allowed because the "Song of Simeon" comes into the category which the Greeks call "domestic". It doesn't have to adhere to the system.' Armed with this official licence, John paid tribute to *Stimmung*, a choral work of the 1960s by Karlheinz Stockhausen, which dwells for seventy-five minutes on a single chord of B flat ninth. This so-called sacred chord is the one with which 'The Song of Simeon' opens. After sounding it seventeen times, John moves to another, but he brings back the *Stimmung* chord for the words 'To be a light'. It is all extremely effective, but when John takes detours like this Father Michael Fortounatto shakes his head: 'I have untold reservations about it. When he uses his own melodies, he is a foreigner to the fund of melodies.'

'The Song of Simeon' is followed by The Lord's Prayer: another item classified as 'domestic' by the Greeks. John's setting is the one described in an earlier chapter, when it was premièred by the Tallis scholars at the Wigmore Hall.

In Greek monasteries, the Vigil Service peaks as a spectacle during the 'Polyeleos': the sequence where all the lamps and candles are lit, and the huge candelabra overhead is given a twirl to set it spinning. The words are joyful. John sets them to the melody already used for 'Christ is risen from the dead', but applies a technique which is far from Orthodox: a canon in six parts.

Almost at the close of the service comes 'The Great Doxology': a slow-moving hymn, 'Glory to God in the Highest'. While the appropriate Byzantine chant is carried by sopranos and tenors, a magic square derivative is enjoyed, at various speeds, by other voices and the hand-bells. For increased joyfulness, more sopranos ring the changes on a descending phrase, like a carillon. John's instruction to all the performers is 'Radiant, but with great inner quiet and stillness.' 'The Great Doxology' is the section of his Vigil Service in which he takes most pride. Here, he thinks, he has found 'just the right balance' between Tradition and his own sensibility.

The première of the *Orthodox Vigil Service* in Christ Church Cathedral was to be in May 1985. Before then, we come to other matters of great moment.

*

Ever since reading the Thekla translation of *The Life of Mary of Egypt*, John had known that this would be his next opera. But who would write him a libretto about the whore of Alexandria turned Desert Saint? He did not think it would be right to unleash Gerry McLarnon on her. He sought everybody's opinion. Years went by. In the end, it was Cecil Collins who came up with a possible candidate. His suggestion was the Byzantinist Philip Sherrard, who used to teach at London University. Sherrard still kept a house at Highgate, but now lived on a Greek island, writing books. The man was no artist – he turned out translations and moralizing tracts – but he once sat at the feet of a Russian sage on Mount Athos and would certainly know his Orthodox stuff. He had been involved with Kathleen Raine in setting up the magazine *Temenos*, and he had written a book of essays on sexual love, entitled *Christianity and Eros*. So perhaps *Mary of Egypt* would suit him. To flesh out Cecil's picture of Sherrard, Elizabeth Collins described Philip the ladies' man.

John wrote to Philip Sherrard and a correspondence blossomed. Sherrard was evidently tickled to be asked to write a libretto and John was warmly invited to visit the Sherrard island hideaway. This invitation was gratefully acknowledged, but it came at a very bad time. John's mother had been diagnosed as suffering from cancer and was undergoing chemotherapy. However, by the end of September she seemed to be making a good recovery. She drove John to the airport, and he began his acquaintance with what looked at first like paradise on earth.

Katounia, on the island of Evia, was once a French mining concession, where they dug magnesite. The mining company went out of business in the thirties, leaving a ghost town of elegant villas, high on cliffs above its own beach, with a view westwards to the mainland and the sunset beyond Parnassus. In the fifties, when Philip Sherrard came along with his Greek wife and some business partners, the site was going cheap. There was no electricity, and the nearest shops were miles away along a dirt road. Sherrard and Co. kept it like that, and let out villas to other connoisseurs of Arcadia. Kathleen Raine came, and Gavin Maxwell, whose brother Sir Aymer was often there for several months of the year. By the time John arrived, Katounia had been the Sherrard estate for nearly thirty years. The natural beauty was intact, but not the Sherrard ménage. Sherrard's Greek wife had become his ex-wife. She occupied one of the most beautiful villas, while Sherrard, now in his sixties, shared a more Spartan residence with a new young wife from England.

To John, Philip Sherrard seemed charming and theologically brilliant. In the evenings, he sat enraptured while the grizzled patriarch, fuelled on home-brewed wine, preached Orthodox Tradition, with emphasis on the tricky concept of Uncreated Eros. Sherrard's daughter, Liadain, had heard it all before. She was twenty-nine years old, fiercely intelligent and deeply reserved. She was also striking-looking: tall, with flowing clothes and long dark hair. In John's eyes, she possessed a beauty which radiated from within: the kind of beauty that Muses are made of. However, her boyfriend was there with her.

During the daytime, John was expected to bring a music notebook and follow where Sherrard led, jotting down material for their operatic enterprise. At the monastery up the road, for example, when the nuns began to chant, he remembers Sherrard instructing him 'Write that down! It will be very inspiring.' Then he was taken to meet a *psaltis* – a practised Orthodox singer – who, at Sherrard's bidding, went through his lengthy repertoire.

John returned to England elated, and with a book full of melodic fragments. But then came the shock of seeing how his mother had declined. November was a grim month. Her condition deteriorated, while the notes arriving from Sherrard about the opera were all disturbingly high-flown.

When the first instalment of the libretto arrived, labelled *The Prologue to Mary of Egypt*, it confirmed John's worse fears, as he explains:

> It began 'Blessed be the Kingdom of the Uncreated Eros, for they are of the Kingdom.' It might be all right for a learned lecture, but no way was it going to take on musical life. No way could I set any of his words. They were too complicated, too philosophical, too intellectual, too dry. My face fell when I first saw them. I still went on corresponding with him, hoping perhaps things might get better, as I was hoping also that my mother might get better. It seemed she was going downhill.

Muriel Tavener was taken into the Royal Marsden Hospital in early December. John watched her leave home. 'It was as much as she could do to get into the car. She sort of crawled into it. I remember I was in my lowest state ever.'

Word came from the hospital that she had about a month to live. She summoned a family conference at her bedside and told John and his father that one of them must marry again. John was awed but not surprised by her strong-mindedness. 'She was, as she always had been, the quiet head of the whole thing.' He was desperate for her to have an Orthodox funeral, although she was still nominally a Christian Scientist. She told him, 'You do it whatever way you want.'

During this dreadful time John cast about him for guidance from those in spiritual authority. He tried Metropolitan Anthony, Bishop Kallistos, Father Sergei Hackel and Father Michael Fortounatto, but he was helped most by his phone calls to Mother Thekla. He had not yet met her, but had kept in touch about *Mary of Egypt*. Now she excelled all others as adviser and comforter. He telephoned her every day.

By 9 January 1985 Muriel Tavener was unconscious and her breathing was changing. Her family gathered round her. John asked his father's permission to send for Father Michael Fortounatto. It was granted, and John attaches huge importance to what happened next.

> My father said, 'Very kind of you to come, Father Michael. Would you like a cup of coffee?' This was in her room. Typical of my father, always carrying on with the show, whatever else is happening. Father Michael said no at first, and then, 'Oh, perhaps I will!' So he did have the cup of coffee, which took up a little bit of time, and this was significant. And then he looked towards her and he said, 'Ah yes, she's very far gone into the next world.' Then he read the Orthodox prayers for the dying. And at the precise moment that he said Amen, blood trickled out of my mother's mouth and she died. At that very moment. I thought this was a miracle.

The funeral service for Muriel Tavener was held in the Russian Orthodox Cathedral. Metropolitan Anthony officiated. Father Michael's choir sang the traditional Russian hymns and then, taking John completely by surprise, the Tallis Scholars stepped forward to sing his *Funeral Ikos*.

John was devastated by his mother's death and said he would write no more music.

PART SIX

*Glory to God for
everything*

§

1 : Ode to Death

Everyone knew that John was deeply attached to his mother, but no one was ready for the force of his grief. Few, apart from Mother Thekla, were able to say the right thing. He was still under the care of Dr Thomas, and reported to him in March that he had had a temporal lobe attack while visiting his mother's grave. For once, the *déjà vu* was welcome. It seemed his mother was still with him and there was no separation between the living and the dead. But the sensation passed and the despair returned. Marco Pallis, the Buddhist, recommended solitude and the restorative power of the landscape in Greece. John had booked his flight, when disaster struck his dear friend Clive Wearing.

On 29 March 1985 Clive was rushed to St Mary's, Paddington, and into Dr Thomas' care. John joined Clive's young wife Deborah at the bedside. Clive's GP had diagnosed severe influenza, but the symptoms had escalated to fluctuating consciousness and seizures. He was suffering from herpes simplex encephalitis and his chances of survival were slim. In a desperate attempt to haul him back from the brink, recordings were played to him of music he loved. John dashed home for tapes of pieces he had discussed with Clive at every stage of their composition. There was no response.

At first John thought he should cancel his flight to Greece and stay to support Deborah, but the pull of Aegina was too strong.

*

During the centuries when Aegina was a target for pirates, the island's capital was on a hill at its centre. In the 1820s, when the threat of piracy had passed, houses were moved stone by stone back to the coast, leaving the hillside with the ghostly shells of twenty-seven Byzantine chapels, linked by paved lanes overgrown with wild flowers. This atmospheric location, called Paleochora, had attracted John from the first. During later visits, he became curious about the gaudy new buildings at the bottom of the hill. Here lay the relics of St Nektarios, a modern saint, who died in 1920. Nektarios had been a bishop with a brilliant mind and simple tastes. His favourite pastimes were gardening and communion with nature. After his death, he became a legendary miracle-worker, especially famous for healing injuries to the brain.

When John got to Aegina this time, he went straight to the shrine of St Nektarios and began to pray for the soul of his mother, and for the recovery of Clive Wearing. He returned to the shrine every day, and after each session of prayer he phoned Deborah. In the end she was able to report that Clive was out of mortal danger, although his brain had been permanently damaged.

John went on struggling to accept his mother's death. While praying to Nektarios, he always kept his forehead pressed against the casket which contained the head of the saint. This never failed to bring a general sense of release. One day, his prayers brought him something more:

> I heard a voice saying, 'Where your treasure is, there will your heart be also.' That seemed to comfort me tremendously. I was missing my mother so much, and this seemed to be a kind of affirmation that I will see her again when I die. Those words spoke very deeply to me. So did the landscape of Greece. I can't disconnect the two. The landscape of Greece had a healing effect.

Marco Pallis had been right. Now at last John could contemplate his mother's death with a measure of calm. His mind went back to the plan he had started to form when she lay dying.

*

For the Tavener family, the Christmas of 1984 had meant Muriel's hospital bedside. No one had given much thought to presents, but John's aunt Brenda did manage to find him something he appreciated. It was a book by Philip Sherrard: a collection of essays on modern Greek poetry, including 'Ode to Death' by Andreas Kalvos, which Sherrard had translated. This long poem is set in a graveyard at midnight. A man kneels in prayer beside his mother's tomb. To his joy, the phantom of his mother rises from the vault, assuring him she has found peace.

John loved not just the poem itself, but Sherrard's interpretation of it, in which the mother is the archetypal comforter: the endlessly feminine, without whom no man is complete. He took Sherrard's book to read while he was keeping vigil at the hospital. During one of his mother's last days, while she lay with her eyes closed, he used her bedside telephone to call a specialist bookshop. He wanted the Greek text of the Kalvos poem, and he described it over the phone: 'The one about a son who lost his mother and his life was shattered. She appeared to him again, and his life was comforted.' He felt sure his mother was listening. 'She must have heard me say all this, and I must have realized that she wouldn't mind me saying it.'

★

John found the Greek text of the Kalvos poem, and now he had it with him on Aegina. He also had the notebook of Byzantine musical fragments, collected when he was staying with Philip Sherrard. In the late spring of 1985 he began a composition in his mother's memory.

Eis Thanaton ('Ode to Death') is a music drama in Greek, to be sung by soprano and bass, each with their own group of instruments. It is in three sections.

First to be written was the long middle section, which sets the words of the mother to her son. The musical material is derived entirely from the Byzantine fragments, which have been elaborated and woven into a continuous melodic line.

For the response of the son to his mother, John again uses Byzantine chant. Then he departs from the Kalvos poem, transforming the mother into the Mother of God, heard from on high, singing the Alleluias from the Orthodox Funeral Service.

The opening section of *Eis Thanaton* – the sorrowing of the son at his mother's tomb – also draws on Byzantine chant. It was written later than the rest: after John had received a visit on Aegina from his friends Margaret and Sarah Long, who had themselves suffered a shocking bereavement.

★

John had got to know Viscountess Margaret Long and her daughter Sarah because of *Thérèse*. Lady Long had seen him on television, talking about the heroine of his opera, and had decided he belonged in the book she was writing, called *Special People*. She got in touch with him and they arranged to meet. In the end, the *Special People* book did not materialize, but John and the Longs became friends. Margaret and Sarah came to concerts. John was invited for meals. In October 1984 Sarah's younger sister, Charlotte, was killed when a juggernaut smashed into her parked car. Sarah and her mother were overwhelmed with grief. John recommended the balm of Aegina. In the late spring of 1985, while he was composing *Eis Thanaton*, they joined him there. He led them up the hillside of ruined churches. They lit candles in each one. He took them to the tomb of St Nektarios, where they found a marvellous sense of peace. He introduced them to Petros Morosinis, who talked to them about the Desert Fathers. Back in England, John arranged for them to have a private meeting with Metropolitan Anthony. After a series of such meetings, mother and daughter were received into the Orthodox Church.

★

In May, John was in Oxford for the performance of his *Orthodox Vigil Service*. The choir of Christ Church had been meticulously rehearsed by Francis Grier. Bishop Kallistos declared, 'This is the kind of music that we ought to be singing in the Orthodox Church in England today!' But he warned John not to hope for acceptance from England's Orthodox establishment during his lifetime. It had to be remembered that this unique occasion depended on the virtuosity of an Anglican choir and the enlightened patronage of an Oxford college.

And indeed, the Russian Cathedral was not strongly represented, although Father Michael Fortounatto came as an observer. The music critics, too, decided this was none of their business. It was left to the BBC to acknowledge the magnitude of John's achievement. The *Orthodox Vigil Service* was broadcast in its entirety on Radio 3, and the BBC recording was later issued as a double LP.

Now that he was back in England, John found the absence of his mother almost unbearable, but with *Eis Thanaton* the creative process had re-started. More music welled up in response to an Orthodox text addressed to the Mother of God. He called the result *A Hymn to the Mother of God* and dedicated it to his mother. Like *The Lamb*, it was 'music which came to me fully grown − a spontaneous reaction to the words. It's a celebration of the Mother: not just my own mother, but the Mother of God, the Earth Mother, the Feminine.'

A Hymn to the Mother of God is in block chords, sung by two choirs, with the second shadowing the first in strict canon, producing dense harmonies and fierce clashes. There are three sections. The first, rejoicing in the 'Woman full of Grace', ends on F major. A long pause allows the rich sound to clear, then comes a dreamy middle section in A flat. Here, the Mother is 'sanctified Temple' and 'mystical Paradise'. After another long pause, the final section echoes the first. The entire effect is ecstatic.

As soon as *A Hymn to the Mother of God* was finished, John added a companion piece. The second hymn has words from the Orthodox Feast of the Dormition of the Mother of God:

O ye apostles, assembled here from the ends of the earth, bury my body in Gethsemane; and Thou my Son and God receive my Spirit.

This valediction is set three times, with Russian chant as the basis of the setting.

★

No one had commissioned the *Two Hymns to the Mother of God*. They were first performed by Martin Neary's Winchester Cathedral Choir. Neary recognized them as little gems, and was equally delighted with the short choral work he had commissioned from John for the enthronement of Winchester's new bishop. John chose to set 'Love bade me welcome', by the seventeenth-century poet and parish priest George Herbert. He loved this beautiful and mysterious poem which begins

> Love bade me welcome, yet my soul drew back,
> Guiltie of dust and sinne.

As with *The Lamb* and the *Two Hymns*, the music is a spontaneous reaction to the text. There are three verses. At the start of each verse, the melody is supported by just a drone, Byzantine fashion. To bring each verse to a close, block chords move step-wise, in the Russian manner.

The enthronement of the bishop took place on 28 June 1985. John was accompanied to Winchester by Sarah Long. She remembers the calm beauty of the music, and the disturbing evening which followed. At dinner, John drank a lot and toasted death. Next, it was back to the cathedral in the gathering gloom. They processed down the nave, with John singing selections from the Orthodox Funeral Service. Then, before he could be stopped, he was wobbling up the long and dangerous-looking ladder to the organ loft. Sarah was helpless and horrified. At last, with bats flying round his head, John unleashed an organ *impromptu* based on 'I Could Have Danced All Night', which had been the favourite song of Sarah's sister Charlotte.

★

Meanwhile, James Rushton, the New York representative of John's publishers, was approached by a young American conductor called

Rhonda Kess, who was looking for the best in British Music Theatre. Rushton gave her the score of John's *Gentle Spirit*. Rhonda found the piece fierce, frightening and absorbing. She set up a performance at the autumn New Music Festival in Cleveland. John was invited to attend. He was still deeply affected by the death of his mother, but the consensus was that the change might do him good.

Rhonda Kess has been warned to expect someone of extravagant appearance, but she had not been prepared for the kamikaze behaviour which went with it. She can remember John's visit to Cleveland in graphic detail. Her first conference with him was in the coffee shop of his downtown hotel. John's tanned face and sun-bleached shoulder-length hair were set off by a black velvet jacket. His white shirt was largely unbuttoned, revealing a chest of dark hair and a dangling silver crucifix. It was eleven in the morning. He ordered *ouzo*. Rhonda opened a dialogue about how *Gentle Spirit* should be interpreted. John was impatient with reasoned debate. He answered her questions by singing extracts from the score and drumming on the table. When he got to the desperate soprano shrieks of 'Gospodi pomilui', Rhonda became aware that all other business in the coffee shop had been suspended. Later, in the hotel lobby, a hovering talent spotter called Mary was sure John must be an English rock star. She attached herself to him for the remainder of his visit. She even attended his lecture on the Sacred in Art. At the end of his oration, as he was leaving the hall with Mary at his side, John snorted something which sounded to Rhonda like 'the sacred and the profane!'

His presence certainly galvanized the performers, and the Cleveland *Gentle Spirit* was chalked up as a big success. After the show, John was presented with a bottle of vodka, and then the celebration party moved to a local night club, which had a jazz band in the corner. To everyone's surprise, John made his way across to the musicians and asked if they would mind if he took over for a while. They retired to the bar. John adjusted the piano stool, then waded into the deep nostalgia of Noël Coward's 'I'll See You Again'. After singing and playing it through once, he called on the night club audience to join him for a second chorus. He wanted them to sing with feeling, and he conducted them, cutting them off sharply at the ends of phrases and insisting on long, dramatic pauses. They loved it. He did it again, but then he made a rash move. He *segued* into the 'Battle Hymn of the Republic'. His performance of this cherished American anthem was loud and long and increasingly unpopular. There were calls for the return of the jazz band. The mood

turned ugly. John remained oblivious. Rhonda and others from the
Gentle Spirit party discreetly led him away.

★

John was back in England by the end of October, for the first performance of a new work. It had been commissioned to accompany the
unveiling of a stained glass window, designed by Cecil Collins for All
Saints Church in Basingstoke.

Behind the commissioning of both window and music was Canon
Keith Walker, an Anglican clergyman with artistic leanings. Having
established that angels should be the *motif* of Cecil's window, the Canon
was inspired to pen the verses that John should set. Unfortunately, he
was no George Herbert. This is how he began.

> Bright beings from the realm of light
> Messengers from the Lord of Might!
> Silent as dew and swift as sound,
> Your presence shines where God is found.

After that, sad to say, Canon Walker's words do not get any better.
What could John do with them? Nothing at all, was his first thought.
He consulted Mother Thekla. She advised him to transcend the doggerel
and respond to the angels' brilliance. According to Orthodox theology,
angels are 'secondary lights of the Trinity, having a royal glory'.

Good advice, but John had to bear in mind that his anthem would
be sung by the amateur choir of a local parish church. His solution was
to set Walker's words plainly, and to respond to the Byzantine doctrine
of angels with a brilliant organ part: brilliant in sound, but not difficult
to play, being no more than repeated clusters of notes in a high register.

The ceremony in Basingstoke was on 3 November 1985. Everyone
declared the music very fine. The stained glass window, too, made a
strong impression, favoured as it was by the transforming power of
bright sunshine. Each of Cecil Collins' angels held a heart, and within
each heart was a staring eye. Collins himself preached the sermon, in
which he told of the ancient Sufi tradition of the Eye within the Heart.
In all our hearts there is an eye, and we go through life with that eye
shut. It is the job of the artist to cause it to open.

After the service, tea was taken in the vicarage. Among the Collins
crowd on that day was Glen Schaefer: Professor of Ecological Physics
at the Cranfield Institute. Professor Schaefer had brought his daughter,
Maryanna, a first-year student at Oxford. Maryanna was just twenty.

She scanned those assembled for tea and thought them all terribly old, apart from John. He looked interesting – a man apart, and at odds with himself – so she went to say hello. He was startled by this blunt approach from someone so young, and with such a beautiful face. He told her he was coming to Oxford soon, to give a lecture illustrated by some of his music. She said she would be there.

And so she was: in the tiny chapel of Worcester College, where John preached on the text from Ezekiel 'Shall these bones live?' and the college choir sang some of his smaller pieces. In those days, John remembers, he tried to preach in the style of Metropolitan Anthony. Maryanna found the music very beautiful and the lecture a mess. John had clearly been drinking and this style of sermonizing did not suit him. Neither did she like the open-shirted, hairy-chested look, which had become more blatant since Basingstoke. Here, she thought, was someone striving to reconcile a deep spirituality with a surface shambles. What he needed was the right woman, but she was not about to volunteer.

John stayed overnight in Worcester College. Next day, by arrangement, he took afternoon tea with Maryanna at the Randolph Hotel. She told him about herself. Both her parents were Christian Scientists. At school, she had done well at music. Now, she played clarinet in the university orchestra, but she was taking a degree in physics because she wanted to understand her father's disillusion with so-called scientific thinking. At the end of their chat, John remembers, he gave Maryanna a farewell kiss on the top of her head. A patronizing gesture, she thought, but she went away impressed in spite of it. They corresponded. He sent her a little piece he had written for solo clarinet. However, they did not meet again for nearly four years.

*

John was still grieving terribly for his mother. All his favourite photographs of her were now framed and standing on the piano in the lounge at Wembley Park, where incense was kept burning.

He wrote to Metropolitan Anthony, describing the wretchedness of his state and talking once again of becoming a monk. On 27 December 1985 Metropolitan Anthony sent him this concerned reply:

> We must meet and talk about your spiritual way; but let me say that, at this stage, you should not think of professing monastic vows; you are still far too unsettled as a result of your Mother's death; it is from the depth of a great stillness that we must make major decisions about our life.

From what you tell me, you live within your grief at the expense of your Father's feelings, and perhaps his health, as breathing incense in one's own home is not right! Think of him, of his grief. Charity begins at home: cherishing actively, thoughtfully, both the living and the dead.

*

In January, John went to Greece, alone. He stayed in Athens, but not this time at the Grande Bretagne. He had found somewhere less extravagant and more convenient for the coast.

The unlovely Athens Chandris Hotel is a modern block on the main highway to the sea. In summertime, the lobby is full of foreign visitors, queueing to book their sight-seeing tours. In January, it is deserted. John was granted sole use of a tour operator's counter, where he could spread his papers and write his music, oblivious to the passing heavy traffic. The weather was cold but some days were sunny, and then he could take a taxi down to Glifada, the spot where St Paul first set foot in Greece, and now a seaside resort next door to Athens airport. It was not warm enough to sit on the beach, so he would take a table outside a quayside restaurant, drink tea, sketch music and cast his mind back. He was first brought to Glifada by Vicky, more than ten years ago. They had come often, to eat in the fish restaurants. Now, they were legally divorced, at her request, and she had married again.

When the weather was really bad he stayed all day at his counter in the lobby at the Chandris, pressing on with what he was writing. It was the first-ever setting in English of the *Panikhida*: the Memorial Service which is sung for the dead in Orthodox churches. His music is extremely plain and close to traditional Russian chant. His instruction is that it should be sung 'like a Sacred Lullaby'. The front page of his manuscript is set out like a memorial tablet.

SERVICE FOR THOSE FALLEN ASLEEP
PANIKHIDA
'In Blessed Memory'
MURIEL   CHARLOTTE
Eternal Memory!

The 9th of January 1986 was the first anniversary of his mother's death.

2 : The Protecting Veil

When John returned to England, he had several telephone conferences with Mother Thekla before completing his *Panikhida*, and by now he had drawn her into a new undertaking: the setting of an epic poem of thanksgiving, written in 1940 by a dying Russian priest in one of Stalin's labour camps. Translations were in circulation in the West, and John had been presented with one when he visited Margaret Long's local Orthodox church down in Bath.

The poem's full title in English is *Akathist: Glory to God for Everything*. An *Akathist*, in the Orthodox Church, is a thanksgiving service. The author of the poem, Father Gregory Petrov, exactly followed the *Akathist* pattern: thirteen hymns, each hymn in two main parts. It seemed to John to cry out for a musical setting. He sent the English text to Mother Thekla and asked her opinion. She was impressed by its power but anxious to see the original Russian. A copy was found among the Orthodox community in London. As soon as she looked at it, she began a new translation and scribbled John an excited note.

Friday night.
    John – DON'T start or waste time on Akathist – wait till I send it to you. It's EXCITING. You see there are certain word associations and liturgical cross-currents for which you need to know the services. For example, he uses for the sky the word *chertog*, which is the *bridal chamber* of Holy Week. Then he has echoes of Psalms and the Gospels – not direct quotations but hints, half-remembered strains. It's so *delicate*, the poetry – fragrant – an OBSTINATE refusal to fall into cynicism or hatred of the world because of what the world has done to him ...
    P.S. I'm torn with worry. What to do. How to do. Pray for me.

In spite of her anxieties, she worked fast. Her diary shows she started to translate on Thursday 16 January, kept going during Saturday and Sunday, and finished on Monday, 'well into the night'. From now on,

John and his needs loom large in the Thekla diaries. Mother Thekla has kindly opened them to this author.

Her new translation of the *Akathist*, complete with notes on the liturgical references, reached John on 22 January. He started work right away, but three days later told Mother Thekla he had had 'one of his attacks'. They spoke again on the 28th, which was his birthday. He was 'a little better', but the *Akathist* had been set aside. Durham Cathedral had asked him to write something for the 1300th anniversary of the death of St Cuthbert of Lindisfarne. Mother Thekla put him in touch with an expert on St Cuthbert, but this was not what he wanted, as she came to realize. On February 19 she wrote in her diary, 'It seems as if I'll be writing the words of St Cuthbert for him.'

They agreed not to provide the expected Anglican anthem. Instead, Mother Thekla versified St Cuthbert's life according to the rules of a Byzantine canon. After the statutory introduction, eight verses tell the saint's story, punctuated by the refrain 'Holy Father Cuthbert of Lindis-farne, pray to God for us.'

John's setting of Mother Thekla's text, for unaccompanied choir, was finished by the middle of March. The music is in the same spirit as the words: sober and mindful of tradition, yet contemporary. Block chords create a Russian atmosphere, but the hints of *Znamenny* chant are not specific. John and Mother Thekla called their creation an *Ikon*, and wrote an explanatory foreword to the score:

> This *Ikon of St Cuthbert*, an ikon of music and words in the place of wood and paint, seeks to recall, in its stylised form, the personal aura of Cuthbert, Saint of Lindisfarne.

*

As soon as *St Cuthbert* was finished, John returned to the *Akathist*. During the next four months, Mother Thekla logged many calls about it: some seeking clarification or reassurance, some reporting good progress. By the end of June the first draft had been completed, and John declared he could go no further without meeting his collaborator. Mother Thekla invited him to pay her a visit. On 23 July 1986, feeling extremely nervous, he was driven by friends to the Greek Orthodox Monastery of the Assumption, in North Yorkshire.

Alerted by the sound of the car struggling down her lane, she who had filled the void in his life was standing waiting for him in the yard. She was physically imposing, with strong features and a ruddy complexion, which glowed in the summer sun. The gusty wind snatched at her black robes, making her even more impressive.

John's friends said, 'We can see you are in safe hands,' and drove away. His hostess exuded energy. Her accent was Oxbridge and she smiled a lot, displaying a striking absence of teeth. John asked how he should address her. She said he could call her anything he liked, except 'The Abyss', which was how she had been addressed on a recent parcel. After showing John the goats, she took him indoors and introduced him to Mother Katherine, who was gentle and dignified and immensely tall.

John talked *Akathist* with Mother Thekla for the rest of the day, but to demonstrate his music properly he needed a piano. He spent the night at the local inn, and next morning he was taken to the home of Mother Thekla's friend Daisy Hardy, in Fylingthorpe. Mother Thekla drove. Her style at the wheel of her Morris Traveller, and much else about her, brought back memories of his godmother, Rhoda Birley.

At Daisy Hardy's, John found a Blüthner upright piano, in mint condition. He placed his score on the music rest: nearly two hundred loose pages of manuscript paper. The *Akathist* was written for two choirs, nine soloists, a large string orchestra, organ and tuned percussion. Somehow, John's demonstration was going to represent all these forces. Mother Thekla was not familiar enough with music to turn the pages for him, so, as he reached the end of each one, he simply snatched it from the pile and let it fall to the floor. Mother Thekla dropped to her knees to keep the falling leaves in order. The first dozen had come into her hands when Daisy Hardy bounced in, calling out, 'Who would like tea or coffee?' John signalled 'No thank you' with a shake of his head, and continued the performance. Mother Thekla dared not speak. This was her first close-up of John in action. Daisy retired. The performance continued without further interruption for more than an hour and a half. John remembers that by the end there was blood on the keyboard. Nothing surprising about that, he says: his fingers often used to bleed when he was demonstrating big pieces. There is no record of what Daisy thought.

Back at the monastery there was more work on the score. A diagram John drew has survived from those sessions. It shows that, as with *Ultimos Ritos* and *Ikon of Light*, the layout of the performers was to carry a symbolic charge. The main choir and the soloists were to be on a raised central platform, approached by thirteen steps, one for each hymn in the *Akathist*. The second choir would surround the platform at a distance: boy sopranos to the east, basses to the west, tenors to the north, altos to the south. The orchestra would be in the dome, creating a 'halo'.

*

The *Akathist* had been written without a commission, and more than two years passed before a performance could be arranged. When it finally happened, practical considerations modified John's conception. Here is the place to outline the work as originally written.

The large structure is built in steps. The first of the thirteen hymns rests on the pedal note A, the second on B, and so on up the white notes until Hymn number seven, which is on G. Number eight drops back to A, and then there is another step-by-step climb, ending on the pedal note F. These pedal notes are really *isons*, or eternity notes, since John is thinking not in keys but in Byzantine tones.

Father Gregory Petrov followed tradition and divided each of his hymns, except the last, into *Kontakion* and *Ikos*. And he opened each one of them with the traditional invocation 'Slava Tebye Bojhe' ('Glory To You O God'). John takes these invocations and fashions them into sonorous curtain-raisers, each one rising through its chosen Byzantine tone (although the words are Russian).

The first *Kontakion* uses a Tavener technique familiar from the *Vigil Service*. While some voices carry the chant-like melody, various others sing only its first two, three, four or five notes, and then sustain their last note, so that clusters form. Beneath the clusters bass voices supply a constant drone.

The 'Glory to You's which end each hymn have their own distinct melody, and the final *Ameen* is always a distant echo, heard from any one of four directions, while up in the dome a bell tolls the eternity note and the strings spell out the Byzantine tone.

'Kontakion II' includes the first of Gregory Petrov's allusions to the Troparion sung during the Russian Orthodox services for Holy Week:

Behold the Bridegroom comes at midnight,
And blessed is the servant whom he shall find watching . . .
Beware, therefore, O my soul, do not be weighed down with sleep,
Lest you be shut out of the Kingdom.

The text of the *Akathist* is studded with such references, and John's music picks them up every time.

'Kontakion XI' is the climax of the piece. The text begins 'Across the frozen chain of centuries, I sense the warmth of your breath Divine,' and John's response is a thick wall of sound. The main melody, sung by tenors, is unembroidered Russian chant. Beneath it, baritones and basses have a lilting tune, which they sing in canon, while the organ and the timpani unfurl a 25-note palindrome. Then silence. Then a counter-tenor solo, whose melodic line comes from the Russian chant 'Thy Cross we adore'. After the solo, the same chant is restated with maximum force by the chorus and orchestra.

'Kontakion XII' has the melody from John's *Funeral Ikos*.

Father Gregory Petrov's thirteenth and final hymn consists of *Kontakion* only. John treats it quite differently from the others. He begins with the cellos, whose expressive melody is a 25-note palindrome. Out of this grow choral Alleluias, which envelop Gregory Petrov's last lines. Then back comes the cello palindrome, while the violins slowly climb higher and higher, in a mood of devotion. After a final *Slava* from the choir, the eternity note in the double-basses tapers away to nothing.

*

When John got back to London after his first visit to Mother Thekla, the news from Cecil Collins was that Maryanna's father, Glen Schaefer, had died of Hodgkin's disease. The pioneering ecologist and committed Christian Scientist was fifty-six years old. John wrote to Maryanna, full of empathy. Since he did not know where she was spending the summer vacation, he sent letters to all the addresses he had for her. There was no reply.

The condition of his friend Clive Wearing remained unchanged. Clive had entirely lost his episodic memory: he could recite facts, but was blank on experiences. He accepted Deborah as his wife, but had no recollection of the wedding. If she left the room for a short time, then he greeted her return with rapture, forgetful of her recent presence. John's face was recognized, but there was no meaning in the welcome. At every moment, Clive's perception was that he had just woken up. The horror of his situation sometimes reduced him to violent despair. He could never be released from medical supervision.

Deborah had been visiting him every day for fifteen months in the psychiatric wing of St Mary's Hospital. At the same time, she was holding down her job as a press officer, and helping charities for the brain-injured. She feared that if she stopped all this she would collapse and go mad. John campaigned for her to try Aegina and the shrine of Nektarios. In the end, she agreed to take a short break.

Before he left for Aegina with Deborah, at the end of August 1986,

John set Mother Thekla a daunting task. She was to provide a libretto for an opera based on the life of St Mary of Egypt. She was not told that Philip Sherrard had already tried and failed.

*

As soon as she landed on Aegina, Deborah Wearing felt a sea-change. As she puts it: 'Suddenly the enormity of what had happened to Clive simply melted into the landscape. Something about Greek Orthodoxy, or the Greeks, or the place, or all three, made Clive's condition seem natural, and in the scheme of things.'

By a strange coincidence, Deborah had studied music under John's old mentor, David Lumsdaine. Now she could see the other side of the coin, as she reports:

> John's music is just rushing through him all the time. That's why he used to drink so much and take stacks of Night Nurse, because that was the only way he could sleep. He would hear music constantly. Maybe we would be in a taxi, and there'd be some snatch of a Greek pop song that would stick like a burr in his head. For three days we'd be singing variations on it. He would sing with the taxi drivers and the waiters, and he was drinking large amounts of *ouzo* and falling flat on his face. Fortunately, all the taxi drivers on Aegina know him and love him. If they found him drunk they would take him home to the hotel. Everyone knows where he stays . . .
>
> When we were on the beach – and there is no doubt John is very drawn to the sea there – he would sing some line, when I thought he was dozing, and he would develop it, and I would pick it up, and there were times when we would sing some phrase at the tops of our voices, over and over into the sound of the waves.

John himself remembers a moment from that holiday which led to a composition:

> We were in a taxi, being driven to a restaurant in Perdika, right at the end of the island. The taxi driver was tuned to a station which plays the folk music of northern Greece. I heard this young girl singing a traditional song, over a drone. Not exactly Byzantine, but certainly Middle Eastern in flavour. I jotted it down on a paper handkerchief.

Next morning, he looked at what he had got and saw a use for it. He had been commissioned to write a *Magnificat* for the choir of King's College, Cambridge. 'So I thought I'd see if I could make something of the young Greek girl's song that the boys at King's would be able to sing.'

The Tavener *Magnificat* is in contrasting sections. First, there are the verses of Mary's song, developed from the folk song fragment. Then, between each verse, there is the refrain, 'Greater in honour than the cherubim', which John has set in triads. This refrain is *de rigueur* whenever a *Magnificat* is sung at Orthodox services, but alien to the Anglicans. John wondered if there might be a problem. Back in England, he rang the choirmaster at King's, Stephen Cleobury, who thought it was probably all right but advised checking with the Dean, since this was a doctrinal matter. The Dean was magnanimous, in the way deans are. 'That's fine,' he said. 'We take a very Jungian view of these things.'

★

By the autumn of 1986 John had a new companion. She was Liadain Sherrard, whom he first met in Katounia, when she seemed happy with her boyfriend. That romance was now over, Liadain was in London, and John had been asked by Philip Sherrard to take care of her. Before long, he was being seen everywhere with the stately, silent girl, and people were saying they looked the perfect couple. When he was invited to America again, for a performance of *Ultimos Ritos*, his father put up the funds for Liadain to travel with him.

The venue for *Ultimos Ritos* was the massive Cathedral of St Paul, Minnesota, and the event was broadcast by Minnesota public radio, which also transmitted a long interview with John, covering the whole of his career. The performance was an exciting one: much wilder than those in England. Chester Music's man in America, James Rushton, was moved to tears.

After Minnesota, John and Liadain moved down to Texas, where the university choir in Dallas sang a set of the smaller choral pieces. Last stop was Rochester, New York, to hear a performance of *To a Child Dancing in the Wind*.

★

On Sunday, 14 December 1986, Mother Thekla wrote in her diary, 'FINISHED St Mary – has been hanging over me for 4–5 years!! Enveloped and stamped and ready to go tomorrow.' She was not to know that three more years of re-drafting would go by before John was satisfied. When he telephoned her on 17 December, he 'seemed very pleased about St Mary'. He also made her promise to borrow a radio for Christmas Eve, so she and Mother Katherine would be able to listen to the Nine Lessons and Carols from King's College, Cambridge. *The Lamb* was to be included, and John and Liadain were going to be in the congregation. Just before *The Lamb*, John told her, he would give a loud cough. According to the diary for Christmas Eve, 'We thought we heard John's cough at the right moment – his Lamb was lovely.'

Early in the New Year there were less happy exchanges, about the performance of *The Ikon of St Cuthbert* in Durham Cathedral. It was set for 20 March and John badly wanted Mother Thekla to be there. She declined to go. She also insisted that her name should not appear on the score. John said his publishers would be reluctant to remove it. After more debate, Mother Thekla wrote in her diary, 'The idea now is to put "Anon" or "Anon Monastic"!!' The eventual compromise was that her authorship would be concealed but the score would carry a dedication. And so it does, simply and mysteriously: 'To Mother Thekla'.

Over 2000 people were packed into Durham Cathedral for the cele-bration of St Cuthbert's anniversary. John's *Ikon of St Cuthbert* was at the heart of the proceedings. Michael Tumelty in the *Glasgow Herald* described 'radiantly lyrical lines, like a Greek folk song, alternating with a softly intoned chant'. In the enhancing acoustic of Durham Cathedral, he found this music 'quite ravishingly beautiful'.

John was there with his father. Next day, *en route* for London, they visited Mother Thekla. Her diary records, 'Quite a lot of talking! First to father, then to John.'

John wanted to talk about a call he had received from the cellist Steven Isserlis, asking if a piece could be written specially for him. John's first instinct had been to say no, he didn't write instrumental works for the concert hall any more, but Steven was difficult to refuse. He said his family was from Russia and he had always loved Orthodox chant, particularly the ancient, *Znamenny* variety.

John had asked for time to consider. Mother Thekla said he should not reject the concert hall, where his music and his message would reach beyond the converted. He wondered if he might write an instrumental *Hymn to the Mother of God*, taking material from his two choral Hymns to Her. Mother Thekla drew up a list of the relevant Feasts in the Orthodox Church calendar. There was Her Nativity; Her presentation in the temple; the Annunciation; the Incarnation; Her Lament at the foot of the Cross; the Resurrection; Her Dormition. And there was one more Feast, very important to the Orthodox, which John should know about. It might give the music its title. It was the Feast of the Protecting Veil, which commemorates the miraculous appearance of the Mother of God to the Christians of Constantinople in the tenth century. The city was besieged by the Saracens and their situation seemed hopeless until She intervened. Standing in the air high above them, She spread Her veil as a shelter and a comfort. Heartened by this vision, the Christians withstood the siege and drove the Saracen army away. The Feast of the Protecting Veil is kept by the Orthodox Church on 1 October, but Mother Thekla pointed out that consciousness of the Mother of God's power of intercession permeates Orthodox worship throughout the year.

John had heard exactly what he wanted to hear. Back in London, he began writing *The Protecting Veil*. Steven Isserlis was expecting something about ten minutes long, to be played with a small ensemble. What he eventually received was forty-five minutes of continuous music, for cello and large string orchestra. But this is to get ahead of our story.

*

On 11 April 1987 John phoned Mother Thekla to say goodbye until June. He was off to Greece for two months, taking his work with him. His flight was on Palm Sunday – the start of Orthodox Holy Week – and the very next day he wrote to Deborah Wearing from the Nafsika Hotel, where she had stayed with him:

> This morning I went to the shrine of St Nektarios and thought of many things – especially of Clive. The weather is wild – torrents of rain and now sunny. Hot and cold. Earthquakes: elemental-spiritual forces of this Week.
>
> I began to look at Orthodox churches – how rounded they are, how gentle, how unlike those Western mathematical masculine edifices. And I thought, yes, the Church is FEMININE – the Church is the Mother of God. Then I thought – this is why the Western Church has gone all wrong with its insistence on masculine precepts, and why the Roman Catholic Church misinterprets the Mother of God, making her sentimental and nurse-like. She is *eternal wisdom*, which is also feminine: *Sophia* in Greek . . .
>
> I rarely think like this in England!

Holy Week on the island of Aegina peaks on Friday evening, when processions from three churches converge on the waterfront. Church bells toll behind a bleak lament, which the priest delivers with fierce intensity.

> Today He is hung upon the tree
> Who hung the earth upon the waters.

The Resurrection happens at midnight on Saturday, in a darkened church. The priest brings to the altar the new Easter flame. Candles are lit from it, until the church is full of light. Outside, on the stroke of midnight, the priest proclaims 'Christ is Risen', and is then overwhelmed by pealing bells and exploding firecrackers. Eggs are smashed. The Lenten fast is broken.

When Holy Week was over, John went from Aegina to Katounia, where Liadain and her father were waiting for him. From here, he wrote to Deborah again.

My Dearest D.
Christ is risen!
It is like an earthly Paradise here. I write from a veranda that overlooks Mount Parnassus. Here you really sense that unearthly *connection* with *everything* . . .
Evenings spent around log fires, oil lamps, listening to 400 frogs, Byzantine and Hindu chant. I wonder if you could bring Clive here. The quiet is almost unearthly, and the air so clear and clean . . .
I have just written a long letter to Mia Farrow – sometimes she comes up with great wisdom.
My love to Clive (I wrote to him).
I am peaceful here (you can't be anything else).

There was no piano in Katounia, so John composed without one. *The Protecting Veil* evolved steadily, while Sherrard's other guests marvelled at the procedure. In the mornings, John would lie on the beach in the eye of the sun, allowing the music to flow into him. Sometimes he would hum. Sometimes a hand would wave in the air. In the afternoons, he would sit at a table on the veranda of his villa, writing it all down.

Since the death of John's mother, Sherrard had never pressed the subject of *Mary of Egypt*. Now, he became enthusiastic about a new idea. He urged John to set 'The Tiger' by William Blake, as a companion piece to *The Lamb*. A choral setting came to John fairly swiftly, and he dedicated it to Sherrard on his sixty-fifth birthday. It has Byzantine drones and palindromes and an air of menace. There is even a musical quotation from *The Lamb*, but not the same magic.

*

In July 1987 *Eis Thanaton* was premièred at the Cheltenham Festival. The bass Stephen Richardson was new to John's music, but ideal as the grieving son. Alison Gough, the pure soprano from the Tallis Scholars who had given the first performance *To a Child Dancing in the Wind*, took the role of the mother. The location was the Victorian chapel of Cheltenham College. The son says his opening lament up at the altar, and his mother made her entrance from the shadowy rear of the building. The performance won enthusiastic applause, but John stayed motionless in his pew, thinking of his own mother.

★

By the beginning of October *The Protecting Veil* was finished. Steven Isserlis still had no idea what was coming. The only clue had been a call from John asking 'What is the highest note you can play on the cello, in a singing way?' To which he had answered 'I suppose the E two octaves and a bit above middle C.'

In John's musical scheme, the cello represents the Mother of God, singing her unending, cosmic song, while the string orchestra acts as a vast resonating chamber. He imagined the performance in the cathedral of St Sophia in Constantinople. The work is in eight sections. Like the *Akathist*, it moves step by step, this time through the scale of F.

The first section, John says, 'represents the cosmic beauty of the Mother of God and her power over a shattered world'. He has marked the score 'Transcendent, with awesome majesty.' Eight double basses lay the foundation of the opening F chord, which then climbs in slow motion through all parts of the string orchestra. Out of it comes the solo cello, at the very top of its range, playing a theme related to the Russian chant 'We magnify Thee'. Meanwhile, double basses sustain the drone, and the rest of the orchestra spells out, immensely slowly, John's first *Hymn to the Mother of God*, 'In You, O Woman full of Grace . . . all creation rejoices.' This first section ends, as do they all, with an effect of Russian church bells.

A linking passage shifts the tonality from F to E, and ushers in Section II: The Nativity of the Mother of God. Its basis lies in *Znamenny* chant, but the ornate melodic line sounds more Indian than Russian. To use John's own word, he has taken the original and 'raga-ized' it.

A linking passage shifts the tonality from E to D, and ushers in Section III: The Annunciation. Here again, John has taken the relevant *Znamenny* chant and produced something sounding Indian.

A linking passage shifts the tonality from D to C, and ushers in Section IV: The Incarnation. The melody here has Byzantine connections.

A linking passage shifts the tonality from C to B flat, and ushers in Section V: The Lament of the Mother of God at the Cross, which is sung by the cello on its own. The melody is *Znamenny* chant, but tossed and turned and heavily ornamented, until it takes on a Middle Eastern character.

A linking passage shifts the tonality from B flat to A, ushering in Section VI, the climax of the piece: The Resurrection. 'A traditional racket,' is what John says he wanted. The cello plays the 'Christ is Risen!' tune which he composed for his *Orthodox Vigil Service*. Select bands of strings follow the cello in canon, or let fly with 'Christ is Risen!' in its Russian and Coptic versions. Elsewhere in the orchestra there is a blazing chord of A major.

A linking passage shifts the tonality from A to G, and ushers in Section VII: The Dormition. This is an exact transcription for cello and orchestra of John's second *Hymn to the Mother of God*. After the three verses of the Hymn, a linking passage shifts the tonality from G back to F, where we began.

Section VIII recapitulates Section I, then adds 'The Tears of the Mother of God', which slide up and down the minor ninth between F and E, creating an apocalyptic atmosphere. Finally, the cello soars heavenwards and dwells alone, on a top F that seems impossibly high.

*

As soon as *The Protecting Veil* had been delivered to his publishers, John returned to setting texts on sacred themes. Two in particular had been haunting him, and he wondered if they could work as a pair. Both were from the early days of the Christian Church in Egypt. One was an anonymous fragment from the third century:

> Let not the Prince be silent
> Nor bright stars . . .
> Sources of rushing waters . . .
> Let all powers call out: Amen. Amen.

This had been found, with musical notation, on the back of a corn account. Scholars describe it as the earliest-known Christian hymn.

The other text was by Clement of Alexandria, a Church Father of the second century. John loved the Christian writings of Clement, because they echoed the more ancient cultures of Greece and Egypt. There was 'Divine milk', for instance, which flowed from 'the sweet breasts of the bride of grace', and there were 'Sacred fishes from the sea of vice'.

He sent both texts to Mother Thekla, who then produced a composite. Her construction called for two choirs. The music John created for the 'Let not the Prince' choir is massive and monolithic: a slow-moving canon, spread across eighteen parts. The music for the 'Clement of Alexandria' choir is austere and Byzantine.

John called the whole piece *Let Not the Prince Be Silent*, and thought it an ideal vehicle for the Tallis Scholars, but there was no sponsor on the horizon. He set it aside and took up a specific assignment, from Richard Hickox, for the summer festival he ran down in Cornwall. Hickox spelled out the new commission carefully. He wanted something thirty to thirty-five minutes long, playable by a first-class local music society, and fitting the tiny church of St Endellion.

John took this as his opportunity to write a sequel to the *Ikon of St Cuthbert of Lindisfarne*. The subject he chose was the most famous holy man of nineteenth-century Russia, St Seraphim of Sarov, who spent years as a hermit before being hailed for his miracles. Mother Thekla demurred at St Seraphim. She thought him too well known. But on 14 November, bowing to John's wishes, she began to arrange his life into the form of a Byzantine canon. Next day she wrote in her diary, 'Worked on the Canon like mad! And did it. Enough to send a draft anyway, to discuss when he comes.'

John arrived a week later, bringing the draft for discussion. He also brought Liadain Sherrard. By now, Liadain had moved out of the Sherrard family home in Highgate and joined the Tavener household in Wembley Park. The two ladies in John's life did not warm to each other, and in any case Mother Thekla needed John to herself, as the diary makes clear. 'Worked with John all the morning *quietly* in my cell and went through St Seraphim. He approved of the text.' On Saturday John's *Panikhida* was sung in the monastery chapel. It drew this commentary from Mother Thekla: 'The *Panikhida* was good. Liadain has a very pure voice and merges into John. But – all a bit too much for old women!' Her spirits were restored on Sunday: 'A very lovely Liturgy. John sang it.' On Monday, after more work with Mother Thekla, John returned to London with Liadain.

★

The *Ikon of St Seraphim*, for choir, soloists and orchestra, was finished at the end of January 1988. It is more dramatic and surreal than the *Ikon of St Cuthbert of Lindisfarne*, and less bound by the guidelines for Byzantine Canons. As John puts it, 'Mother Thekla was beginning to *dance*: out of Tradition and back in again.'

Like the *Akathist* and *The Protecting Veil*, the *Ikon of St Seraphim* moves in steps. The first of its eight sections rests on a droned A, the

second on B, and so on up the white notes, until Section VIII comes
home to A again. The drone comes from a group of musicians in the
distance: bass voices, who chant the Jesus Prayer in Church Slavonic,
accompanied by a tam-tam, low trombones and high violins.

Seraphim's story is told by the choir, while a baritone soloist
represents the Saint himself. At the climax, the Devil appears in the
guise of a counter-tenor. His shrieks of 'Throw yourself down', 'Feed
the hungry' and 'Bow down and worship' are so horribly at odds with
the drone that the choir is shocked into abandoning syntax.

> Voices enticing, voices pleasing, voices mocking,
> Tug, praise, shriek, flatter, smell of swine . . .
> Demons, devils, jigging imps.

Orchestral 'flashes of lightning' burst across the combat between
St Seraphim and his tempter, until the saint is victorious. Then the drone
stops, like a missed heartbeat, and St Seraphim himself takes over the
Jesus Prayer, surrounded by silence.

> Lord Jesus Christ, Son of God
> Have mercy upon me a sinner.

*

Tavener and Thekla were now a writing team, but Mother Thekla still
refused to take any credit. This worried John's publishers, who needed
to establish copyrights. The diary entry for 10 December 1987 shows
how it was done. 'Chester Music telephoned – wanted to pay me for
the Akathist!! We compromised on some of John's tapes!'

So the relationship became a professional one, although Mother
Thekla did not have a tape-recorder. And one awful implication of being
involved with John did not dawn on her until later. Here is the diary
entry for 17 December:

> Most distressing conversation with John – television looms. Obviously
> he cannot lie – must mention me – but I WILL NOT speak, nor
> appear. He agrees. But they may come to the monastery with him.

The planned programme was for a Channel 4 series called *Art, Faith
and Vision*.

Mother Thekla slept badly and reviewed her situation. Orthodox
monasteries have no strict rules, so she could not be accused of breaking
them. In any case, she was the Abbess, with local autonomy. But John
was pulling her life seriously out of shape. Was his music worth serving?

Yes, of course it was. It was music which explored the Divine without claiming to fathom it. In her words:

> John has the ultimate humility before the 'Goal', which he knows he cannot reach. I couldn't work with anybody who did not understand human limitation ... But he is totally ruthless where his music is concerned. He doesn't mind whom he turns inside out. I know, and I do it with my eyes open. Only a monk or a nun could cope: we aren't concerned with personal ambition. I take it as my monastic obedience. It's not John: there is something here which I have been told to do, so I do it.

*

As soon as *St Seraphim* was finished, John announced a huge new undertaking. Mother Thekla's diary notes it flatly. 'Feb.3rd. John tel. – wants to write The Passion. So that's my next job.'

The ambition was to match the great Passions of the German tradition – Bach's *St Matthew Passion* in particular. Just as Bach had created a unified work of art from chorales and arias, so John would draw on the traditional chants and texts of Orthodox Holy Week.

With her usual high energy, Mother Thekla produced a first draft in ten days: a synthesis of the Prophetic utterances, the Four Gospels and the Orthodox commentaries. On 15 February the bulky manuscript reached John by post. He phoned to say he liked it, but it seemed to him that this text, set to music, would run for at least six hours. Mother Thekla's diary for 29 February records his arrival at the monastery. 'Snow – but John did come and we worked very hard after supper. Passion "tamed" into 6 Cantatas to be sung separately – or two or so together, as people please.'

Next day, the deputation from Channel 4 arrived for a preliminary meeting. 'Television people – convinced them I could not be filmed – but perhaps my words about John's work could be recorded?'

John returned to London, and the dialogue about the Passion continued by telephone. Although the text was already immensely long, Mother Thekla kept insisting it was incomplete. To be properly Orthodox, it should not stop at the Crucifixion, like the Protestant and Catholic Passions. It had to have a Resurrection. By 5 March, John had been persuaded. Three days later a seventh cantata was sent to him, and a formal running order. I: The Conspiracy. II: The Last Supper. III: The Betrayal. IV: The Trial. V: The Crucifixion. VI: The Tomb. VII: The Resurrection.

Although there seemed no prospect of a commission for it, *Resurrection* (as it became known) took the main part of John's creative energy for the next twelve months: a period also crowded with distractions and excursions.

★

On 14 May 1988, after three weeks of sunshine and Philip Sherrard in Katounia, John was in Washington DC with Liadain, for the American première of his *Vigil Service*. The performance, in Washington Cathedral, opened a week of celebrations of the Millennium of the Russian Orthodox Church (founded in 988). Among the congregation, John counted 'at least five archbishops and seven bishops from the Soviet Union, and Metropolitan Theodosius of all the Americas'. He was thrilled by the dramatic voice of the Orthodox priest who led the service, and thought the choir of the Episcopalian Cathedral did wonders.

He had also been booked to give a talk. He wrote the text in Katounia, and it has a whiff of Sherrard about it, but its central statement is pure Tavener:

> The whole purpose of sacred music must be to lead us to the threshold of prayer or to the threshold of a true encounter with the living God. Because the Sacred is prior to art and totally unaffected by anything art can do. An Ikon, for instance, is not art. It is beyond art – a real presence that we venerate, looking tenderly at us, helping us to pray, and lifting our minds and hearts above this earth (where we are in exile for a short time) into Heaven, our true 'Homeland'.

★

While John was away in America, the health of Mother Katherine took a sharp turn for the worse. She had had an operation for cancer back in 1984, but now the malignancy had broken out again. On some days she could not walk and had to stay in bed, deprived of the consolation of reading because her sight was failing. Mother Thekla arranged a cell for her on the ground floor of the monastery, and went out and bought her a portable cassette player – the latest thing, bright yellow in colour, which they called 'Buttercup'. Now they could play the cassettes from Chester's of music by John. The other composer whose music Mother Katherine wanted to hear was Beethoven, particularly his late string quartets. Mother Thekla brought her a selection of tapes.

Mother Katherine had been following the progress of the composition of *Resurrection* with intense interest. Knowing that John would soon be coming to see them again, Mother Thekla made a bold move. The details are in her diary.

> MAY 16. Decided to buy a piano for John. He's back safely. America was good – warm, enthusiastic. We're getting a tape of his talk and the service.
>
> MAY 17. Quite mad – bought a piano.
>
> MAY 23. 'Music room' completed – piano due Tuesday next week.
>
> MAY 31. PIANO came! – Very nice one.
>
> JUNE 2. John arrived in the evening – we stayed up late.
>
> JUNE 3. Worked with John in the morning – a lot to do.

Mother Katherine's cell was opposite the 'music room', and the doors were left open so she could lie in bed listening to John singing and playing the piano. He was working on the central section of *Resurrection* – 'The Trial' and 'The Crucifixion' – and she was deeply moved by what she heard. He promised he would play it all to her when it was finished. She told him, 'If I live to hear it, it will be good, but if I die it will be even better.'

On the third day of John's visit, there was extra work for Mother Thekla, when Deborah Wearing arrived, at John's invitation. The diary notes there was a lot of talking and then, at two o'clock in the morning, 'John improvised at the piano. "Baa Baa Black Sheep" as Bach would have written it! Etc. So *tired*.'

After the service on Sunday morning, John and Deborah left. John was needed by the Channel 4 people, who had started making their film. There had been sessions in London and at Christ Church Cathedral in Oxford, and now the whole team was off to Greece. Philip Sherrard had given permission for filming on his property, and would be making a screen appearance.

By the middle of July, the television team had reached the monastery. At Mother Thekla's insistence, they brought no film camera: only a tape-recorder and a stills photographer. According to the diary, the visit was still bad enough.

> JULY 18. Television (NOT cameras!) – talk – talk – talk. HOURS! (My 70th birthday).

★

On 8 August the *Ikon of St Seraphim* was premièred in the little church of St Endellion. Richard Hickox says of it, 'The piece speaks from the heart. It's when I came to appreciate what a great composer John is.'

It also seemed to Hickox to have been tailored to suit the building. The group chanting the Jesus prayer was placed in the belfry tower at the back. The main choir and orchestra were up near the altar. Stephen Varcoe, in the title role, sang from halfway down the nave. 'He did it wonderfully. Like a priest at Evensong, kneeling facing the same way as the congregation. And then we had the Devil in the pulpit! Simon Gay, the counter-tenor.'

Next evening, the *Ikon of St Seraphim* was done again, this time in Truro Cathedral. Hickox thought the impact had been lost in the big space, but John much preferred the grander acoustic. Someone presented him with a tape of this performance, and he took it to his next evening *chez* Cecil and Elizabeth Collins. Elizabeth had told him that Arvo Pärt would be there. She looked forward to sitting John down with the cult composer from Estonia. Unfortunately, Pärt's response when the tape was played to him was extremely limited: partly because he spoke virtually no English and partly, Elizabeth remembers, because he had a raging toothache.

*

In September, John and Liadain were back in Katounia, where John continued to be fascinated by Philip Sherrard's views. *Mary of Egypt* had long since dropped quietly from the agenda, but the Uncreated Eros stayed a favourite log-fire topic. John understood Sherrard to be talking about the ideal erotic relationship: as it was in the Garden of Eden, before the Fall. If he were to write a piece of music around it, John wondered, which text might he use? Sherrard said take it from Genesis: the words describing the creation of Eve, while Adam was asleep. During that sleep, the theory ran, Adam meditated on the concept of Woman and so brought her into being.

The Uncreated Eros is a four-minute choral piece of extreme formality, quietness and solemnity. Bass voices set up a drone, and then more basses chant, 'And the Lord God caused a deep sleep to fall on Adam, and he slept.' Their chant forms an ornamented palindrome, in Byzantine tone I. It is followed by a long silence. Then the drone builds up again and the text is continued, to the same chant, but now in Byzantine tone II. Another silence, then the drone again, then the chant, but this time given to women's voices, celebrating the creation of Eve. Finally, all voices join to proclaim, 'And they were both naked, the man and his wife, and were not ashamed.'

*

Soon after he got back from Greece, John was again up at the monastery, working on *Resurrection* and discussing the nature of music with Mother Katherine. He did not tell her that when Philip Sherrard heard about her passion for Beethoven's late String Quartets, he decreed that these were not Sacred Music. Nor did he tell Mother Thekla about *The Uncreated Eros.*

His next public engagement was at the October 88 Temenos conference at Dartington Hall. Kathleen Raine had booked him to give his illustrated lecture. She had also booked the Dagar Brothers: performers of the Indian classical and devotional repertoire. Their music had everything John admires: ritual, repetition, and immensely long-breathed melodic lines. Moreover, it was not projected outwards, but drew the audience in, so listeners and performers achieved a state of harmonious vibration. Recordings by the Dagar Brothers became the most played in John's collection.

★

Without doubt the prime Tavener occasion of 1988 was the première of the *Akathist* in Westminster Abbey. It had become a possibility when Martin Neary moved to the Abbey from Winchester, bringing his keenness with him, but sponsors remained elusive and the BBC showed no interest. The Taveners decided to go it alone. The family firm put up the money and John's brother Roger took charge of logistics. A date was set – Monday 21 November – and the English Chamber Orchestra was booked to perform with the Abbey Choir.

Even before the rehearsals began, Martin Neary felt sure the *Akathist* was too long. At more than one hundred minutes, with no interval, it would tax the stamina of performers and audience alike. He was particularly concerned about the young choristers and, choosing his words with the greatest care, he suggested to John that cuts might be considered. John was appalled. He believed the traditional Akathist scheme of thirteen hymns should remain inviolate. There were telephone conferences with Mother Thekla. She advised that if shortening would benefit the performance, it should be done. And she offered the consoling thought that T. S. Eliot, on the advice of Ezra Pound, had hacked great lumps out of *The Four Quartets.*

The only place where a cut could be made without upsetting the stepwise progression was after Hymn VII. Here, the pedal note, which has climbed step by step from A to G, drops back down to A. John offered Martin Neary the possibility of eliminating Hymns VIII and IX, and starting the second ascent on the pedal note C. The offer was accepted, and so the *Akathist*, as performed and published, is in eleven sections only.

Also less than ideal was the placing of the performers. First of all, John's notion of a platform reached via thirteen steps was not even considered. Secondly, the geography of Westminster Abbey, which has its choir screen to the west of the transepts, foiled his plan to station singers at the four points of the compass. Thirdly, the attempt to put the orchestra in the organ loft, so it would be heard from on high, had to be abandoned as unworkable.

All seats in the Abbey were sold and, compromises notwithstanding, the evening was a hit with the critics: John's first triumphant première in London since the *Celtic Requiem* nearly twenty years earlier. His only disappointment was that there was no professional recording of the performance. All we have is a low-fidelity tape, made on a machine perched on John's father's knee, which begins with worries expressed by Kenneth about the crack in the windscreen of his car.

★

A few days after the performance, John went up to the monastery with the imperfect tape, which they played on 'Buttercup'. He also took a tape of Mozart's *Magic Flute*, which he recommended to Mother Thekla as the model for *Mary of Egypt*: child-like and yet profound. She could not concentrate on this radical new idea. Mother Katherine was now extremely ill: there were strange lumps on her collar bone, and her nose was bleeding.

John returned to London. After the success of the *Akathist* he was back in vogue. He had a commission for a String Quartet; an invitation to visit Moscow; interest from the City of Glasgow in *Resurrection*; and a request from BBC Television (Department of Religious Affairs) for a ten-minute Passion, which they would turn into what they called an 'Easter video'.

The surge of popularity coincided with domestic unhappiness and heavy drinking. Liadain wanted him to leave Wembley Park and set up home with her and have children. His alarm bells were ringing. He phoned Mother Thekla to say he wanted to come to the monastery at Christmas, on his own.

He had started thinking about the String Quartet. It would be a set of meditations derived from *Resurrection*, and it would be dedicated to Mother Katherine. She was sinking fast, and *Resurrection* was still not finished. He arrived at the monastery on Christmas Eve, just before she lost consciousness for the last time. Her only words to him were, 'Oh, John, you've come.' He sang to her softly: some Byzantine hymns, and even some Gregorian chant, such as she would have heard when she was still Benedictine Dame Mary Thomas. She did not respond. Mother Thekla urged him to join the Vigil Service being held in the monastery chapel. She would call him if there was any change. Several times during the night he was called from the chapel. He was in Mother Katherine's cell when she died, at 6.45 on Christmas morning.

There were no undertakers available during the Christmas holiday, so Mother Thekla did the washing and the laying-out. John marvelled at her naturalness in the face of death. The funeral was held on 29 December. Bishop Kallistos took the service. John did all the singing. Then the coffin was carried from the chapel up the grassy slope behind the monastery, to be buried beside the grave of Mother Maria. John was chanting all the way. The low winter sun shone straight into his face.

3 : Paradise promised

In her grief, Mother Thekla busied herself working for John on what she called 'the sequence of the string quartet in Mother Katherine's memory, out of *Resurrection*'.

Her scenario reached John through the post on 11 January, and he was making good progress with the music when Philip Sherrard phoned him from Greece with news of another death. Liadain's close friend Sophie Royde-Smith, a young painter, had been killed in a car accident on the Athens road. The body would be flown home and the funeral would be in London. John conveyed the dreadful news to Liadain, who was staying with friends in Scotland. She hurried back to Wembley Park. Encouraged by Mother Thekla, who thought his endless shilly-shallying was cruel to the girl, John chose this moment to tell Liadain he could never marry her. She moved out, and the last time they saw one another was at Sophie's funeral. Philip Sherrard's fury over the way his daughter had been treated was delivered in a blitz of scathing letters. From now on, the gates of Katounia were closed to John Tavener.

★

On 1 February he was at the monastery, with the completed draft of *Resurrection*. It was in seven sections, but the idea of treating them as separate cantatas, one for each day of Holy Week, had been dropped. John sang and played the whole thing in one sitting at the monastery piano. Mother Thekla timed it. It lasted just over two and a half hours. They spent several days making final improvements, then turned their attention to *Mary of Egypt*. John was slightly disappointed that none of Mother Thekla's efforts so far had 'come out right'. He wondered if she would mind trying again, and went back to London.

After a week, he received through the post the latest draft, to which was attached a short note: 'This is the fifth AND FINAL version of *St Mary of Egypt*.'

Three days later he was back at the monastery, this time with the team from BBC Television's Department of Religious Affairs. For their Easter video, John had supplied a ten-minute *Ikon of the Crucifixion*, adapted from *Resurrection*. Now they wanted to shoot a documentary introduction. John obliged the camera by striding on the moors and playing the monastery piano. Mother Thekla took against the producer and would only allow herself to be filmed from behind.

On 10 March John was at the monastery again, for a meeting with the person from Glasgow who was interested in *Resurrection*. By an odd coincidence, this man's name was also Tavener, and it seemed he and John might be distantly related.

Alan Tavener was Director of Music at Strathclyde University and artistic director of Cappella Nova, the leading choir north of the border. He came to the monastery with his wife, Rebecca, and John gave them one of his extraordinary performances: two and a half hours of orchestral and choral piano, with his voice taking the solo parts, from bass to soprano, and the whole thing radiant with religious commitment. When it was over, Alan and Rebecca Tavener swore that, whatever the difficulties, *Resurrection* would be heard in Glasgow Cathedral during 1990: the city's year as Cultural Capital of Europe.

★

In *Resurrection* the musical language John cultivated while writing his *Orthodox Vigil Service* comes into full flower.

To Mother Thekla's design in seven sections he has added a prologue and an epilogue, to be sung by an unaccompanied choir, barely audibly, 'from the highest possible gallery'. This element, called 'Paradise', is none other than the short choral work *The Uncreated Eros*, in which the text from Genesis has been replaced by chanting of the Greek word *Ameen*. John offers this explanation of the function of Paradise in his grand design:

> I wanted to frame *Resurrection* with the Paradise we know about (the Paradise of Adam and Eve), and the Paradise to which we are called, about which we know only that it was promised by Christ to the thief on the cross.

After the Paradise music, the Mother of God (soprano) makes her opening statement of obedience and humility:

Be it unto me according to Thy word.

Her descending musical phrase, from A to A in Byzantine tone I, is to be her *leitmotif*.

Next comes a melodic fragment played on the viola: a hint of what will finally emerge as the *Znamenny* chant celebrating the Resurrection. It is followed by a string quartet playing a 25-note palindrome, which is the principal *Resurrection* theme.

When the main choir makes its entry, it is singing the Orthodox hymn 'Thy Cross we adore': first in Greek, to a Byzantine melody; then in Russian, to a *Znamenny* chant; then in English, to a melody of John's with Byzantine origins.

A restatement of the palindrome by the string quartet leads to Section I: The Conspiracy. Mother Thekla's text draws on the Gospels, the Orthodox commentaries and the Old Testament Prophecies. When John sets the words of the Prophets his starting point is Hebrew chant, which comes out as wild and fierce, underlined by timpani and trombones. At the end of this Section the Mother of God is heard again, with Her characteristic musical phrase. Her words this time are 'Woe is me my child'.

Section II: The Last Supper opens with a hint of the *Znamenny* chant celebrating the Resurrection, this time on trombones, followed by the 25-note palindrome, played here by the trumpets. The narrative then moves forward, using the Byzantine text 'Of Thy mysterious supper', set to music from Byzantine sources, treated polyphonically. When Christ Himself sings, He insists, with supernatural deliberation, on the low A which is the eternity note. Beneath him, this note is softly echoed on the organ. A tam-tam provides the pulse, and up above trumpets of royalty proclaim the 25-note palindrome. Higher still, the string quartet projects the eternity note, which, John instructs, should be 'shining with light'.

At the end of the supper, when Christ pours water into a basin and begins to wash His disciples' feet, John sounds the joy-sorrow chord which we know from *The Lamb*. Here it becomes identified with the apostle Peter and His emotional outburst: 'Thou shalt never wash my feet.' After gently reproving Peter, Christ says one disciple will betray Him. Above the chorus of 'Lord, is it I?' a single voice stands out: the counter-tenor voice of Judas, which clashes horribly with the eternity note. After this, all the forces, instrumental and choral, come together to sound the joy-sorrow chord and sing the words 'And it was night.'

The section closes with the Mother of God and Her lament, 'Woe is me my child', now in a different Byzantine tone. Then comes a Meditation, Eastern in character, for two alto flutes.

Section III: The Betrayal opens with a hint of the Resurrection chant, this time played by recorders, followed by a sombre statement on trombones of the 25-note palindrome. The dramatic climax of this section is the moment when Jesus is identified by Judas, whose piercing shriek of 'Master!' is excruciatingly at odds with the drone. After the drama comes the Old Testament refrain:

> O my people, what have I done to you?
> Wherein have I wearied you?

John's music for it elaborates a Jewish melodic fragment to produce a slow-moving chorale, tender and sad. The section ends with the Lament of the Mother of God (again in a different tone), after which there is a second Meditation played by the two alto flutes.

Section IV: The Trial begins with a hint of the Resurrection chant, this time on the organ, followed by the 25-note palindrome, now played by a string trio. When the High Priest demands to know if Jesus is the Son of God, the sound of Paradise is heard briefly and faintly from on high. The joy-sorrow chord reminds us of the presence of Peter. When it is put to him that he is one of Jesus' disciples, Peter's passionate denial wrenches the notes of the chord into a feverishly intense vocal line. Christ is taken before Pilate, who asks is He the King of the Jews. The sound of Paradise is again heard from on high. The shouting of the crowd, 'We have no King but Caesar!', achieves an awful significance, as the instruments join the chorus in a hideous distortion of the melody 'Thy Cross we adore'.

Section V: The Crucifixion opens with a fierce chant for solo tenor, based on the one sung by priests all over Greece during Holy Week:

> Today He is hung upon the tree
> Who hung the earth upon the waters.

All that relieves the bleakness of the lone voice is the occasional sounding of the eternity note, on a single bell.

Woven throughout the rest of the Crucifixion scene is an extended Lament of the Mother of God, whose music moves through several Byzantine tones, while steadily rising in pitch.

When Christ tells the thief, 'Today thou shalt be with me in Paradise,' the sound of Paradise is again heard from on high, and it is the melody of Paradise that Christ uses. But when He comes to His last words, 'Eli, Eli, lama sabachthani', He sings entirely without accompaniment, and His long, tortured vocal line goes beyond Middle Eastern melisma into primordial howling.

A third Meditation for the two alto flutes leads into Section VI: The Tomb. Here, John has dispensed with Mother Thekla's text. Instead, two violins in canon hint at the *Znamenny* chant which honours the myrrh-bearing women, while wordless sighs from the choir slowly rise in pitch. Then words burst forth with great force: 'Rise, O God, and judge the earth.' Which is the cue for all the lights to go out.

Section VII: The Resurrection is to be performed while all the singers process towards a central point, carrying candles. It begins with the *Znamenny* chant for Easter Sunday, which has been hinted at all the way through the piece. Now at last it comes into its own, sung in Russian, and punctuated by the ecstatic sound of Easter bells. Then the trumpets of royalty and the Old Testament trombones explode 'like lightning flashes of joy'. They introduce the final, triumphant appearance of the 25-note palindrome, sung by the choir, which delivers the message 'Christ is Risen!' simultaneously in three languages.

Next, Greeks, Russians and English go their separate ways and take it in turns to sing, in their own languages and with their own music:

> Christ is risen from the dead,
> Death He trampled down by death,
> And to those in the tomb He has given life.

The music for the English language version was composed by John, originally for his *Orthodox Vigil Service*.

The joyful sequence of musical events brings us suddenly to the dialogue between Mary Magdalene and the risen Christ, outside the tomb. Christ's 'Woman why weepest thou? Whom seekest thou?' comes with the trumpets of royalty. Mary Magdalene's confused reply comes with the joy-sorrow chord which previously characterized Peter. When recognition dawns, her long-drawn-out cry of 'Rabboni!' echoes the feverish music of Peter's denial. John's intention here is to convey 'the ecstasy of the risen Christ bubbling up inside her'.

Easter bells bring back the triumphant singing in three languages, which breaks into a dance of uncontrolled joy. Then the music of Paradise is heard again, complete, as at the beginning. But this is not quite the end. There is a final statement of obedience and humility, delivered by the Mother of God on behalf of us all: 'Be it unto me according to Thy word.'

★

John's first String Quartet, written in Mother Katherine's memory, can be properly considered as a pendant to *Resurrection*, or better still as a meditation on its principal themes. It owes nothing at all to the Germanic tradition.

The opening theme, marked 'Fragrant with the innocence of Paradise', came to John in a dream. Played by the cello, with a drone-like accompaniment from the others, it grows from a rising five-note phrase, and becomes a distended palindrome, not entirely obedient to the laws of the magic square. It is followed by another palindrome, but this time an exact one: the one heard throughout *Resurrection*.

Next comes the Greek chant 'Ton Stavron' ('Thy Cross we adore'): the first of a series of *Resurrection* flasbacks. These are linked sometimes by a hint of Paradise played on the cello, and sometimes by a restatement of the palindromes.

The end of the quartet is as the beginning, except that now the Paradise theme on the cello is heard simultaneously on the violins, who play it in canon, very fast and high. 'Shimmering like gold dust' is how John puts it in the score. It was this high, fast version which came to him in his dream – a dream triggered, he believes, by the deaths of Mother Katherine and Liadain's friend Sophie.

He called this mysterious quartet *The Hidden Treasure*, after the title of a book by Mother Maria, which refers to the riches of the Kingdom of Heaven.

★

Ten days after the demonstration of *Resurrection* at the monastery, *The Protecting Veil* was played through at Wembley Park. By now it had been commissioned by the BBC, for the 1989 season of Promenade Concerts. Steven Isserlis had pronounced the cello part demanding but not unplayable. As a matter of fact, he was thrilled with it. He brought his wife Pauline to Wembley Park with him. Also present was an ex-student of John's, Pamela Moody, to whom *The Protecting Veil* is dedicated. Although John was rarely seen with Pamela in public, they had been lovers on and off for fifteen years. After leaving Trinity she became a cello teacher, and made her home in North London, so she could be near him. She was always there for John when he needed her.

In his words, 'We went through heaven and hell together.' The inscription 'To Pamela' on the score of *The Protecting Veil* was intended to make up for a lot.

Accompanied by John at the piano, Steven gave an interpretation which made light of the technical difficulties and much of the lyrical intensity. John thought it came near to definitive, but Steven had suggestions for improvements. The main change he recommended was to Section IV: The Incarnation. Here, for the first time, John takes the cello towards the bottom of its range. Steven said what was written could not be played without sounding 'growly'. He wondered if John might agree to raising it an octave, and he showed what he meant. According to Steven, John stayed unconvinced until he had quizzed the others present. 'They both said, "It's better up an octave, John," and in the end he bowed to the general opinion, and became very happy about it.'

Then he gave Steven a valuable insight into the long central section for unaccompanied cello, 'The Lament of the Mother of God at the Cross'. As Steven tells it:

John sat down at the piano and said, 'If you play this slowly enough, it will bring tears to the eyes of all the old Russian women.' And he harmonized the statement that appears over and over again in the Lament, and I got a sense of the phrasing and the underlying feeling. John likes the purity of just one line, but I'm sure that when he writes he's got the harmonies in the back of his mind.

*

On Good Friday 1989 the BBC showed John's 'Easter video', which they called *The Cry of the Ikon*. First came the documentary film, featuring John looking holy and Mother Thekla's rear view. Then Alison Gough sang the *Lament of the Mother of God*, against a colourful background of electronic jiggery-pokery.

Mother Thekla, of course, had no means of viewing the transmission of this extravaganza, but friends made sure she caught up with it. Someone brought what her diary called 'A Video (only playing) box and a television set that doesn't receive signals – so no licence.' Then someone else arrived with *The Cry of the Ikon* on tape. She found the music altogether lovely and the pictures altogether vulgar.

*

On 13 May 1989 *Let Not the Prince Be Silent* received its première. It had been commissioned by Lady Digby, the principal patron of the

Tallis Scholars, and the performance was in Sherborne Abbey, Dorset. The programme also included *Spem in Alium*, the spectacular forty-part motet by Thomas Tallis, but what should have been a splendid occasion turned out unhappily and marked the parting of the ways for John and Peter Phillips.

Peter maintains that Lady Digby was entitled to expect John's piece to be singable by the forty voices employed for *Spem in Alium*. Yet it became obvious at rehearsal that two hundred would be a better number for the massively slow canon, with its high notes held for page after page. He dared not ask his patron to pay for more singers. His only option was to tamper with John's intentions. He quickened the tempo, for example.

John could not understand why difficulties were being discovered so late in the day. As usual, he had delivered his score a long time before the event. In his view, *Let Not the Prince Be Silent* is one of his major pieces, still waiting for its authoritative performance.

*

The weekend following the miserable première was spent at the monastery. This time John took Pamela Moody. By the time they left, Mother Thekla was exhausted. As well as cooking all the meals and digesting new ideas about *Mary of Egypt*, she found herself in the role of agony aunt for John and his devoted companion.

On 1 June, John rang the monastery to say goodbye. He was flying to Moscow next morning for a five-day visit, which would climax with a performance of his *Akhmatova: Requiem*. His father wanted him looked after, and was paying for a companion to travel with him. John had chosen Sarah Long. Sarah was an English aristocrat and an Orthodox convert. He thought her ideal. Mother Thekla found herself on the receiving end of an anguished call from Pamela.

*

In the Soviet Union of Mikhail Gorbachev, the writings of Anna Akhmatova had been unbanned, and Gennady Rozhdestvensky's proposal to perform John's *Requiem* was good politics in line with *glasnost*. At Moscow airport, John and Sarah were greeted with flowers by Madame Voronova, Chairlady of the Charity Council of the Cultural Foundation of the USSR, whose bright pink lipstick and matching nails came as a bit of a surprise. Ivetta Voronova turned out to be an incurable romantic. Her first responsibility was to take her guests to their hotel and see them comfortably installed. Beaming with anticipation, she escorted them to what looked like the bridal suite. In the centre of a large space was a king-size bed. Madame Voronova tried to slip away, leaving the couple together, but John stopped her and told her she did not understand. Sarah and he could not possibly share sleeping quarters. 'Yes, yes!' protested Madame Voronova. 'She is such a beautiful young girl!' She would not accept that this opportunity was to be wasted until John finally raised his voice and demanded single rooms. Very unhappily, Madame Voronova led Sarah away to mean quarters in the attic.

The day-to-day guides were Paul Pritykin (an English speaker from the Cultural Foundation) and Boris Kulikov, Rector of the Moscow Conservatoire, who spoke no English at all. On the first morning, the car John and Sarah had been told to expect was extremely late reaching their hotel. It took them to a church, but when they got there they were faced by padlocked gates. Their guide for the day was Boris, who seemed to have been drinking. He disappeared, and when he came back he was carrying a sledge-hammer. Amazed by his assault on the padlock, a passer-by pointed out that the church had a door at the back. It was open. They went in and found themselves up at the altar, among the priests. The nave below them was packed, Sarah remembers. 'Masses of old ladies with head-scarves on. Hundreds of candles. The whole of the church inside was golden. A real surprise, after the outside.' They had been led to believe that the Patriarch of Moscow and all the Russias would be there, but it seemed he had already left.

The main event of the day was at the Danilov Monastery. For years, the Communists had used this building as a prison. Now, it had been restored to its former glory, as the Patriarch's headquarters. John and Sarah were to attend a banquet. As they were driven through the monastery gates, they heard joyful Russian bells and could see the monks in the bell-tower, pulling on the ropes. Inside the crowded hallway they spotted the Patriarch, who looked to Sarah like a wedding cake. 'White head-dress, white and blue robes, white face. He was too ill to walk, so he had to be taken up the staircase on a sedan chair. Then he was placed on a throne, like a sacred object, and we all had to prostrate ourselves before him.'

After that, all processed into the banqueting hall, for what seemed routine to the Russian clergy, but astounded John and Sarah. The shops in Moscow were bare, but here was another world. Sarah made a list of what they consumed:

Caviar (red and black), suckling piglets, salmon, sturgeon, wild garlic, pickled garlic, soup, chicken Kiev, fish, pork, prunes, chestnuts, strawberries, almonds, chocolates, wine, champagne, vodka, brandy.

They seemed to be celebrating a Patriarchal anniversary. Between each course, vodka was downed and the Russian hymn 'Mnogaya Lyeta' ('Many Years') was loudly sung. The most impressive voice belonged to Metropolitan Filaret, the Archbishop of Minsk and Belorussia, who sat at the Patriarch's right hand. During one of the vodka sessions, this magnificently bearded figure stood up, pointed a finger at John, and called upon him to address the Patriarch. There had been no warning and by now the alcohol count was high. John thinks he managed to convey greetings from the Russian Cathedral in London.

When the consumption of food and alcohol was finally over, the Patriarch was carried away and John and Sarah were taken for a private audience with Metropolitan Filaret, who turned out to be a connoisseur of music and the arts. John described his plans for *Mary of Egypt*. The Metropolitan said yes, let it be an ikon in notes instead of colours. The gravity of their conference was upset by the monk assigned to the guests as their guide. Apparently the worse for drink, he crashed violently against Sarah, causing her to cannon into the Metropolitan's ample stomach. Sarah remembers this fellow's name. It was Brother Seraphim. He grabbed John by the arm and dragged him down miles of corridors, past the Patriarch's emerald throne and his private chapel. Sometimes Brother Seraphim danced, sometimes he sang, sometimes he gave Sarah and John hugs and kisses. When they reached the foot of the bell-tower, Sarah said no, John was not well enough to go up there. She was told yes, that was exactly where John was going, but women were not allowed. John tried to explain that he had had a stroke. Brother Seraphim was not interested. John remembers how it ended. 'Getting up there was a nightmare. Then this bear-like monk started clanging all the bells. I thought my ears had gone for ever.'

By next morning John's hearing was back and he was looking forward to Sunday service in the Zagorsk Monastery outside Moscow, which is famous for its ikons. Unfortunately, Boris found it hard to start his day, so they did not reach Zagorsk until long after the service was over. Madame Voronova said never mind, she had a better idea. With meaningful looks, she laid on a trip round the town for John and Sarah in a horse-drawn carriage.

Back in Moscow, dinner was at a Chinese restaurant with a gypsy piano trio. Sarah documented the evening in her travel diary:

An hysterical meal, with masses of toasts. Madame Voronova toasting 'Men!' 'Women as nature's miracles!' John toasting 'Anna Akhmatova!' Me toasting 'Russia!' Madame Voronova toasting 'Love!' Boris making a long toast in Russian. Then spontaneous dancing from Madame Voronova. Boris also did a lot of proper Russian dancing. Then Boris took over playing the piano. He could play like a concert pianist, and then he'd suddenly imitate a black soul singer, all in Russian. Then John did his set piece, playing 'Baa Baa Black Sheep' in the style of Mozart, Bach, and so on. Everyone was dancing. All this celebration building up to our first meeting with the conductor, Rozhdestvensky.

That meeting, in Rozhdestvensky's office next morning, was horribly sobering. Their interpreter, Paul, turned white while the conductor ranted and raved. Odd bits were translated. 'A disaster.' 'There will be no concert.' 'There is no soloist.' What it all meant was that Rozhdestvensky was furious because the English soprano, Penelope Walmsley-Clark, was not yet in Moscow. Her flight did not arrive until the evening. The concert was the next day. Rozhdestvensky was not known for his keenness on rehearsals, but he was insisting on a full one with the orchestra today. Moscow was providing someone to sing the bass solo, but the soprano had by far the most important part. He needed to hear her. No rehearsal: no show. Or perhaps John would like to take the place of the orchestra and accompany Walmsley-Clark on the piano?

Calls were made to the Cultural Foundation, to the British Embassy, to John's publishers in London. John felt desperate and cried out for champagne. In the end, Rozhdestvensky fixed a night-time rehearsal with the orchestra, which Penelope Walmsley-Clark would have to join straight from the plane. During the pandemonium, a telegram arrived from England telling John that Cecil Collins had died. John and Sarah went back to their hotel in a state of utter misery.

Penelope Walmsley-Clark duly arrived. She had been travelling since six in the morning, but was taken from the airport to the rehearsal room unfed and unwatered. By all accounts, she acquitted herself brilliantly. A car took her back to the hotel with John and Sarah, where they were told sorry, no food, even though the restaurant was still in full swing. On Penelope's behalf, Sarah stood in the middle of the restaurant and made a terrible scene, until the management was embarrassed into providing a table. But nothing to drink, not even water. In Sarah's account, rescue came from a party of deaf and dumb students at a table nearby, 'who were communicating in whooshing noises, really enjoying themselves. They took pity on us and gave us some water. Then they toasted us in vodka and gave us some champagne.'

There was a further rehearsal next morning, then a TV crew took John and Sarah to the tiny flat where Anna Akhmatova had lived. They were shown the sofa where she sat and listened to Pasternak reading the first draft of *Dr Zhivago*; the window from which she watched the KGB on constant guard; the bed where she died.

The concert was an elaborate and emotional affair, in the Tchaikovsky Hall at the Moscow Conservatoire. First there were excerpts from Rachmaninov's *Vespers*. Then Rozhdestvensky's wife, Victoria Posnikova, gave a brilliant account of Prokoviev's 7th Piano Sonata. During the interval, she began the campaign, which still goes on, to persuade John to write some music for her. In the second half, a tape was played of Anna Akhmatova reading her own poetry, as a prelude to *Akhmatova: Requiem*, in which Rozhdestvensky found depths John barely knew were there.

After the performance, bouquets and honours were heaped on John, on Rozhdestvensky and on a big personality called Kirill Sokolov, an exiled Russian painter living in the north of England. John remembered meeting him at Mother Thekla's monastery.

*

On Wednesday, 7 June 1989, the day after the concert, John was back in London. He contacted Elizabeth Collins and arranged to play the organ at Cecil's funeral. He also had to face the news that one of his favourite ex-students, the flamboyant Giles Hewlett-Cooper, who once shocked the conservatives at St John's Presbyterian Church in Kensington, was now close to death. As his cancer had advanced, Giles' faith had grown stronger. His religion was a highly personal mixture of Hinduism and Christianity. He had taken a close interest in the *Akathist*, had corresponded with Mother Thekla, and had taken to signing his letters 'Glory to God for everything, for absolutely everything'.

On 9 June John went to be at Giles' hospital bedside in Southampton. He was driven there by Penny Turton, who had known them both since her young days in the choir at St John's. John and Penny were with Giles during his last hours. John read to him from the Gospels. Penny stroked his head. She was deeply affected by his attitude to his own suffering and death. 'He was radiant with acceptance. He saw everything as an opportunity for transformation, and was able to welcome it with faith and love.'

On 13 June John was in charge of the music at Cecil Collins' funeral in Chelsea. At the end of the service Alison Gough sang the unaccompanied lament 'All the heavy days are over', from *To a Child Dancing in the Wind*, while John intoned Orthodox Alleluias. Two days later, he attended the crematorium service for Giles Hewlett-Cooper. Giles had said there should be no priest, so John officiated. As the coffin came in, he chanted *Aghios O Theos*, while other friends of Giles hummed the *ison*. Then there were readings from the Hindu scriptures, interleaved with more Greek chant.

After all that, John worked on *Mary of Egypt* with fresh creative energy: an energy which always seemed to come to him after the death of dear ones. The opera became dedicated to Giles. Taking a break from it one day, he browsed through the collected poems of George Seferis. One *haiku* in particular caught his eye, and he rang Mother Thekla to read it to her:

> In the evening
> And at dawn's first light
> The jasmine stays eternally white

Without a pause, Mother Thekla added some free verse of her own:

> He asked for bread and we gave Him a stone
> Do whatsoever He bids you.
> *Gospodi pomilui.*
> Remember me, the thief exclaimed . . .
> The house where I was born . . .
> This night in Paradise.

When she stopped, John repeated the *haiku*. Through what seemed to him a supernatural process, he now had a text to set in memory of Cecil Collins.

The little choral piece which emerged is called *Eonia*, which means 'Eternal'. Orthodox chant is the basis of John's music for Mother Thekla's lines. Before and after them comes the *haiku*, rocking gently back and forth on two chords which sound familiar. They are the first two chords of 'The Departure of the Guests', from Tchaikovsky's *Nutcracker Suite*, and for John they are packed with associations. First, *The Nutcracker* was a ballet Vicky loved to dance. Secondly, a Russian production of it was on the television in his mother's hospital room during the Christmas just before she died. She opened her eyes during

'The Departure of the Guests' and whispered, 'How beautiful.' Thirdly, Stravinsky loved these two chords of Tchaikovsky. He quotes them towards the end of *Petrushka*. Finally, it was *The Nutcracker* that was being piped through the loudspeakers of the Indian restaurant in Manchester, which was used as a haven late one night by John and Mia Farrow.

According to John, Cecil Collins would have been tickled by the first London performance of *Eonia*:

> It was in a church in the City. The score is marked 'With unearthly stillness', and the choir sang it very, very quietly. But outside the church, all the way through, there was an Irish drunk singing his head off. Elizabeth is rather deaf, and I'm not sure if she knew which was which.

Since then, without benefit of the Irish *obbligato*, *Eonia* has become one of John's most popular small choral pieces.

★

An event of great consequence during the early summer of 1989 was the recording of *The Protecting Veil* in the BBC Maida Vale studios. This recording was the standard BBC preliminary to a live première at a Promenade Concert. The orchestra was the BBC Symphony, conducted by Oliver Knussen, who found the music affecting and amazingly frugal with notes. Knussen seemed wary of John and asked him if he lived in a monastery. John said not exactly, and suggested they share a few bottles of wine. He knew that Knussen was Artistic Director of the Aldeburgh Festival, and decided to strike while the iron was hot. During the drinking, he told him all about *Mary of Egypt*, and wondered if such an unusual opera might find a place on the Aldeburgh programme. Knussen thought it might. He promised to put it forward, and he was as good as his word.

Next time John went to the monastery, he took a copy of the BBC recording of *The Protecting Veil*. After Sunday Service, all gathered round 'Buttercup' to listen to it. Mother Thekla had been unprepared for its beauty. She wrote in her diary, 'So strange to be sitting with John – who wrote it. A nearly frightening thought.' Others present included the painter Kirill Sokolov, whom John had come across in Moscow, and a young lady called Charlotte Callus, who worked for Chester Music and was being used by John to fill the gap left by Liadain.

After *The Protecting Veil* tape, John had another surprise up his sleeve: a videotape of the Ingmar Bergman film of Mozart's *Magic Flute*. He wanted Mother Thekla to study it. Now that a commission from Aldeburgh was in prospect, he was keener than ever to get *Mary of Egypt* finished.

*

On 26 July, the Channel 4 programme about John was televised. His father threw a celebration party, but the film featured Katounia heavily, and it was no fun viewing the Eden which was now out of bounds. John felt he needed a sunshine holiday before *The Protecting Veil* at the Proms. Denied Katounia, he took up an invitation from Dave Gilmour, guitarist with the psychedelic rock group Pink Floyd. Gilmour kept a villa on Rhodes, and had said John could use it at any time. They had been friends since they had played together at a charity Christmas concert. That concert was John's last public appearance as an organist, so it earns an entry here.

Dave Gilmour's wife Ginger was a devoted pupil of Cecil Collins. She was also a disciple of the guru Lily Cornford, and the Christmas concert in Westminster Central Hall was to raise funds for Lily Cornford's Maitreya School of Healing. The top attractions were an all-star rock group led by Dave Gilmour, and a choir which sang music by John. When the programme had run its course, John improvised some exit music on the Central Hall organ: a solo *fantasia*, full of quotations and modulations. Dave Gilmour was impressed, and his villa on Rhodes stood waiting. At the end of August 1989 John went there with Charlotte Callus.

*

After his week on Rhodes, John was back for the première of *The Protecting Veil*. The BBC build-up included radio interviews with him and with Mother Thekla and then, on 4 September – the night of the Prom broadcast itself – a *Protecting Veil* preview on Radio 3, by a panel of musicians who had heard the Maida Vale tape. They were unanimously ecstatic. Far greater than the music of Philip Glass and Arvo Pärt, they said. The young composer Steve Martland thought it 'one of the most unbelievably beautiful and moving pieces I have ever heard. It's going through my head now. I've never stopped thinking about it. It's a magic piece.'

While the radio audience was having its appetite whetted, those with tickets for the concert could meet the composer in person, at a pre-Prom talk in the Royal College of Music opposite the Albert Hall. Among those who went along was Maryanna Schaefer. She remembers finding John at the door 'greeting everyone in his usual way'. John remembers the moment too. He had no idea Maryanna was coming, he had not seen her for four years, and he did not immediately recognize her. She accosted him with 'You don't know who I am, do you?', followed immediately by 'I'm Maryanna Schaefer.' Cheeky as ever, he thought. She could see he'd had a few drinks. 'He swooped down from his heights and gave me kisses on both cheeks and took my telephone number.'

The Protecting Veil caused the same sort of sensation as *The Whale* twenty-one years earlier, but the dedicatee was not there to share the excitement. Rather than attend the Albert Hall and be ignored, Pamela chose to stay at home and listen to the performance on her radio.

Three days later there was more Tavener on the air, when the BBC relayed the first London performance of the *Ikon of St Seraphim*, from Christ Church Spitalfields. At the weekend John went to the monastery, with another companion for Mother Thekla to meet. This time it was Susan Vaughan, one of his earliest girlfriends, who had designed the set for *The Cappemakers* at Charleston. Mother Thekla seems to have found Susan a bit on the boisterous side. 'It was good to see John,' she wrote in her diary, 'but a little noisy!!'

Back in London on Sunday night, John was shown the pile of rave reviews for *The Protecting Veil*. On top was the one by Nicholas Kenyon in the *Observer*, who set John's piece alongside Messiaen's *St François d'Assise*, Górecki's Third Symphony, and Arvo Pärt's *St John Passion*, 'each in its different way a masterpiece'.

On Monday morning John heard from the BBC that letters of appreciation from listeners were pouring in. In the afternoon the Maida Vale recording of *The Protecting Veil* was on the radio, then at 10 p.m. there was a late Prom, broadcast from Kensington Town Hall, which included yet more Tavener: his eight-year-old *Trisagion*, performed by London Brass, in an arrangement for double the number of players he first thought of. John was in the audience and was pleasantly surprised: both by the effectiveness of the arrangement and because here at Kensington Town Hall was Maryanna Schaefer again. She had not told him she was coming. After the concert they took a taxi to her flat and shared a bottle of wine. By now, Maryanna had her physics degree and a job with the Central Electricity Generating Board. September 18, one week after the *Trisagion* adventure, was her twenty-third birthday. With surprising thoughtfulness, John sent her a huge bunch of flowers. Then he rang to say he was going to Greece: could he take her out to dinner before he went?

Maryanna has no problem remembering that dinner. It was at the swanky San Lorenzo restaurant in Knightsbridge. John assured her they might well bump into Princess Diana. They sat down at the bar, and then he flabbergasted her with his style of wooing. 'He said, "How can a Christian Scientist understand the Incarnation of God?" I wasn't really thinking of the Incarnation at that point, but I tried my best.' Over dinner he explained that the evening was a sort of celebration: he had just finished an opera he had been writing for many years. It was called *Mary of Egypt*. He made it sound fascinating. He said he'd call her as soon as he returned from Greece. He was going to the island of Aegina, to get away from it all after the Proms.

He was back on 6 October, feeling poorly, but keen to see Maryanna again. During the last three months of the year, she says, 'We saw each other all the time, and fell in love. I was concerned with John the person rather than John the musician and composer. A lot of people probably didn't concentrate on him as a person in the way that I did.'

John was impatient to show her to Mother Thekla. He took her to Yorkshire for the first time in early November. They stayed at the local inn for the weekend, and went to the monastery for their meals. He drove her back to London on Sunday night, so she could get to work, then he returned to the monastery on his own in the middle of the week. The final version of *Mary of Egypt* needed checking, and he wanted a text for a large new choral work, which was being commissioned for the 900th anniversary of Chester Cathedral.

It was decided to base this new piece on events in the life of Christ as seen through the eyes of the apostle John. It would be called *We Shall See Him As He Is*. He and Mother Thekla spent several days planning it, then Maryanna joined them again at the weekend.

Mother Thekla was left to provide *Mary of Egypt* with just one more thing: a warning notice for producers, emphasizing that this was not an opera but a 'moving ikon'. She drafted the following headings:

NOTHING operatic, dramatic, realistic.
TOTALLY stylized.
PRESENTED impersonally, for the audience to draw its own conclusions.
FUNDAMENTAL primary colours in the music, movements, clothes, words.
A REPETITIVE interrelationship between music – words – movements – clothes.

She sent them off to John on 27 November and wrote in her diary, 'St Mary – after all, *all* these years – completed! Seems odd.'

But the première of *Mary of Egypt* was still several years away. The next big occasion in the diary is Christmas 1989. The build-up began on 16 December. 'John telephoned. Is bringing video tapes and crackers and I don't know what!!' December 23 was 'A somewhat overpowering day . . . Arrival of John and Maryanna. Putting up Christmas tree!!!' The 24th is described as 'unbelievable', and so is Christmas Day, when the victuals included a turkey and a crate of Greek wine. '11 for dinner – NOISE – TALK – FUN – John insisted on *ghastly* video film. Dr Zhivago!!! But it was good to have him, and Maryanna is growing on me.'

On the 27th, they listened to a service on the radio from Westminster Abbey, which included a new Thekla/Tavener carol: a jolly one, called 'Today the Virgin'. Mother Thekla had written the words back in the summer, with no prompting from John. They have Mary explaining to her worried husband Joseph that 'God in His mercy' has taken flesh in her womb. John's melody is folksy and brazen.

★

After Christmas at the monastery, John took Maryanna to Aegina and proposed to her. She accepted and, naturally enough, remembers every detail. The question was popped in a tiny taverna in the seaside village of Perdika. 'He couldn't wait. He was planning to do it as we walked to the top of the Holy Mountain at Paleochora, but he couldn't wait. We walked up the hillside next morning.'

Back in England, the engaged couple began to look for a house away from London. John liked the idea of living near the monastery, so estate agents in North Yorkshire were put on alert, and Mother Thekla was drawn into the search. When John and Maryanna next came to visit her, much of the time was spent viewing local properties. One was found – a large house with a nautical atmosphere, overlooking the sea – which John liked very much. Maryanna did not like it at all. Meanwhile, John's brother Roger, who regularly scanned the property columns, saw that the Old Rectory at Down Ampney in Gloucestershire was for sale. This beautiful house was where Vaughan Williams was born. Perhaps the firm of Tavener could buy it as an investment and let John and Maryanna live there? Maryanna thought this a wonderful idea, but it turned out to be too expensive.

John complained that house-hunting was a strain. By the second week in February he felt he had earned a break and flew to the south of France, to be on his own for a little while. He was pleased to find the sun quite hot, and lay on the beach all day. While he dozed, a short piece came into his head, not much more than a melodic fragment, in the style favoured by the *clarino* players of northern Greece. Back in his hotel, he wrote it down and decorated it with the inscription 'To Maryanna. Happy Valentine's Day.'

When he got home, he invited Maryanna to come round with her clarinet. She had hardly played since leaving Oxford, but he coaxed her into performing her Valentine present, high notes and all. Her tone, he thought, was agreeably un-English, and it occurred to him that what he had written could grow into a concert piece, perhaps for the London Symphony Orchestra, who had asked him for a showcase for one of their members. He checked and found that something for clarinet would suit them nicely.

On 1 March he arrived at the monastery in thick snow, to devise a plan for the clarinet piece which would make sense theologically. He and Mother Thekla worked out something which incorporated two of their favourite themes: the Holy Fool and the Paradise promised. They called it *The Dance Lament of the Repentant Thief.* Just as the cello takes the part of the Mother of God in *The Protecting Veil*, so here the clarinet represents the thief crucified beside Jesus; the one who asks 'Remember me, when You come into Your Kingdom' and is told 'Today you will be with Me in Paradise.' Accompanied by strings and percussion, the clarinet/thief performs a set of dances and laments. He is comic and pathetic by turns, like the Holy Simpleton of Russian literature, dancing blindly towards salvation.

*

By now, Maryanna was visiting the monastery every weekend, to take instruction in the ways of the Orthodox Church. Teaching duties were shared between Mother Thekla and a new resident: a monk called Father Ephrem, who had been given his own, strictly segregated quarters in exchange for performing priestly functions such as administering the Sacrament.

On Saturday, 24 March 1990, Maryanna was baptized by Father Ephrem in the monastery chapel. Those present were John, Mother Thekla and Maryanna's own mother. The scene Mother Thekla describes in her diary is a beautiful one. Outside the window there was deep snow. Inside, Maryanna was lit by a shaft of bright sunshine.

Dressed in white, she stood in a shallow tin bath while Father Ephrem anointed her with water and oil.

★

Rehearsals for *Resurrection* started in early April, under a confident Alan Tavener, who quickly made his choir and the Scottish Chamber Orchestra feel at home in John's extraordinary sound world. Two of the main soloists were already familiar with the mature Tavener style. The bass Stephen Richardson, who sang Christ, had taken the lead in *Eis Thanaton*. The counter-tenor Simon Gay was just right for the role of Judas, having been perfect as the Devil in *The Ikon of St Seraphim*.

The sounds of Paradise were pre-recorded, so they could be played from loudspeakers up in the roof. At the suggestion of Mother Thekla, Glasgow Council had been persuaded to commission a painting on the grand scale from Kirill Sokolov. In spite of complaints from local Protestants, his free-style magnification of a Russian Ikon of the Resurrection was given a candlelit place of honour.

On the night of Tuesday, 17 April 1990, the narrow nave of Glasgow Cathedral was packed with a highly expectant audience. Mother Thekla stayed at the monastery, but Father Ephrem was there, with John and Maryanna, and John's father, to whom the work is dedicated. From the rehearsals, Alan Tavener knew the performance would last two hours and forty-five minutes. John was opposed to having an interval, but three five-minute pauses were conceded: after Parts II, III and VI. Part VII: The Resurrection had a visible effect on the Greek Orthodox delegation, headed by Archbishop Gregorios. Each time the Greek version of *Christ is Risen!* came round, they got to their feet and sang along.

At that moment, and for a long time afterwards, John believed *Resurrection* to be the finest of him. The Glasgow performance was broadcast by the BBC, but, sad to say, there have been no further performances.

★

As soon as Glasgow was over, John went to Aegina on his own. He finished *The Repentant Thief* and worked on a new composition: a setting of words by St Ephrem the Syrian, the fourth-century poet and mystic, whose symbol-laden writings had been recommended by the new resident at Mother Thekla's monastery. The chosen text was an allegory of the Incarnation, beginning 'Thunder entered her and made no sound.' John imagined it sung in procession, married to the Russian refrain 'Velichaemtya' ('We Magnify Thee'). Mother Thekla made him a composite text. His setting is for organ and two choirs – one of them in the distance, with a single handbell.

Thunder Entered Her was just one product of the extremely fertile summer of 1990, during which John made frequent solo trips to Aegina. Mother Thekla was called upon to expand the text of *We Shall See Him As He Is*. She sent the revised edition out to Greece with John's father. Back came another request, noted in the diary for 21 June: 'John has ideas about The Apocalypse!!!' What happened, John says, was that he found himself thinking about the message his brother Roger had left on his pillow all those years ago, after the performance of *Genesis*. Roger had prophesied that one day *Genesis* would be followed by *Revelation*, and now John was hearing the faint sound of trilling trumpets, 'far off and very very high'. Some trumpets were fluttering around topmost E flat, while others were down below on D. This interval of a minor ninth was the sound image which spurred the request for an apocalyptic text.

All through July and August John worked on the score of *We Shall See Him As He Is*, while Mother Thekla distilled a text from the Book of Revelation for his next *magnum opus*. It became clear to Maryanna that house-hunting and marriage had slipped from John's list of priorities. She appealed to Mother Thekla. The judgement was that nothing could be done. In the end, she made the journey to Aegina, to remind John of his promises. She did not find him responsive, so she broke off the engagement. She remembers the precise date of this encounter. It was 4 September 1990: one year to the day after the première of *The Protecting Veil*. By this time, privatization had ended her job with the CEGB and she was working for British Nuclear Industry Forum. Soon after that unhappy trip to Greece, her new employers offered her a secondment to Vienna, as part of a United Nations team studying the effects of radiation from the Chernobyl accident. She took it.

John came back to England at the end of September and went straight to the monastery. According to Mother Thekla's diary for 1 October, 'He played and sang *We Shall See Him As He Is* right through. I think it's probably the most magnificent thing he's ever done – not a stray moment.'

*

We Shall See Him As He Is is a montage of events in the life of Christ, taken from the writings of St John, which have been freely adapted by Mother Thekla. There are eleven scenes, or Ikons.

The music is for solo tenor, who sings the role of St John; two more soloists (soprano and tenor); large chorus; trumpets; timpani; organ; and strings, with not less than ten cellos, one of which has an important solo part.

The first sound is an unaccompanied statement, by the solo cello, of the Russian chant heard during Holy Week, when they sing

> I see Thy bridal chamber adorned, O my Saviour,
> And I have no fitting garment that I may enter therein.

This glimpse of Paradise is followed by a choral statement of the title phrase 'We Shall See Him As He Is', sung in Greek, in a traditional Byzantine tone, while the strings hold the eternity note, which is D.

Each Ikon is introduced by St John. At the start of Ikon I he sings the two words 'I heard', extending them into a melodic line of Byzantine beauty. Then the bass voices, chanting canonically, meditate on the mystery of Creation. The Ikon ends with an ascending five-note phrase from the strings, which will recur throughout the piece, sometimes expanded into a 25-note palindrome by means of the magic square.

In Ikon II the choir, singing tenderly, makes a chromatic descent to suggest the baptism of Christ, when the Holy Spirit came down like a dove.

Ikon III has trumpets and timpani heralding the wedding feast at Cana, where Christ turned water into wine. The atmosphere of the feast is created by soprano and tenor soloists and two solo violins, all in unison, sounding very Middle Eastern. Then to celebrate the miracle, chorus, orchestra and organ combine to create a sound from a completely different world; a blazing, Bach-like chord of D major. The Ikon ends with a restatement of the opening Bridal Chamber theme, this time on four cellos, and then a reprise of 'We Shall See Him As He Is' by the chorus.

Ikon IV has the atmosphere of an oriental bazaar, with busy music played in octaves by the strings. The scene is the temple, which Christ finds defiled by the money men. When he sings 'In my Father's house', he projects pathos rather than anger, and it is the Bridal Chamber melody that he uses.

Ikon V celebrates the union of Christ and His church:

> He that has the Bride
> He is the Bridegroom.

John's setting, marked 'Massive', is for chorus, orchestra and organ. It begins in a Byzantine tone, but ends with a great burst of D major. This

D major chord is sustained by the violins, while the solo cello soars upwards and quotes the Lament of the Mother of God from *Resurrection*. The Bridal Chamber theme comes back, now played by seven cellos, and then the chorus sings 'We Shall See Him As He Is', this time in a different Byzantine tone.

Ikon VI features the much-married woman from Samaria, who remembers meeting Jesus at the well, where He asked her for a drink of water. Her simple melody, Byzantine in character, starts soberly but moves to a spectacular conclusion: rising from bottom G to a sustained top D. Her strange companion on her journey of remembrance is a solo violin, which keeps quoting a fragment of the Aria 'Have mercy Lord' from Bach's *St Matthew Passion*.

Ikon VII starts as a pale reflection of Ikon III. Where before trumpets proclaimed the wedding feast at Cana, now the same notes are heard as eerie harmonics on the double basses, introducing the diseased multitude around the pool. When Christ orders one of the cripples 'Take up thy bed and walk,' chorus and orchestra clamber slowly up the chromatic scale, until they arrive at another triumphant chord of D major. The Ikon ends with the Bridal Chamber music, played now by ten cellos, and 'We Shall See Him As He Is' sung by the chorus in a new Byzantine tone.

Ikon VIII represents the Last Supper. At the words 'But one shall betray me', the melody clashes with the drone, like the singing of Judas in *Resurrection*.

Ikon IX starts with St John's memories of the Crucifixion. His 'I saw', many times repeated, goes through all eight Byzantine tones, while the chorus details those things which were seen: 'body crucified; blood; water'. Then comes the Tomb, represented by the canon for high violins which also served in *Resurrection* and *The Hidden Treasure*.

Ikon X is the climax of the piece: a meditation on Christ's words from the Cross:

> Behold thy Mother!
> Behold thy son!

The words symbolize the establishment of the Church on earth, so John uses again his music for Ikon V. And, as before, there is an outpouring from the solo cello, which this time quotes from *The Protecting Veil*. The drama is heightened by a series of flashbacks, and the Ikon ends with four massive and apocalyptic statements of 'We Shall See Him As He Is', each one in a different tone.

Ikon XI begins with a canonic passage for St John and the bass voices, reflecting on Time and Eternity, mirroring Ikon I. It ends with a solo violin, playing as quietly as possible and without vibrato the Bridal Chamber music with which it all began.

★

After the play-through of *We Shall See Him As He Is*, John and Mother Thekla looked at other projects. It was agreed that the text for *The Apocalypse* should be re-written once more, at a quarter of its present length. And John wanted a text for another new piece: a music drama based on the ancient narrative of the Falling Asleep of the Mother of God and Her burial by the Apostles.

On 19 October he went to Aegina again, to write out the final version of *We Shall See Him As He Is* and make sketches for the new pieces. He found himself working at fever pitch and could hear his heart thumping. Maryanna rang from Vienna. He complained to her that he was unwell and depressed, which was strange and frightening: he had never before been depressed when the music was flowing. She took to phoning him at the Nafsika Hotel every evening. Counselling him to go to bed. Warning him not to drink too much. Long-distance mothering. The proprietor, John's old friend Dimitri Poulakos, was indignant. He classed this as conduct unbecoming a young girl who had broken off an engagement.

During the daytime, John composed without let-up. As well as working on the major pieces, he produced a couple of miniatures: *O, Do Not Move*, on words of Seferis, dedicated to Penny Turton, whose marriage had ended unhappily; and *A Christmas Round on a Greek Text*, dedicated to Dimitri Poulakos, with whom he had long gloomy talks in the evenings. The weather was foul, and John was the only guest in the hotel.

Although Vicky Maragopoulou had remarried, John was still in touch with her and sometimes they met when he passed through Athens. Her father, Costas, had remained a dear friend. When John's mother was dying, he spoke to Costas frequently. Now, his ex-father-in-law was blind and bed-ridden and not far from the end. On 9 November John felt a compulsion to be with him. The sea was rough and he was advised to travel on another day, but he waited on the quay until the ferry re-started. Vicky met him in Athens in the pouring rain, and they went to the hospital together. Yet again, John asked forgiveness for the mess he had made of marriage, and yet again Costas and Vicky forgave him. When he got back to Aegina, he set about composing a lament for his dying friend: *Thrinos*, a five-minute cello solo, based on a Greek funeral chant. Vicky phoned him before he had finished it, to say her father was dead.

Tormented by the past and feeling physically wretched, John made a desperate prayer to the Mother of God. He reviewed the disaster of his marriage and all the other failed relationships. He prayed for a sign – anything – to show him what to do. He said even death would be better than the present misery.

He finished *Thrinos*, left Aegina and went to stay at the Athens Chandris Hotel. Vicky spent some time with him, but her new husband was her priority, so mostly he was on his own: either in his hotel room, staring at the mounds of music he had written, or down at Glifada, touring the tavernas, muttering 'I wish I could die,' like he used to do when he was a teenager.

After three days of this he flew home. In a spirit of defiance, he threw a party in Wembley Park, inviting friends like Penny Turton and Michael Buckland. His aim was to get seriously drunk. Talking to his brother Roger, he mentioned the loudness of his heart. Roger asked, did he feel thumping in his neck? Yes, he did. Was he short of breath? Yes, he was. Roger said the symptoms sounded horribly familiar. Next day, he arranged for John to see a specialist.

The diagnosis was not good. Marfan's syndrome had struck again and John had a leaking aorta. There would have to be heart surgery, after more tests to establish the extent of the degeneration. When he got home from the hospital, he called Mother Thekla, Vicky and Mary-anna. Then he worked on *The Apocalypse*, propped up on pillows. Maryanna came back from Vienna.

By the end of November it was clear that the operation would have to be a big one. He kept working on *The Apocalypse*. On 14 December there was more bad trouble. A large cyst, possibly malignant, was discovered beneath one of his wisdom teeth. It would have to be removed before the heart operation could take place. He continued to work on *The Apocalypse* and made good progress.

On 23 December he and Maryanna arrived for Christmas at the monastery. The diary notes that on 28 December, at a ceremony in the monastery chapel, John was anointed by Father Ephrem 'so that he is safe for what follows'. In other words, he received Holy Unction. Back in London, at John's request, the ceremony was repeated by Father Michael at the Russian Cathedral.

*

Through January, John waited for surgery and worked on *The Apoca-lypse*. By the 22nd he had reached Ikon IX: The New Jerusalem. On the 25th, he was in the Middlesex hospital, for the extremely unpleasant operation on his jaw. Skin was removed from his leg to patch the wound. Archbishop Gregorios came to give him a blessing, thinking they had operated on his heart. The Archbishop's English was not good, and he was bemused and appalled by the battered state of John's face.

What most concerned John was how to represent musically the New Jerusalem, where there would be no death, no sorrow, no crying, no pain. Where God would wipe away all the tears. It was impossible to imagine what that would be like. As a gesture of humility and not-knowing, he elected to set 'The New Jerusalem' entirely on one note – the eternity note of D – arranged into a gigantic canon, with all the voices and instruments singing and playing as quietly as possible. Since there was to be no variation in pitch, all the interest would be in the shifting rhythmic patterns. As a basis for these, he took the 4, 3, 2, 1 formula he had been using since *The Whale*. Each of the vocal and instrumental groups would work its way through the twenty-four poss-ible permutations, each from a different starting point, but all ending together. He was too feeble and distracted by pain to work out the mathematics of it, so he called on Maryanna to bring her young mind to bear. Not pleased to be cast in this clerical role, she nevertheless obliged with the sets of figures, for which he was immensely grateful.

On 3 February he was home, and the long wait began. He had to be fit enough for heart surgery, and a suitable valve had to be available: a human valve, because a mechanical one would be too noisy for him.

By the end of February the first draft of *The Apocalypse* was finished, and his thoughts reverted to the Falling Asleep of the Mother of God. Mother Thekla had already turned the story into a libretto for a music drama, but now he was hearing it as a purely instrumental piece, played from a great distance by a string quartet and handbells. This new piece became known as *The Last Sleep of the Virgin*.

On Thursday 21 March the call came. John was to report to the hospital next day. Professor Magdi Yacoub would be the surgeon, and he would operate at night. Maryanna took John to Harefield and booked herself into a nearby hotel. Friday night came and went, with no oper-ation. So did Saturday. The surgical team was not satisfied with the quality of the valve available. John and Maryanna went out into the countryside for their meals. By Monday there was still no valve, and John was sent home. He phoned Mother Thekla next day and worried her by saying his nerves were in shreds and he might now refuse the operation altogether. He also reported good progress on *The Last Sleep of the Virgin*.

On Friday 12 April he was called into hospital again. In the front room at Wembley Park, stacked on his composing table, he left the completed manuscripts of *The Apocalypse* and *The Last Sleep of the Virgin*, all in faint pencil. Into hospital with him he took yet another text by Mother Thekla for the music drama about the Falling Asleep of the Mother of God. At his urgent request, she had reworked it as 'a singing tableau for young people'. They called it *Let's Begin Again*, 'because we must all begin again and become as children'. He wanted it at his bedside, so he could work on it as soon as the operation was over.

Magdi Yacoub carried out the surgery on Saturday night. He managed to patch the aorta with Dacron, so no transplant was necessary. When John was wheeled from the theatre into intensive care, Maryanna was there to watch over him. Magdi Yacoub left the hospital. And then John started to haemorrhage. He was rushed back into the theatre and opened up again. Magdi Yacoub gave advice from his car phone. Roger arrived to keep watch with Maryanna. On Sunday morning John was again moved from the theatre to intensive care. He seemed to be holding his own. Maryanna relayed the news to the monastery, where Mother Thekla had been waiting by her telephone. It was the Sunday following Orthodox Easter Sunday. She found herself tremulously singing the climax of John's *Resurrection*. 'I could hardly sing it – but I did sing his "Christ is risen!"'

PART SEVEN

Let's begin again

§

Let's begin again

After two days on the critical list, John was moved from intensive care to a room of his own. It seemed he was safe, but his temperature refused to go down. Favourite ikons were installed, and, whenever the coast was clear, he got Maryanna to burn incense. The nursing staff turned a blind eye to the scorch marks on the carpet, but, as more and more composing days were lost, John became increasingly agitated. He studied the text of *Let's Begin Again*, called for his manuscript paper, and wrote the opening bars. They begin with a low A, given to the Voice of God, while choir and instruments sustain the chord of A minor seventh. This chord, John remembers, was plucked from the air. He had been hearing it all around him ever since he woke up from the operation. It turned out to be the humming of assorted hospital machinery. After that, progress on the piece was painfully slow, and he put it to the hospital staff that for his temperature to settle he needed to be at home.

On Friday 3 March, three weeks after the operation, he was back in Wembley Park. His father's health was not good, so Mother Thekla had found somebody to take care of them both. She was Elreda Kidd, the widow of Mother Katherine's brother, and she moved in for the duration of John's convalescence. Maryanna came every evening, after work at British Nuclear Industry Forum. John's clearest memory from those days is of his first, shuffling journey to the lounge and the reunion with his piano. During the wait for the operation, the thought of dying had been less awful than the possibility that afterwards he would no longer be able to compose. He placed his fingers on the keyboard. 'I was very anxious to see if I still had something coming through me.' The answer was that the music did not flow freely. Praying, too, had become difficult. When he told Mother Thekla, she reassured him that composing and praying were similar acts, and both would become easier as he grew stronger.

An exciting distraction was the commercial recording of *The*

Protecting Veil. In spite of the success of the broadcast with the BBC
Symphony Orchestra and Oliver Knussen, Steven Isserlis's record
company, Virgin Classics, preferred the more glamorous London
Symphony Orchestra, under Gennady Rozhdestvensky. The company
also sought financial inducements before it would embark on what it
said was a risky venture. The Arts Council obliged with a subsidy of
£10,000, and another £10,000 came from Roger Tavener.

Escorted by Maryanna and leaning heavily on his stick, John struggled
from the car to the recording studio and sat down exhausted. He hoped
Rozhdestvensky would make the journey worthwhile, and he was not
disappointed, although it seemed the *maestro* may not have done much
homework on the score. He began by wondering what time the woodwind section was arriving, but then he produced exactly what John
wanted: an Orthodox interpretation, an insider's view, tuned to the
qualities of chant and the sound of Russian bells. 'Darlings, it is so
beautiful,' the *maestro* kept telling John and Steven, as he wrapped up
the recording with ample time to spare.

*

The next landmark in 1991 was 4 June. On that day, in the garden at
Wembley Park, John and Maryanna again became engaged. Maryanna
says the decision this time was taken 'quietly and soberly, unlike the
previous desperate and frantic occasion'. John gives all the credit to
Maryanna:

> I wouldn't have asked her. I thought 'Here is this incredible girl, who
> has given up all this time. What the hell does she see in me?' I was
> old. I was ill. I didn't want to have children. And at that time I wasn't
> earning much money, either. It almost broke my heart, her devotion
> to me. I couldn't understand it. But she was adamant.

The hunt for a house was resumed, with particular emphasis on
Sussex. The drive there from London was not too taxing for John;
Maryanna would be able to commute to her office; it claimed to be
England's sunniest county; and it contained Charleston Manor, of
blessed memory.

John had been travelling the same route from London to Charleston
since he was twelve years old: down the Brighton road, then across
country through Hurstpierpoint and Lewes. On one of their searches,
he and Maryanna stopped for a pub lunch in Hurstpierpoint, scanned
the local paper, and saw that part of a large manor house was for sale.

They went to look. The property, called Naldretts, stood at the end of a long private drive. It was bulky, pebble-dashed, built in 1906, and now divided into three units of accommodation. The one for sale was the west wing. John liked it immediately: large rooms, high ceilings, the proper environment for the concert grand piano that had been promised as a wedding present by Philip Pilkington; and for Kirill Sokolov's large painting of the Resurrection, which was coming from Glasgow Cathedral, in exchange for a new choral piece. A further bonus was the presence in the area of Father Sergei Hackel, John's collaborator on *Akhmatova: Requiem*, who held Sunday services for the Orthodox of Sussex in a converted parish church. Maryanna did not like Naldretts at all. She thought it unhomely, but it was what John wanted so they put in an offer.

*

As soon as he was mobile enough, John was back on the concert scene. Looking dramatically frail, with cape and stick, he came on to the platform at Spitalfields to take a bow on 12 June, after Steven Isserlis had played *The Protecting Veil* with Richard Hickox and the City of London Sinfonia. Three days later he was at St Albans Abbey for the première of *Thunder Entered Her*. All the while, he was slowly moving forward with *Let's Begin Again* and complaining of a lack of energy. At the end of June, anxious for hot sunshine but not strong enough to travel to Greece, he went with Maryanna to the South of France. They stayed for ten days, and as soon as they came back they drove to North Yorkshire, to see Mother Thekla for the first time since the operation. The diary records their welcome.

> *Saturday July 13.* My two arrived for supper so of course we were very late. Maryanna's 'grown up' quite a bit – but what she's been through! John not as dreadful to look at as I feared – but *very* long and thin – and gets breathless. The *tiniest* scar – after all that.

Maryanna returned to London after the Sunday service, but John stayed for a week, working with Mother Thekla on *Let's Begin Again*, and inviting ideas for a new orchestral piece. The Bournemouth Symphony Orchestra was starting to talk about a Tavener commission to celebrate its centenary season in 1994. Mother Thekla suggested basing it on Psalm 104, which rejoices in God's presence in every aspect of His creation: humans, animals, landscape and seascape. She divided the Psalm into sections, which might correspond to the sections of the orchestra. This new work would be called *Theophany*.

★

Mary of Egypt looked set for the 1992 Aldeburgh Festival, and planning meetings began. Aldeburgh appointed Lionel Friend as conductor, and a young director called Lucy Bailey. The first concern of these two was the casting of the title role. John was keen to give it to Patricia Forbes, who sang on the recording of his *Panikhida* for Ikon Records and impressed him with her seriousness and the non-operatic purity of her tone. Conductor and director, however, both baulked at her lack of theatrical experience. Lionel Friend had known John since *Thérèse*, when he was called in to prepare the vocal score. He remembered the crisis over Elise Ross.

Lucy Bailey made the trek north to confer with Mother Thekla. Having established that the most important quality expected of Mary was 'radiance', Lucy put forward Patricia Rozario, a young soprano from Bombay with a brilliant voice, a wide range and a rising operatic reputation. An audition was held in Wembley Park. With her husband at the piano, Patricia first sang some Mozart, at the request of Lionel Friend. She remembers John's lack of interest. 'He got up and went to pay someone who was washing his car.' Then he took over the keyboard and guided her through the part of Mary. 'He wanted to see if I could get it sounding improvised and almost Middle Eastern, which was no problem!' Neither were the high notes. But the extreme low – a sustained, unaccompanied G flat – was tough. 'John wanted it to sound really strong and rasping. I'd never sung a G flat before. Not in performance.'

She was offered the part and, although her agent said it was the wrong career move, she took it. Devoutly Catholic, she had never felt brave enough to parade her Christianity among the opera set. John's forthright allegiance uplifted her, and she loved *Mary of Egypt* for its message as well as its music. For her, it was 'a large proclamation'.

The other principal role – that of Zossima, the holy man – went to Stephen Varcoe, who had shone in *The Ikon of St Seraphim*. That left one solo singing part to be filled: the disembodied Voice. For this intensely melismatic, unwestern vocal line, John said what was needed was a Greek nun, who could sing in a chest voice. Or perhaps an Indian. When he became persuaded by Lionel Friend that his suggestions were impractical, he remembered an acquaintance from Dartington days: Chloe Goodchild, daughter of the Bishop of Kensington. Chloe loved ancient and ethnic musics, and had spent years studying Indian vocal styles. She was recruited.

*

Because the Orthodox Church was persuaded to annul John's first marriage on the grounds of non-consummation, he was entitled to a second wedding ceremony with all the trimmings, including the crowns of joy and martyrdom. He quite liked the idea of the Russian Cathedral again, but Maryanna preferred to avoid a replay of the past. And in any case, John had come to appreciate the more earthy qualities of Archbishop Gregorios, the head of the Greek Church in Britain, to which Mother Thekla's monastery was affiliated. So it was to Gregorios that application was made, and his Eminence kindly offered to perform the ceremony himself, in his private chapel in Bayswater, which had a garden they could use for the reception afterwards.

The date chosen was Sunday, 8 September 1991: the Feast of the Nativity of the Mother of God. The service was to be at 5.30 p.m., and family and friends, including this author, were assembled in good time on a warm summer afternoon. The bridegroom waited at the door, the young bride circled the block in the wedding limousine, but of Archbishop Gregorios there was no sign. An anxious hour passed. And then the Archbishop arrived, beaming and unabashed and wanting to know 'Where is the girl?' To relieve the tension, the limousine driver had been instructed to take her on a leisurely cruise round Hyde Park. She was back at 6.45, looking radiant, and the full Orthodox ritual, complete with crowns, unfolded without further hitch.

Late that evening, after the banquet in the Archbishop's garden, John drove away with his bride in his latest conveyance: a second-hand black Mercedes 280 CE. The three-day honeymoon was at a hotel in Alfriston, near Charleston Manor, and after that, since the purchase of Naldretts had not been completed, Maryanna moved into Wembley Park to start her married life.

Just one week after the wedding, Marfan's syndrome issued a grim reminder that it was a family member. On Saturday evening, at Harefield hospital, Professor Magdi Yacoub performed heart operations on two Taveners: John's brother Roger and Roger's son Simon. The pig's valve which had served Roger for eleven years was failing, and had to be replaced with a mechanical one. Simon had to have his valve strengthened. He was twelve years old.

*

On 19 September came the première at the Barbican of *The Repentant Thief*, with Andrew Marriner taking the clarinet part and Michael Tilson Thomas conducting the London Symphony Orchestra. It sat strangely in a programme which began with Bernstein and ended with Beethoven. John went home before the Beethoven, wondering if his clarinet-as-Fool had meant anything to the LSO audience. Ideally, he would have liked the music to be used for a short ballet, with a set designed by Cecil Collins. He was badly missing Cecil, and in a state of rising anxiety about the coming change to his way of life. His father, too, seemed agitated at the prospect of such upheaval after forty-seven years. On 18 October, contracts were exchanged with the vendor of the house in Sussex. That same day, Kenneth Tavener complained of heart trouble. He was rushed to hospital, where it was confirmed that he was the carrier of Marfan's syndrome. However, his condition did not justify an operation at the age of seventy-eight.

Maryanna took charge of the logistics of setting up the new house, and got strong support from Mother Thekla. The two women knew that dislodging John from Wembley Park was going to be a tricky business. Vicky and Liadain had both failed, and he still might refuse to go. Mother Thekla knew his rituals, and how much it mattered to him that conditions for composing should be exactly right. Having established that a good-sized room in the Sussex house had been set aside as his study, she commissioned the construction of a sturdy work-table of antique appearance: more fitting, she said, than the round dining table in Wembley Park that had done duty as John's writing surface for over thirty years. This was to be her wedding present. She would have it sent directly to Sussex, along with some other useful items: Mother Katherine's desk, for example, which she thought might do for Maryanna. The generous load was delivered on Saturday 9 November. John and Maryanna went to Sussex for the day to receive it, and to see the progress being made with bookshelves by the local carpenter, who had been recommended by Father Sergei Hackel. John complained that the house was too cold to live in. Maryanna said 'leave it to me'.

★

Let's Begin Again and *Theophany* had been set aside in order to work on two small pieces: both new commissions, needed for the following year.

For Steven Isserlis and the Australian Chamber Orchestra, John expanded his solo cello lament, *Thrinos*, and made it a meditation in three sections, which he called *Eternal Memory*. The first section, described as 'Remembrance of the Paradise Lost', sets out the chant-like material plainly and serenely. The middle section, representing life's blind alleys, plays variations on the theme, from the comic to the pathetic. The last section returns to the serenity of the first, but this time looking forward to the 'Paradise Promised'.

The other composition was to be sung at next summer's Vale of Glamorgan Festival by the Hilliard Ensemble. For them, but more particularly for Maryanna, he chose to set 'Village Wedding' by Angelos Sikelianos. Using the Philip Sherrard translation, he raided this long poem for *haiku*-like fragments, to which he added a refrain, taken, words and music, from the Orthodox Wedding service.

O Isaiah, dance for joy, for the Virgin is with child.

To convey the Greek atmosphere of the Sikelianos, there are hints of folk music. To acknowledge the poem's sense of lost innocence, the joy-sorrow chord from *The Lamb* is sounded. To begin it all, John has a dedication which comes from neither Sikelianos nor the Orthodox service. It is a direct address to Maryanna, set to music:

To my beloved, who breaks my heart.

*

As soon as *Village Wedding* was finished, there was something else to divert attention from the looming move. Rhonda Kess, who had championed *A Gentle Spirit* in America, was now in London, teaching Music Theatre at Trinity College of Music, where John was still nominally a professor. With his permission, she was to present his opera *Thérèse* as the college Christmas production, in a scaled-down version prepared by herself. John was intrigued and slightly alarmed by her plans for this pocket edition, which was to happen on the tiny stage of the Rudolf Steiner Theatre. The title role was to be split between two characters: a bed-ridden Thérèse, and a Thérèse who moved through dreams. The vocally acrobatic Rimbaud was to become a cross-dresser, played by a girl with good stage presence and a powerful contralto voice. The action was to be set in a circus.

When Mother Thekla was told what was afoot, she thoroughly approved of the circus. She had heard a tape of the Covent Garden *Thérèse*. It was the one work of John's about which she had reservations.

The libretto was not true to her idea of the saint. No staging of it could be too surrealistic.

Apart from a few chance encounters at the Russian Cathedral, John had not seen Gerard McLarnon for years. He phoned him with the news of *Thérèse à la* Kess, and got a vivid response which sounded just like old times. 'Excuse me,' said Gerry, 'while I vomit on my jam.'

Thérèse was performed twice, on the 5th and 6th of December. John and Gerry attended both performances. Their opera had not seen the light of day since 1979, and they applauded what Rhonda and her students had achieved. So did this author, who filmed an extract for inclusion in a new portrait of John he was preparing for BBC television.

★

Three days after *Thérèse*, and exactly three months after the wedding, came the removal to Sussex. John was not required to take part. A faithful friend of the monastery, Ann Gotteri, was despatched to London by Mother Thekla. She spent a night under the Tavener roof, then journeyed to Sussex next morning with Maryanna and the last load of furniture, including the Wembley Park grand piano and a crate of more than one hundred ikons.

Maryanna had undertaken to have Naldretts in perfect order before John arrived. By now central heating had been installed and the rooms had been freshly decorated. The painting of the Resurrection had arrived from Glasgow, and dominated the dining room. The concert grand piano from Philip Pilkington looked very fine in the sitting room. John's favourite and essential piano – the grand from Wembley Park – was to go up into his study, next to the new composing table. To Maryanna's horror, the removal men were unable to manoeuvre it up the stairs, and she finally had to accept it in the dining room. She and Ann spent the rest of the day making everything else immaculate. They dusted until their noses were red with sneezing. They filled the shelves with books. Lady Birley's music stands were decorated with ikons and hung with incense holders. More ikons were formed into a shrine on the landing. Manuscript paper was placed on the composing table. At the end of the afternoon, full of trepidation, Maryanna telephoned Wembley Park to confess the disaster of the grand piano, and to arrange urgent transport for the little upright which lived in John's Wembley Park bedroom. As far as she could tell, John was not bothered. He seemed not to take it in.

With Ann for company, Maryanna spent Monday night at Naldretts. Next morning, the little upright piano arrived and was put in the study.

At noon came John himself. He made no comment on the disposition of the three pianos, except to say they should all be tuned. After a light lunch, he went to his study, sat at his new composing table, and began working.

Next morning, Maryanna took the London train to her job at British Nuclear Industry Forum. When she got back in the evening, there was a surprise. Feeling homesick, John had been out and bought himself a pet. In Wembley Park, he had been used to the company of a pedigree Burmese cat. Here, he had settled for an ordinary black and white kitten, which he called Pushkin.

Some days later, in accordance with Orthodox tradition, Father Sergei Hackel came to the house and gave it a ceremonial blessing. After prayers at the shrine on the landing, he sprinkled holy water on the walls of each room in turn, followed everywhere by Pushkin, and by the Taveners' new neighbours, who had been invited to share the occasion.

When the time came for Mr and Mrs Tavener to drive north to the monastery for Christmas, Pushkin went too.

*

What concerned John most at the beginning of 1992 was *The Apocalypse*. January was spent studying the score and deciphering the faint pencil marks. Some of what he had written was incomprehensible to him and had to be re-composed. By the end of the month it was all making sense, and he was ready for the meeting which had been set up at the BBC, where he would explain to John Drummond (now in charge of the Promenade Concerts) how this huge work had been precisely designed to fit the Albert Hall. His ambition was to hear it performed at a Prom during 1994, the year of his fiftieth birthday. He had not realized that this was also the year of the 100th Promenade Season, and John Drummond had already planned for all the concerts to be retrospective in character, with no new commissions.

He made his pitch to Drummond nevertheless, explaining that, apart perhaps from St Sophia in Constantinople, the Albert Hall was the only place which could accommodate what he had conceived. The Voice of God and the Woman Clothed with the Sun would be heard from the top gallery. Seven trumpets, six trombones and heavy percussion would be up there too, 'raining disasters down'. In the middle level of the universe, that is to say in the choir stalls flanking the Albert Hall organ, would be the 'messengers between Heaven and Earth': seventy treble voices, seven counter-tenors and a consort of recorders. The organ would play its part, particularly at the time of the Last Judgement. On the platform would be the 'terrestrials': St John; the Whore of Babylon; a saxophone; violins and double basses; handbells; and seven male-voice choirs, each with seven singers, to represent the Seven Churches on Earth. Directly underneath the dome of the Albert Hall ('directly underneath God, as it were'), on the spot where the fountain usually plays, would be a string quartet, which would never cease from sounding the eternity note of D. At the end of two and a half hours, the Albert Hall would be turned into the New Jerusalem, with every singer and instrument taking up that same note.

When John had entered his office, John Drummond had been quite confident that his answer was going to be no. By the time the meeting was over, he found that *The Apocalypse* had become his only new commission for the 100th season. Here is his explanation of how it happened:

> Right from the start of his career, John has forced the world to take him on his own terms. There's no way in which I could say, 'Look, John, I'm extremely busy, will you talk a little faster please, I don't have time for the twenty-minute sentence.' That is John. That is his persona as a man and a musician.
>
> I have been tempted in some works of his to say, 'Oh, couldn't we have a modulation? Or a bit of *allegro* or something!' But I know what I'm in for. And what I have to recognize as a concert promoter is that here we have a composer whose work is of tremendous interest to the audience. So when he comes to me with a proposal which is imaginative and impressive, for something he cares very much about, which is tailored to the building in which we perform, I think, although this is a very expensive operation, and although it is the 100th season, I think, 'Let's go ahead.'

The score of *The Apocalypse* is dated 'Second week in Great Lent 1992', which means John finished inking it around the middle of March. By this time he had also inked in *The Last Sleep of the Virgin*, which was to be premièred by the Chilingirian Quartet at the 1992 Cheltenham Festival.

*

The other-worldliness of *The Last Sleep of the Virgin* brings to mind the unearthly middle movement of Beethoven's String Quartet in A minor, Opus 132, which is headed 'A Holy Song of Thanksgiving to the Godhead, by one recovered from an illness.' John and Mother

Katherine used to listen together to Opus 132, but, although *The Last Sleep* shares a feeling and an atmosphere with it, the two works have no procedures in common.

The trills high above the eternity note of D, which began *The Apocalypse*, also feature in *The Last Sleep*, but John's main source of inspiration here is the Greek Orthodox Feast of the Dormition of the Mother of God, where texts about Her falling asleep and burial are chanted in each of the eight Byzantine tones.

The work is sub-titled 'A veneration for string quartet and handbells', and each of its sections is introduced by a softly played handbell solo, followed by the trills on the violins. Some sections unfold their main material polyphonically; others have solo violin or cello playing a long, flowing melodic line, against sixths played on the handbells. The hybrid quality of these *cantilenas* might be called Byzantine Bach, so it is not surprising to learn that Bach's suites for unaccompanied cello were often on John's record-player while he was waiting for heart surgery.

The way *The Last Sleep of the Virgin* found its form was a mystery to John, and still is. He knows the prospect of death was a potent factor, and he remembers the music was difficult to receive, like tuning in to a faint radio signal. That is why the score includes an instruction that the performance should be given 'at a distance from the audience, and with the sound at the threshold of audibility'.

*

While he was fair-handing *The Apocalypse* and *The Last Sleep*, John had a surge of energy which produced a new short choral work, for a concert in Westminster Abbey. Called *Annunciation*, it is a setting of the dialogue between the Archangel and the Mother of God, designed to take advantage of the Abbey's architecture. The Mother of God is represented by a quartet of voices, singing from high up in the Henry V Chantry. The part of the Archangel is taken by massed choirs, who thunder down below.

Martin Neary thought this a wonderful piece, and very beautiful, not least because the voices are harmonized in parallel seconds, 'which gives the thing a richness, a tang, and makes it true to the end of the twentieth century'. What matters to John about the dissonant seconds is that they feature prominently in the church music of Georgia, and thus are fully sanctioned by Orthodox tradition.

*

Mary of Egypt moved into rehearsal rooms in North London in early
May. By this time the director, Lucy Bailey, had paid three visits to
Mother Thekla, who was impressed by her eagerness and her keen young
mind. John, meanwhile, had been introduced by Father Sergei Hackel
to a brilliant young Russian ikon painter, Sergei Fedorov, who was
living in London in a council tower block. The serene beauty of Sergei
Fedorov's ikons moved John to propose him as the right person to create
a *Mary of Egypt* set. He took Lucy Bailey to the tower block. The lift
was out of order, so, defying doctor's orders, he led the marathon climb
up the stairs to the fourteenth floor, where Sergei Fedorov was waiting
with his ikons and his interpreter and his vodka. The occasion was an
intoxicating one, but John's dream of an Orthodox ikon painter as
set-designer got no further. The job went to Lucy Bailey's nominee,
Jeremy Herbert, a young professional whose answer to the challenge of
Mary of Egypt was a modernistic canopy of gauze panels on metal
struts.

John had taken longer over *Mary of Egypt* than over anything since
Thérèse, and it mattered to him desperately that it should receive a
fitting performance. He attended almost all the rehearsals, gave frequent
demonstrations to the cast, and insisted on the importance of the
Orthodox thought behind both words and music. One morning he
offered the inspiration of a favourite tape. It contained the voice of
Father Dionysios Fifiris, still singing in his nineties, and known to the
faithful as 'the nightingale of Mount Athos'.

★

In the foreword to her libretto for *Mary of Egypt*, Mother Thekla gives
us the essentials. The protagonists are the monk Zossima, a Holy Man
'on the road of lovelessness and death'; and the harlot Mary, 'on the
road of love and life'. The moral of this double narrative, in which
'seeming virtue' comes to salvation through 'seeming vice', is 'Judge not,
that ye be not judged.'

The drama is in five acts. During Acts I and II the lives of Mary and
Zossima move forward in parallel, but miles apart. Act III takes place
forty-seven years later, when they meet in the Jordan desert. Acts IV
and V set out the consequences of that meeting.

The singers, besides Mary, Zossima and the Voice, are a boys' choir,
representing the Angels, and a mixed chorus, which represents everybody else. The orchestra is small, and purpose-built by John, not so

much for the sake of a *tutti* sound, as for the individual colours within it, and what these colours symbolize. There are flutes, trumpets and trombones; tuned and untuned percussion; harp; two violins, viola, two cellos and a double bass. The most unusual of the percussion instruments is the *simantron*, a roughly fashioned wooden plank, about five feet long, which is struck with a wooden mallet to summon Greek Orthodox monks to prayer. To supply the constant drone, or eternity note, which in this case is F, two muted violins, playing without vibrato, were pre-recorded and then tape-looped.

Although it is never quoted directly, the Byzantine Hymn to the Mother of God, 'Tin Oreotita' ('Awed by Thy beauty'), is the musical inspiration behind the whole of the tightly knit score.

The opening of Act I, headed 'With unearthly stillness', is a 25-note palindrome played on the handbells, in the third Byzantine tone, which is the tone of 'Tin Oreotita'. Then come *melismas* on the flutes, using the same tone.

What happens next makes it abundantly clear that John has no intention of meeting the expectations of regular opera-goers. While the stage remains empty, the Voice (disembodied) chants the message 'The ways to salvation are more than one', extremely slowly, for more than seven minutes, accompanied only by the drone. The vocal style, with characteristic 'breaks' in the voice and much emphasis on the leading note, is unremittingly Eastern.

When the action begins, it is split between Mary and Zossima, who occupy separate halves of the stage, each with their own grotesque attendants, called 'Swine-men' and 'Swine-women' by Mother Thekla. While the Swine-men dance attendance on Mary, the Swine-women cavort around Zossima, whose theme when he sings is self-congratulation:

> Is there one to rival me
> In what an ascetic monk should be?

Zossima is always accompanied by a trombone, and by the rigid rhythm of the *simantron*. Mary's singing is always accompanied by the flute, and to begin with is wordless and alluring. Her seductive 'Ahs' pivot on the eternity note of F, while Zossima's music rests on E. The gulf which separates the protagonists is symbolized by this interval of a minor ninth, which is also heard in the Swine-men's cries of 'Come and buy' and the Swine-women's shouts of 'Grunt and groan'.

In a dramatic development, young men announce the start of their pilgrimage from Alexandria to Jerusalem, quoting from the chant 'Ton

Stavron' ('Thy Cross we adore'). Oblivious at first, Mary continues her wordless *melismas*, but then something changes in her and she sings her first words: 'Take me.'

Simultaneously, Zossima succumbs to doubt and sings, 'Where is salvation? Where is the way?', using the same music as Mary, and abandoning his *simantron*. The Voice answers him, and he is instructed to go to a monastery beside the river Jordan.

Act II begins with the 25-note palindrome on handbells and the flute *melismas*, as at the start of Act I, but now in a different Byzantine tone. After the Voice has spoken again, an orchestral chord is the signal that we have come to the desert.

On Zossima's side of the stage, we meet the desert monks, whose chanting is rigidly underpinned by the *simantron*. When Zossima's voice takes over, the music becomes slower and gentler, with the *simantron* less emphatic.

On the other side of the stage, Mary and the pilgrims have assembled in Jerusalem. A church congregation is heard singing 'Ton Stavron'. Mary wants to enter the church, but some hidden power is blocking her way. Her sinuous 'Ahs' turn into 'Help me', which starts on top F and slowly descends to bottom G flat. The Voice tells her she will find her salvation in the desert beyond the river Jordan, and Act II ends with Mary chanting 'Save me' over and over again, to represent her many years of solitude and repentance.

Act III is set in the desert, forty-seven years later. During the opening handbells and flutes, Zossima comes into view. In accordance with the tradition of his monastery, he is spending Lent out in the desert on his own. But he has spotted a figure dressed in rags, whom he feels compelled to follow. His opening plea

> Why run from me, an old and sinful man?
> Why shun the one who sought you from his youth?

uses exactly the music of Mary's 'Save me' (the *simantron* has been banished). When Mary answers him, she brings us back into the third Byzantine tone (the tone of 'Tin Oreotita'), where we began. Her rising five-note phrases, doubled by the flute, also conjure up *The Magic Flute* of Mozart.

Zossima begs Mary for a blessing. She calls on him to bless her first, and a radiant duet develops, in which the single word 'Bless' is passed to and fro and given all kinds of expressive melodic contours, as John '*raga*-izes' 'Tin Oreotita'.

After the duet, Mary sings a humble prayer, 'Blessed is God', during which she is joined by a choir of Angels, who sing Alleluias and hold her aloft. Zossima, deeply moved, asks who she is. As she tells her life story, she reverts to the *melismas* she sang in Alexandria, but now they are sharp-edged and objective. At the end of her long confession, she asks that in one year's time Zossima should come to her again, bringing the bread and wine needful for Holy Communion.

Act IV takes place one year later, and is entirely wordless. There are five episodes, which form an arch, held together by the Angels, who hum throughout. Their thick cluster of sound is made up of all the notes in 'Tin Oreotita'.

Episode 1 has Zossima searching for Mary, while a trombone with a Harmon mute wails a despairing lament. Episode 2 has the approach of Mary, who is walking on water, while flutes recall what she once sang. Episode 3 is the Communion, which combines the orchestra's 'desert chord' with Mary's flute and Zossima's trombone. Episode 4 has Mary going away across the water, while the flute music of Episode 2 is played in reverse. Episode 5 is the departure of Zossima, while the lament from Episode 1 is played backwards on the trombone.

Act V takes place one year later. Mary has died. A flute solo recalls chronologically all the events in her life. When Zossima finds her body, and the message she has left, asking him to bury her, he collapses in despair. But he is rescued by the desert animals, led by the lion, who bury the body and perform a joyful song and dance. Their intoxicating music, called 'Love's Whirligig' in the score, rings the changes on what we heard in Alexandria, and even adds some delicious harmony to it. Their text insists on the moral: 'Judge not.'

When they have finished, the Voice, very distant, is heard for the final time:

The ways to salvation are yet more than one.

Last of all, the handbells restate the palindrome, just as it was at the beginning.

*

The Aldeburgh première of *Mary of Egypt* was in the Snape Maltings Concert Hall on 19 June 1992, and the reactions of the music critics ranged from quiet enthusiasm to puzzlement. But all were agreed about the singing of the two principals. As Edward Greenfield put it: 'Patricia

Rozario produced tone of heady beauty in Mary's radiant *melismas*, finely matched by Stephen Varcoe as Zossima.'

For John, too, Patricia Rozario was a revelation: the ideal interpreter of his music. He could not imagine writing again for any other soprano. As for the critical reaction to the opera, it was less important to him than the presence in the audience at Snape of an Orthodox delegation, including Bishop Kallistos from Oxford, who had helped with the *Vigil Service*. The Bishop was delighted John had progressed from providing music for the converted. As he puts it:

> I think it best for John to be on the frontiers, as it were: drawing on Orthodox spirituality and traditional motifs, but presenting them in a freer form. I thought it courageous to have such a strongly religious piece played before a very mixed audience. A few people couldn't take it, and went out after about twenty minutes, but the bulk of the audience was enthralled. And therefore John is a kind of missionary, spreading understanding of these Orthodox themes.

The scene from *Mary of Egypt* I chose for my film was the ravishing 'Bless' duet. The first thought had been to film on the set at Aldeburgh, but the combination of those shiny metal poles and the bare brick wall at the back of the platform was distinctly lacking in camera appeal. I decided instead to take the soundtrack of the Aldeburgh performance up to North Yorkshire, and film the scene, mimed to playback, on the moorland behind Mother Thekla's monastery. By now, I had made two wooing expeditions to the monastery, pleading for a Thekla appearance in the film. By the end of the second, chinks were appearing in the armour she puts on for media folk, and her good nature was shining through.

Once she had agreed to the filming, her co-operation was total. If it rained, she said, we could bring the scene indoors. In the event, the weather for filming was brilliantly sunny, with a good breeze, so the lighting truck and the generator and the wind machine which had been welcomed on to monastery territory all stood idly by. The scene was shot at the base of a fifteen-foot-high cross, constructed for me there and then and erected on the skyline by Mother Thekla's carpenter, whose name happened to be Mr Edmund Cross. Patricia Rozario projected Mary as a fiercely intense image, helped by the wind, which snatched at her hair and her plain dark cloak. Stephen Varcoe was reverent and tender as Zossima. Panchromatic film stock removed the drama from the particularities of time and place.

Filming took all afternoon, and John stayed nearby, flat on his back, eyes closed, soaking up the sunshine and waving a hand in time to the 'Bless' duet, which was pumped out ad infinitum by the heavy-duty loudspeakers. Towards the end, Mother Thekla joined us, dressed in the full regalia of an abbess, and agreed to be filmed witnessing the desert scene which had lived for so many years in her imagination.

When it was over, John requested that the big cross be transported to his Sussex garden. And so it was.

★

These were hectic times for the Taveners, with more premières to be attended at the summer music festivals: *The Last Sleep of the Virgin* in Cheltenham (where, respecting John's wishes, the Chilingirian string quartet and the handbells were hidden from view in the high gallery above the Pittville Pump room); *Village Wedding* in the Vale of Glamorgan; and *We Shall See Him As He Is*, first in Chester Cathedral, and then a week later at the Albert Hall, as part of the 1992 season of Promenade Concerts. The tenor John Mark Ainsley mastered the Byzantine inflections of the apostle John, and sang the part beautifully. Patricia Rozario was spectacular as the Woman at the Well. Richard Hickox conducted the BBC Welsh Symphony Orchestra, with the Chester Festival Chorus, the Britten Singers and the BBC Welsh Chorus. The Albert Hall performance, which received what the *Financial Times* described as 'a vociferously warm ovation', was recorded by Chandos Records and issued as a CD.

Threaded among the festivals, John had more days of being filmed by me: down memory lane at Charleston Manor; singing in the choir of Father Sergei Hackel's Sussex church; conducting *The Lamb* in Cambridge; dreaming a performance of *The Protecting Veil* in the Greek Cathedral in London. And for a weekend I had my camera crew inside John and Maryanna's Sussex home. A deeply disruptive visit, no doubt, but with one lasting benefit: John's favourite grand piano was finally hoisted upstairs to his study, as originally intended. It looked good up there, dressed with all his favourite photographs. And space had been liberated in the dining room, where we filmed a candlelit supper, over-looked grandly by the painting of the Resurrection.

★

The CD of *The Protecting Veil* was released in February 1992, a year after it had been recorded, and two and a half years after the première at the Albert Hall. To the astonishment of the reluctant record company, it went straight to the top of the classical music charts, and there it stayed. The intriguing title, the haunting sound, and the exotic beliefs of the gaunt composer were all good copy for the newspapers. It was *The Whale* all over again. In the *Guardian*, a spread by James Wood came with a lurid cartoon, clinching Wood's word-picture of 'long, wild hair and a face of rather clumsy beauty'. The headline was 'Chant of the mystic musician'. The *Independent on Sunday* had a colour photo of John, captioned 'The sacred and the tanned'. Underneath, the question was posed: 'Where have you seen this man before?' And the answer given: 'On a cross.'

The CD won the Gramophone Award for 'Best Contemporary Recording', and was shortlisted for the Mercury Prize: a brand-new invention of the music business. Eight of the ten albums on the Mercury shortlist were from the world of pop music, including the latest from Simply Red, U2 and Primal Scream. The two outsiders, both quoted by William Hill at odds of 20–1, were an album of South African jazz, and *The Protecting Veil*. All the candidates attended a presentation dinner at the Savoy Hotel on 8 September, and speeches were called for before the winner was announced. John used the opportunity to speak up for the Mother of God, but this cut no ice with the assembled captains of the music industry. Some sniggered. Some openly scoffed. The £20,000 prize went to Primal Scream, for their hit album *Screamadelica*, which, said the judges, 'reflects what 1992 is about'.

Twenty thousand pounds would have bought a very decent second-hand car, but John's disappointment was soon overtaken by a new distraction. He was invited to become patron of the Cricklade Music Festival, in Wiltshire, and the organizers wanted him to write something for next year which would showcase Patricia Rozario and Steven Isserlis, with a piano part for himself.

He ruled out the piano. It no longer suited him as a composer. The sound was too impure. But a duet for his favourite soprano and cellist was an inspiration. He chose six short poems from the translated works of Anna Akhmatova and sent them to Mother Thekla, saying he would like to set them in Russian. She first of all made fresh translations, more faithful to Akhmatova's terse style, then she provided parallel texts in English and transliterated Russian, as Father Sergei Hackel had done for *Akhmatova: Requiem*.

Guided by the sounds of the Russian words and Mother Thekla's map of their meaning, John wrote six beautiful songs. Their atmosphere is strongly Russian, although the music owes something to Byzantium and there is even a quotation from an Indian *raga* (a musical thank you to Patricia Rozario).

★

When the *Akhmatova Songs* were finished, early in October, John felt exhausted and ready for a sunshine holiday. He booked a fortnight for two at a hotel in Khania, Crete, then found that Maryanna could be with him for only a week. He had forgotten she was a working wife. Not caring to be alone when she left, he paid for his old friend Michael Buckland to fly out and join him.

A potent ingredient of that second week was *tzikoudia*: a clear spirit, claimed by the Cretans to cure all ills. Large quantities were consumed, first of all for John's sore throat, and then to lubricate the session he and Michael spent with Ross Daly, an expatriate musician of Irish descent, who collected and played the ancient instruments of the Middle East. Amongst the arsenal assembled by Daly for his concerts in Khania was a *bandir* drum, the unique sound of which impressed John deeply. He was told that in Sufi music it represented the heartbeat, never deviating from certain sacred patterns. This was exactly what he needed to kick-start a composition which had stalled: *Theophany*, the wordless setting of Psalm 104 for the Bournemouth Symphony Orchestra. So far, the task of writing for symphonic forces had seemed stale and unprofitable, but with the *bandir* drum all that would change. Ross Daly promised that when he was next in London he would take John to an ethnic instrument shop near Covent Garden, where *bandir* drums and suchlike are on sale.

More conviviality and another musical bonus followed a visit to Martin Stebbing, a former pupil of John's: the one who had introduced him to Peter Phillips. Stebbing had fallen in love with Greece, and had come to live here. He took John and Michael to a taverna in the mountains, where they experienced the novelty of dining on camel, washed down, of course, with *tzikoudia*. Then it was back to Stebbing's house and his massive collection of CDs. Tonight he chose to play his guests a new recording of Mahler's 10th Symphony.

In his tired and fragile state, John was devastated by the loveliness and the languor of Mahler's music. Up welled the tears, and then came the guilty feeling, as he recalled the stern warning of his friend Petros Morosinis: 'We must be on our guard against Mahler. He is a great temptation. He never had a spiritual experience in his life!' In spite of

Petros, he asked Stebbing to play the CD again: not all of it, just the *finale*, with its melting flute melody and doom-laden thwacks on the bass drum.

Back in England, feeling distinctly unwell, he visited the specialist, who told him his blood pressure was up and his heart was weakening. Mahler's 10th preyed on his mind. Hoping no one would recognize him, he sneaked into a record shop in Brighton and bought the CD. Back home at Naldretts, he took to playing it in the evenings, with his wine, hoping his weakness for it would wear off. He even made a tape of it and sent it to Mother Thekla.

On his doctor's advice, he was making fewer visits to London. There was one on 26 October, for the West End preview of my film about him. And then there was the shopping expedition with Ross Daly. As well as a *bandir* drum, John bought an expensive Chinese wind gong, because it too had a sound which belonged in his *Theophany*. The writing of this piece picked up speed, and at the same time he was giving serious thought to a new opera. Its subject had been chosen a year before, from the book *The Soul After Death*, by a Californian Orthodox monk, Father Seraphim Rose. The crucial chapter for John, called 'The Aerial Toll Houses', draws on ancient teachings to describe the trials of the soul as it climbs the sky after leaving the body. Mother Thekla had been sent a copy back in February, with a request that she turn it into a libretto. She wrote in her diary 'The next horror – John wants an opera on the after-life. What can beat that?' In her opinion, Father Seraphim Rose was too confident and too specific about what lies in wait for us. Like her mentor, Mother Maria, she believed in the Platonic doctrine of the limitation of the human mind: 'We do not know.' In the end she devised a libretto which, rather than adapting the American, ran surreal rings around him. It was sent to John without her usual helpful notes in the margin, and was received with bafflement and dismay.

It would be premature to reveal details of Mother Thekla's libretto, since it stays the subject of what will be a lengthy dialogue. Suffice to say that it includes bridge-playing ladies from Knightsbridge; and there is a trip to an aerial zoo.

★

Nineteen ninety-two ended fruitfully. As well as reaching the end of *Theophany* and exploring *The Toll Houses*, John delivered to his publishers a new work for voices and strings. The commission had come from the London Festival Orchestra, who wanted something to perform with a cathedral choir. He turned again to the poetry of St Ephrem the Syrian. This time he chose St Ephrem's *Hymns of Paradise*, which paint a picture of the joy beyond the final Resurrection. John found the images 'absolutely stunning', and allowed his music to be guided entirely by the words. Although the choir of St Paul's Cathedral and a full orchestra were available to him, he chose to write only for bass solo with just the trebles and the altos, plus six violins. 'I thought boys' voices, with the piercing sound of very high violins above them, would give a shining quality: a sense of joy we can never experience on this earth. A kind of piercing joy, which we can't quite *get*.'

The climax of the piece is a joyful Dance of Paradise. The blind and the deaf take part. Cripples leap around. The deformed who have never even crawled fly through the air. John thought of *The Magic Flute*. Taking his cue from Mozart's stuttering love duet for the fools Papageno and Papagena, he offers us 'Pa-pa-pa-pa-Para-para-para-para-para-para-para-Paradise', all perched on a plain chord of G.

The Christmas of 1992 was the first for several years not to find John at the monastery. Instead, Mother Thekla received some momentous news. Maryanna was expecting a baby.

*

At the start of 1993, *The Protecting Veil* was still among the best-sellers, and by now Britain had its first national commercial radio station, Classic FM, pumping out canned classical music around the clock. Once a week, it broadcast 'The Classic Countdown': its own chart show, bringing listeners the tunes the cash-registers were playing, spiced with talk of 'climbers' and 'bubblers' and 'sure-shots'. The station had come on air in September, when *The Protecting Veil* was a ready-made hit. Looking to create hits of its own, it nominated Górecki's *Symphony of Sorrowful Songs* (composed in 1976) as its first 'sure-shot'. Helped by the air-play, the Górecki sold massively and shot to the top. That's show-business. It's also necessary to an understanding of what happened next: the critical backlash and the outburst of musical snobbery. When *The Protecting Veil* was premièred in 1989, critical opinion had been overwhelmingly enthusiastic. Now, Tavener was lumped with Górecki, and the pair stood accused of commercial expediency and conspiring to hoodwink the musically illiterate. Even John's photogenic appearance came under fire. He contrived to look spiritual, it was alleged, as a marketing gimmick. A notably ill-informed and spiteful attack came from Edward Pearce in the *Guardian*. He misspelled John's surname throughout, and alleged that 'Taverner' was 'an ardent member of something called the Ba Hai'.

John was frankly delighted with the popular success of *The Protecting Veil*, and not a little surprised by it. The piece meant much less to him than the *Akathist* or *Resurrection*, so it seemed odd that this one should hit the jackpot. The attacks in the press were dutifully reported to him by his publisher, James Rushton (who had taken over from Robin Boyle as Managing Director of Chester Music). John did his best to ignore them, but he wanted the record put straight about his religious faith. Threatened with legal action by James Rushton, the *Guardian* published a retraction on behalf of Edward Pearce.

The huff and puff of the élitists had done nothing to dent record sales or dampen business enthusiasm. Although James Rushton warned would-be commissioners that John was without commercial guile, and a *Protecting Veil* Mark II could not be anticipated, offers came rolling in. The most attractive was from the London Symphony Orchestra, who wanted something to perform in concert with the viola player Yuri Bashmet. John liked the idea of this star soloist from Russia, but could not face writing again for a symphony orchestra. He asked, could he do it instead for Bashmet and the London Symphony Chorus? The answer was yes.

The piece which emerged was called *The Myrrh Bearer*. Its agenda, as usual with John, was not first and foremost a musical one. The starting point was a ninth-century poem by Cassiane: the Byzantine aristocrat-turned-nun, rumoured to have been the mistress of the Emperor. 'The Troparion of Cassiane', as the poem is known, is about Mary Magdalene, the fallen woman, who brought myrrh and washed the feet of Christ, which she dried with her hair. In John's scheme, Mary is represented by the viola, for which he conceived a long arch-like melody, rising from the instrument's lowest register to its highest, and then falling back again. The essence of this ornate melodic line is the Byzantine chant which goes with 'The Troparion of Cassiane', when it is sung during the services of Holy Week.

Once the viola's role was established, John applied to Mother Thekla for something for the chorus to sing. He expected she would provide a text to complement the beauty of the Troparion, so what came through his letterbox was a bombshell:

I thought when I first saw it, 'It's completely and utterly mad! What on earth can I do with it?' She had things like 'March in step!' and 'Round and round the mulberry bush, hunt the thimble, boo!' The last thing she put was 'We have no king but Caesar! CRUCIFY HIM!' That was the only obviously relevant part. I tried all day long to get her on the telephone, and couldn't. So I thought, 'Right! I'm going to start writing this piece.' I shut myself in my study, wrote out the first stanza for the viola, then I brought in the chorus, with their what seemed to me inane words. And then, as I got going, I thought, 'Yes! This piece is extraordinary. These inane words for the chorus and this ecstatic and repentant line for the viola make absolute sense.' I suddenly realized what she was doing. The chorus symbolizes us: the sins and vanities of this world, and condemnation of God in favour of earthly power. She is far ahead of me, and I just have to catch up.

To the chorus and the viola John added a small percussion section, of bass drum and Chinese wind gong. The gong works with the viola, adding a quiet glow. The thwacks on the big bass drum emphasize the rudeness of the world, and echo the 10th Symphony of Gustav Mahler.

*

The Protecting Veil had passed the peak of its popularity in Britain, but was just embarking on its world travels. Steven Isserlis took it to Finland, New Zealand and Japan. Raphael Wallfisch played it in the Megaron, a new concert hall in Athens. John attended the Finnish and the Greek performances. On 2 April 1993, Steven Isserlis was to set it before the American public in New York's Carnegie Hall. John was going to be there and, since a dose of sunshine was overdue, he and Maryanna treated themselves to a stop-over in Bermuda. Here, he wrote a small work for unaccompanied choir. It had bedded itself in his mind some weeks earlier, in chilly England, when he attended the funeral of a young girl who had been killed in a road accident. Athene Hariades was a family friend. She had loved acting and poetry and the Orthodox Church. Metropolitan Anthony led the prayers around her open coffin in the Russian Cathedral, and then she was buried in Hampstead Cemetery, not far from John's mother. At the graveside, choral Alleluias came into John's head, sung in unison over the eternity note F. As so often, the death of someone dear had given rise to music. Song for Athene was so far formless, but when he told Mother Thekla about it she knew what was required. To complement his Alleluias, she sent him seven one-line verses. Six came from the Orthodox Funeral Service. The seventh was from Shakespeare's *Hamlet*: 'May flights of angels sing thee to thy rest.' In the warmth of Bermuda, melody and harmony were discovered for the verses, and *Song for Athene* was completed.

In New York it was snowing, and the papers and the TV news were full of the courtroom battle between Mia Farrow and her husband Woody Allen. Woody stood accused by Mia of abusing one of their adopted children, and the famous couple, plus their lawyers, had been jousting in a Manhattan courtroom every day for nearly a month, with no end in sight.

John and Maryanna spent two evenings with Mia Farrow, in the apartment on Central Park West where she cared for her brood of eleven children, natural and adopted. Even before the trouble, she and Woody were not living together. His home was on the other side of the park. Mia's morale seemed high. John thought her very brave. She drew a rosy picture of maternity for Maryanna, and said John must not worry: she would be his telephone helpline when the hour came for him to be a daddy.

John's brother Roger flew to New York for the concert at Carnegie Hall, which had been heavily promoted – so much so that Steven Isserlis feared the hype might be counter-productive. Michael Tilson Thomas was the conductor, and the curtain-raiser was Leonard Bernstein's 'On the Town'. Difficult to draw New Yorkers into the world of *The Protecting Veil* after that, Steven thought, but most of the audience came with him, in spite of the loud coughing which savaged the quietest passages. At the end, there was a standing ovation. The reviews were mixed and, as was becoming usual, Steven had to deal with the odd pugnacious character who confronted him personally with the accusation that the piece 'lacked argument'. His stock answer was that complaining about the absence of argument in John Tavener's music was as sensible as attacking Jane Austen's novels for failing to serve up violence. He also recommended a visit to a Russian Orthodox service.

★

Back in England, John discovered that Mother Thekla was in hospital. She had slipped in the goat shed and broken her ankle in two places. Elreda Kidd, who had looked after John, was up at the monastery. When he telephoned, Elreda warned him that Mother Thekla hated being ill and was sounding very fierce. So, he confronted *The Toll Houses* again without benefit of further dialogue. The mundane element in the Thekla libretto was never going to inspire music, but if the piece could be a hybrid, perhaps a film, in which 'terrestrials' spoke and 'celestials' sang, then he would be able to handle it. And if Mia Farrow would play the leading Knightsbridge lady, then that would be perfect. He called Mia and sounded her out. She said she would love to do it. And she wondered how he was preparing himself for parenthood. In that department, he had to admit, he was not doing very well. Maryanna had talked him into going to antenatal classes of the modern kind. These started with all the parents-to-be in session together, after which the future fathers were led away to a separate room, to confess their deepest thoughts. The other fellows in this therapy group all seemed terribly young, and had plenty to say for themselves. Things like 'That'll be the end of going down the pub,' and ''Course, she'll never get her figure back.' So far, John had managed to contribute nothing. There was now talk of him having one-to-one counselling at home.

★

At the end of June John's self-esteem received a boost, when he was doubly honoured by his spiritual homeland. First, he became the only non-Greek to receive an Apollo Award for services to Greek culture. At the ceremony in Athens he made a short acceptance speech in Greek, prepared with the assistance of the ever-loyal Vicky. Secondly, *The Protecting Veil* was performed by Steven Isserlis with the London Philharmonic Orchestra, in the Odeon of Herodes Atticus: the now roofless theatre, built in the second century AD at the foot of the Acropolis. The cello sound did not thrive in the urban atmosphere, and passing police sirens played havoc with the magical opening, but the evening was warm, the setting was majestic, and as a symbolic gesture the performance was a landmark. The cities of Athens and Thessalonika are both now planning Tavener Festivals.

Back in Sussex, Maryanna laid plans for a water-birth at home. The great day was still a month or so away, and John planned to spend this interval on *The Toll Houses* and *Let's Begin Again*, but he was deflected by a commission from John Eliot Gardiner, who wanted a new piece for the thirtieth anniversary of his Monteverdi Choir. Mother Thekla was still recuperating after her accident, and hoping to work in peace on the new book she was writing, about the themes in the novels of Charlotte M. Yonge. John's call for yet another text was not welcomed with great eagerness. It became more interesting when he told her that, although the commission was for something of a celebratory character, he had found the title he wanted in the collected letters of Mother Maria. The piece should be called *The World Is Burning*.

In the scheme she produced, the title phrase is chanted over and over again by the main choir, like a cosmic lamentation, interspersed with prayers to God from a second group of singers. In the distance, apparently unheard by either of them, the voice of Christ insists 'Thy faith hath made thee whole.'

This scheme suited John very well. The opening of the piece has the main choir singing 'The world is burning', extremely quietly and slowly. The music is an ascending phrase of five notes, over an E drone and a low murmur from the tam-tam. The sub-choir takes over, with a prayer whose music seems to come from medieval Russia. Then the bass voice of Christ is heard, 'from a great height', singing a highly decorated line in the Eastern manner.

This sequence of events occurs five times, and each time the lament of the main choir expands, following the rules of the magic square, until it has become a 25-note palindrome.

There is a short coda, for the main choir only. Up to now we have been in E minor, but suddenly we are in E major, and the choir gets no further than 'The world is . . .' before fading away. John has marked this coda: 'Transfigured with the radiance of paradise.'

★

Thursday, 26 August 1993 was the day John Tavener became a father. Soon after the event, Maryanna persuaded him to commit his recollections to paper. What follows draws on that account.

On the evening of Wednesday 25th, Maryanna sipped raspberry leaf tea and warned John there was not long to go. They retired to bed early, and he tried to keep her calm, but at 11 p.m., when the labour pains began, he convinced himself she would be better off without him and made his way to the spare bedroom. Here he slept soundly until 6 a.m., when he slowly became aware that his wife was trying to wake him, and that she was distraught. When he had removed his ear-plugs, he was able to hear her telling him that the midwife had been summoned. Slowly gathering himself together, he made his way downstairs, lit the ikon candles underneath Christ and the Mother of God, and started the incense burning. Then he and Maryanna sat and waited.

The midwife arrived at 7, and John was called upon to direct his mind towards practical matters. First of all, the portable pool, which had arrived in sections, had to be assembled. Luckily, the midwife knew

how this was done, and the wooden frame and the plastic tub were
soon set up in the middle of the sitting room. Filling this large container
with warm water was another matter. The hose reached from kitchen
to sitting room all right, but the hot water supply turned out to
be pitifully inadequate. After four hours, the pool had been filled to
a depth of only six inches. Maryanna waited on the sofa. John did
what he knew best. He played the piano. He began with some Mozart,
but Maryanna let it be known that she would rather hear Bach. So
Bach it was, for a while, until Maryanna announced that what she
really wanted to hear was John's *Resurrection*. He found the tape and
put it on.

Ever since she had heard it in Glasgow, Maryanna had loved
Resurrection, particularly the Lament of the Mother of God. Now
she was in labour, the Lament took on a new dimension, as she explains: '"Woe is me my child" became so much more clear, and more
poignant, because my consciousness was so raised. I didn't have any
pain-killers. My hair is just now growing again, where I pulled it
out!'

The midwife warned John that this could go on until next day, and
he remembered there was no food in the house. He had wanted to invite
his old friend Penny Turton to come and help, but Maryanna had been
adamant: just the midwife and himself. Judging that by now Maryanna
was too far gone to argue, he went and called Penny.

Back in the sitting room, *Resurrection* had reached the awesome
'Rise, O God, and Judge the Earth'. The midwife asked him to turn it
down a bit, because she wanted to conduct an examination. Maryanna was diagnosed as 'fully dilated'. Although the water was
still hopelessly shallow, she clambered into the pool. It felt most un-
comfortable. The next events are best in the words of John's written
account:

Resurrection is continuing, and at the final brass chord Maryanna
moves from water tub to the lavatory. Yeats' line occurs to me: 'The
awful mystery on the bestial floor.' And as if to remind us of the
dignity of the indignity, the Ikon of the Nativity watches over us in
the lavatory. I always knew that Nativity Ikon would justify its place
in here one day. The birth pangs begin, Maryanna requiring me no
longer. I wonder if she ever did. She was rude enough. Anyway, it is
her time, and I sit on the stairs and observe, with a kind of stunned
love. A head appears, and then a body, without noise. Then the beginning of the screaming that proclaims every birth. The pouring of the

blood, the cutting of the umbilical cord by me, which adds some kind of ritual, especially as it takes me three snips at it. It is a girl – Theodora. She has found her way, amid candles, incense, prayers, blood and stench, into the world. Glory be to God for everything.

Theodora Alexandra was born at 12.10 p.m. She was a tall, thin baby, weighing 7lb 10oz. While he was cutting the cord, John began singing to her: the Russian chant 'The bridegroom comes at midnight'. During the last weeks of the pregnancy, he had often sung this favourite passage crouched over Maryanna's stomach. He wanted to be sure it was the first sung sound the baby heard.

Penny Turton had arrived by now, and was making tea in the kitchen, out of Maryanna's sight. John sent Penny into Hurstpierpoint to buy champagne. Maryanna fed the baby, and then passed her to John. It was a warm summer's day, and too good a chance to miss. He took Theodora into the garden and introduced her to the sun.

In the evening, Maryanna's mother arrived and took charge. John returned to the spare bedroom and inserted his ear-plugs. Next morning, at the usual hour, he went to his study and sat at his composing table. He was worried not just by the practical threat to his routine. He needed to know if the fruit of his loins, by its very existence, was going to block the musical flow. The answer seemed to be no. Immediate progress was made on *Let's Begin Again*, which felt exactly the right piece to tackle. In this telling of the story of the ascent into heaven of the Mother of God, he was seeking to emulate the vivid naïveté of Coptic ikons. It would be sung by adults, but mimed and danced by children. At the front of the score he added the inscription 'To Theodora'.

One week after the birth, in accordance with the Orthodox rule book, Father Sergei Hackel came to the house, to pronounce a healing blessing over Maryanna. By this time, John's euphoria had worn off and he was running a temperature. After another week, and a row with Maryanna's mother, he collapsed to the floor with chest pains. His heart seemed to have gone wild and he could not get up. The GP described what had happened to him as 'an adrenalin rush'. Three days later, he was pole-axed by a violent migraine. Ten days after that, on 21 September, he went to the doctor with sharp pains in his eyes, perhaps connected with Marfan's syndrome.

Maryanna agreed that the best remedy for all his ills would be a trip to Greece, and so, on 30 September, the three Taveners arrived at the Nafsika Hotel. One cabin had been booked for Maryanna and Theodora. Another for John. After three weeks, his morale was restored.

Maryanna brought the baby back to England. She had work to do for British Nuclear Industry Forum, who now employed her as a freelance consultant, operating from home. John stayed on Aegina for another week, much of which was spent with Petros Morosinis, on whom he tested the lecture he was going to give at the Victoria and Albert Museum.

★

On 7 November 1993, during the regular Sunday morning service in the chapel of the Monastery of the Assumption, Theodora Tavener was baptized by Father Ephrem. Present at the ceremony were John, Maryanna, Mother Thekla and Ann Gotteri, who had been appointed Theodora's godmother.

The following Saturday, the large lecture theatre at the V & A could not accommodate all those who wished to hear the Tavener illustrated talk, which he called 'Towards the Sacred in Music'. Those who managed to get in heard John at his most radical and provocative. Those who knew him well detected the hand of his friend Petros Morosinis.

Stravinsky's *Canticum Sacrum* was allowed to belong to the Sacred Tradition, but not Mozart's *Coronation Mass*, which was labelled an 'operatic sweet of sin'. The Papageno-Papagena duet from *The Magic Flute* was part-approved, but rated far below the chosen examples of Byzantine chant, Indian sacred music and Sufi flute-playing. Beethoven was ruled out. Bach was deemed to be a special case, needing a lecture to himself.

The final musical example struck an apocalyptic note: it was the last two Ikons of *We Shall See Him As He Is*. Before cueing the tape, John quoted the words of St John at the close of the Book of Revelation ('Even so, come, Lord Jesus'), to which he added an elaboration of his own:

Come quickly because I cannot bear to be without You one second longer, because without You, my life is meaningless ... Come, fill every note that I write, because unless You do, my music and my whole life are totally absurd.

Near the back of the hall were Maryanna and Theodora. The baby was good nearly to the end, but the organ blasts of *We Shall See Him As He Is* were too much, and she had to be taken out. Just two months later, an extraordinary opportunity arose for mother and daughter to experience the full range of John's output, from *Celtic Requiem*, through

The Lamb to *The Last Sleep of the Virgin*. The occasion was the Festival of the Music of John Tavener, organized by the BBC to celebrate John's fiftieth birthday: four days of performances, in Westminster Abbey, the Barbican and Westminster Cathedral.

The centrepiece of the Festival was a concert at the Barbican by the BBC Symphony Orchestra, conducted by Gennady Rozhdestvensky. They performed *The Protecting Veil*, with Steven Isserlis, and *Akhmatova: Requiem*, with Penelope Walmsley-Clark. But the event which meant most to John was the *Akathist*, conducted by Martin Neary in Westminster Abbey. In contrast to 1988, this performance was both broadcast and properly recorded. And to make the occasion perfect, John's pew was shared by Archbishop Gregorios and a distinguished overseas visitor: Metropolitan John Zizioulos of Pergamon. At the end, this eminent Byzantine scholar thanked John for what he described as 'a taste of Paradise'.

The recording of the *Akathist* (further cut down to ten hymns, to make it fit on to one CD) has now been issued by Sony Records. Eight years after John played the whole thing to Mother Thekla on Daisy Hardy's piano, the slimmed-down version has become a commercial hit. It spent several weeks in the Classic FM top twenty, and at the time of writing is number one in the classical charts in New York and Los Angeles.

*

On Saturday, 29 January 1994, John's fiftieth birthday party was held at Naldretts. One hundred guests were invited and most of us came, in spite of the foul weather. There were friends from as far back as Highgate School. There were patrons and performers of his music. There were writers and broadcasters. There was Father Sergei Hackel, with members of the Orthodox community in Sussex. Bringing memories of Charleston Manor was Doreen Pugh, faithful secretary to the late Lady Birley. Mother Thekla was represented by Father Ephrem and Ann Gotteri. There were delegations from the Russian and the Greek Cathedrals in London. Father Michael Fortounatto led the Russian contingent. At the head of the Greeks was Archbishop Gregorios himself. At least, that was the plan. The champagne buffet was enticingly set out at noon, but at 2 p.m. it remained untouched. Protocol forbade any interference with it until the Archbishop had blessed it, and of His Eminence there was no sign. Hungry guests were on the verge of mutiny when the episcopal conveyance finally drew up outside. On the threshold, John bowed low and kissed the proffered ecclesiastical hand. Then Father Michael Fortounatto, showing a zealous reverence for rank, bulldozed guests aside shouting, 'The Archbishop! The Archbishop!' as he cleared the way from the front door to the dining-room table. After the blessing had been pronounced, John handed to Father Ephrem the *simantron* and mallet, used in *Mary of Egypt*, which was now part of his dining-room furniture. The fierce clatter of wood on wood which Father Ephrem produced was the signal that at last we could eat.

As was usual at parties in which Kenneth Tavener had a hand, the hospitality was lavish. Catering was by one of London's top Greek restaurants, and the supply of champagne was endless. Before the cutting of the birthday cake, Father Sergei Hackel led the assembly in the Russian anniversary song 'Mnogaya Lyeta' ('Many years'). As he took us higher and higher, Father Sergei's face darkened and the veins on his neck stood out. The Archbishop congratulated him on the power of his performance. Then there was a speech from Philip Pilkington, who had been John's friend and supporter (but never a fellow-believer) for more than thirty years. Feeling that the recent Tavener Festival had devoted ample time to John the composer and John the Orthodox Christian, Philip chose to turn the spotlight elsewhere. His speech began like this:

> The first car John bought was an Armstrong Siddeley Sapphire. It was the start of a series of remarkable purchases. I particularly remember number two: a 1947 Bentley mark 6, the doors of which refused to shut when you were in and which refused to open when you wanted to get out. Then there was number 6: the two-tone grey Silver Cloud with the leaking sun roof and the horn which jammed, treating everyone within earshot to a resplendent major third.
>
> To some, John's taste in cars of this kind has presented an enigma. They have problems reconciling his very real absorption in rarefied, spiritual concerns with what appears to them to be a craving for dilapidated ostentation. Fortunately, people are not as simple as some moralists would have us believe.

The speech went on to warn that biographers of John would ignore his cars at their peril, so I went to the garage and took details of the latest incumbent. On previous visits to Naldretts I had been introduced first to a graphite-grey BMW Series 7 coupé; then to a Le Mans blue Rolls Royce Silver Shadow I, with cocktail cabinet; then to a bottle-green F registration Jaguar XJ6, with walnut fascia. This time it was a ten-year-old Bentley Mulsanne Turbo, in a golden colour the makers describe as Cotswold beige. John's father called this machine an

outrageous extravagance. Maryanna agreed it was financially
imprudent, but said John felt he had earned it. After all, he had given
her the baby she wanted.

★

Coming up next was the première by the Bournemouth Symphony
Orchestra of *Theophany*. In its final form, besides the *bandir* drum and
the Chinese wind gong, it incorporated singing parts for God and for
Adam and Eve. John wanted the voices to have a supernatural sound,
which, he imagined, would best be achieved by using tape. The Bournemouth Symphony Orchestra had nothing like this in mind when they
commissioned a piece to celebrate their centenary. What they expected,
not unnaturally, was an orchestral showcase. They declined to pay for
any tape-recording, so the burden fell on John's publishers.

The part of God was tackled first. A studio was booked, with an
engineer and one singer. John had written the part for a chorus of eight
basses, but he accepted the cost-effective solution of using just the deep
bass voice of Jeremy Birchall, multi-tracked, pitch-adjusted, and
enhanced by the similarly treated Chinese wind gong. Blasting from
the big speakers in the recording studio, the aggregate effect easily met
John's requirement for 'God-like power'. At further sessions, Jeremy
Birchall created the voice of Adam, and Margaret Feaviour was brought
in to do the voice of Eve, again with electronic assistance.

★

The taped sound of God, chanting 'Ego eimi' ('I am') forms the bass
and the basis of the whole of *Theophany*. At the opening of the piece
He is heard on His own, slowly delivering His sequence of pitches,
which have been abstracted from the Byzantine chant which goes with
Psalm 104. Then the sections of the orchestra take it in turns to join
Him, and decorate His theme.

Next comes a new event on tape, where the voice of God is joined
by the voice of Adam, also chanting 'Ego eimi'. John notes in the score
that Adam here represents 'man in his paradisal state – an ecstasy of
adoration and contemplation'. Accompanying the tape while Adam
sings are two solo instruments, played 'live': alto flute and *bandir* drum.
The flute enriches Adam's vocal line, while the *bandir* drum beats out
the Sufi rhythm of the human heartbeat. And here ends *Theophany*'s
first block.

The second block begins with another statement by the voice of God.

Then the sections of the orchestra take it in turns to decorate, as before. The drama intensifies when the voice of God is joined on the tape by the voice of Eve, 'in her paradisal state, full of wonder'. Here again, alto flute and *bandir* drum supply a 'live' accompaniment. Adam joins Eve on the tape, 'in an ecstasy of Theophanic adoration'. During their duet, other instruments join the flute and *bandir* drum, until the whole orchestra is playing. Then silence. Then four God-like assertions of 'Ego eimi', increasingly fierce. Finally, a twenty-second silence, intended, says John, to signify the Fall.

★

The première of *Theophany*, on 3 May 1994, was to be part of a double celebration: the centenary of the Bournemouth Symphony Orchestra, and the inauguration of a brand-new concert hall in Basingstoke. Other items on the bill were more obviously celebratory: Elgar's arrangement of the National Anthem, for example, and Verdi's *Anvil Chorus*. This mixed bag was to be repeated in Poole and Southampton later the same week.

In the expert opinion of the engineer who had created it, the *Theophany* tape would not get a proper hearing unless a heavy-duty sound system was hired, of the kind used by rock groups. The hire-cost of this equipment, with an operator, for the three concerts, would be around £8,000. The Bournemouth Symphony Orchestra flatly refused to meet any of it and there was a crisis, not resolved until a few days before the première, when Philip Pilkington found some of the money, and Maryanna persuaded her employers, British Nuclear Industry Forum, to come up with the rest.

John had not written anything involving tape for twenty years – not since the disastrous Dutch première of *Ultimos Ritos*. His nervousness was not eased by the goings-on at the rehearsal in Basingstoke on the day of the performance. While the conductor, Richard Hickox, strove to bring orchestra and tape together, paint in the brand-new building was still drying, and staff were struggling to master the electrics. Some players got paint on their clothes, all had trouble reading their parts in the emergency lighting, and the talk-back between conductor and tape-operator functioned only fitfully. However, in the evening everything worked, including the feed to Radio 3, which broadcast the concert live.

There are plans to issue *Theophany* on CD.

★

John's fifty-first year continued to be an extremely active one. As well as *The Toll Houses*, work in progress on his composing table included *Agraphon* (a setting of a poem by Sikelianos); *Song of the Angel* (for soprano and strings, commissioned for the fiftieth anniversary of the United Nations); and *Innocence* (for choirs, organ, cello and soprano, commissioned to be performed in Westminster Abbey during the unveiling of a statue to all the innocent victims of war).

But what mattered most to him in 1994 was the première of *The Apocalypse*, which was given a Promenade Concert to itself, on Sunday, 14 August. Nine months earlier, to help with the forward planning, he had come into a BBC studio and given a demonstration to the Prom committee, singing and playing the whole thing. The tape of that two-and-a-quarter-hour *tour de force* was used by the conductor Richard Hickox as his essential guide, more useful to him than the score, as he explains:

> It's very difficult for John to set down in Western notation the kind of music that he writes. Future generations will be able to rely on our records and tapes, but from the score it would be hard to know. With most contemporary music, I study the score then discuss the piece with the composer. John is the only person I ask to play it through. Because you learn so much.

Chosen to sing the key role of St John was the tenor Thomas Randle, whom John tried to encourage in the direction of Byzantine wildness. Stephen Richardson, who sang the part of Christ in *Resurrection*, was the Voice of God. And there was a cameo role for Patricia Rozario.

Public interest ran high, and the pre-Prom talk in the Royal College of Music was heavily over-subscribed. Those turned away missed hearing John in fierce mood. Just before the talk began, he was shown the disparaging Tavener Profile which had appeared in that day's *Observer*. The article was published anonymously, but John knew immediately who had written it. A few days earlier, he had received an apparently friendly call from the music critic Tom Sutcliffe, who expressed eager interest in everything John held dear. Information he gave to Sutcliffe was repeated in the article, the main purpose of which, it seemed, was mockery. John's music was likened to a 'spiritual accessories market' and a 'bibulous visit to a monastery the other end of Europe'. To support his case, Sutcliffe quoted two other members of the critical fraternity, but the identity of these brave souls was not revealed. The first was referred to as 'a leading critic'. The second was 'another respected critic'. Small wonder that John opened his pre-Prom talk by firing a salvo at the ignorance and cynicism of the English critics in general.

★

The Albert Hall was full for what John considers the mightiest piece he has ever written, and he looked forward to sharing with the public what he had heard while his heart was in crisis.

John Drummond had ruled that the string quartet could not be situated directly beneath the dome, surrounded by promenaders: it had to be in the middle of the platform. But the remainder of the forces were deployed as John wished. Violins, double basses and handbells were at the front of the platform. The seven male-voice choirs were at the back. Up in the choir stalls, flanking the organ, were a consort of recorders and two choirs of Angels: on the left, seven counter-tenors; on the right, seventy trebles. Far above them, in the High Gallery, picked out by a spotlight, was Patricia Rozario. Also up there, concealed from view, were the trumpeters, trombonists and percussionists; and Stephen Richardson, with the electronics to enlarge his bass voice to God-like proportions.

John's father, Maryanna and Theodora had been at the rehearsals. His brother Roger would join them for the performance. More than thirty years had passed since Roger had left that note on John's pillow, after the performance of *Genesis*, saying 'Perhaps your last great work will be *Revelation*.'

★

The final version of Mother Thekla's text for *The Apocalypse* squeezes the twenty-two chapters of *Revelation* into nine Ikons, bounded by a prologue and an epilogue. The original order of events is preserved, but to accommodate John's demand for an unwordy text, the majestic prose is reduced to telegraphese. For example, in *Revelation* Chapter I, in the King James's bible, St John sees

> Seven golden candlesticks; and in the midst of the seven candlesticks one like unto the Son of Man, clothed with a garment down to the foot, and girt about the paps with a golden girdle. His head and his hairs were white like wool, as white as snow; and his eyes were as a flame of fire.

In the text of *The Apocalypse* this vision has become:

> Seven golden candlesticks.
> The Son of Man.
> His hair – white as snow.
> His eyes – flame of fire.

Just as important to John as the text were the notes and diagrams Mother Thekla sent with it, in which the meanings of the symbols were dissected and a network of cross-references plotted.

The goal was a composition where every note has a meaning beyond mere music and the performers are elements in the apocalyptic landscape. The seven male-voice choirs, for instance, as well as representing the seven Churches on earth, are linked to apocalyptic themes:

Choir I	Heaven
Choir II	Natural calamities
Choir III	Human calamities
Choir IV	Natural and human calamities
Choir V	Rome, Babylon, Emperors, Kings
Choir VI	Satan, Judgement, Hell
Choir VII	Martyrs, Saints, the Elect

John converted these equations into musical terms. Each of the seven choirs was allocated a Byzantine tone (Tones I to VII were used, Tone VIII was not), and each was assigned a characteristic interval, to be sounded, usually by a bell, whenever they sang. Choirs I and VII were both given the note D, so they were perfectly in accord with the eternity note. The others were assigned notes which clashed with the D, to produce varying degrees of dissonance. Choir II was linked with C. Choir III with B. Choir IV with B and C together. Choir V with the extremely dissonant C sharp. Choir VI with G sharp (the tritone, traditionally regarded as the Satanic interval).

The Apocalypse is a landmark Tavener composition, which has dispensed entirely with Russian chant and the Russian tones. This book ends with a journey through its world of symbols.

The Prologue begins with members of the string quartet establishing the eternity note of D, which they will be playing virtually non-stop for the next two and a quarter hours. Then St John sings 'I saw', also on the note of D. He is followed by the trumpets, up in the Heavens, softly trilling their high chords – a mysterious, beckoning sound, setting D against top E flat – and then making a slow descent, which turns into a 25-note palindrome via the magic square. Up in the Heavens with them, bass trombones, backed by gongs, sound the eternity note with great force, and then the Voice of God, confining itself to just that one note, spells out its first message:

I am Alpha and Omega
What you will see
Write in a book
And send to the seven Churches.

Complete with resonant pauses, and expanded by unhurried interjections from the trumpets and trombones, the delivery of these four lines takes more than six minutes. Thus has *The Apocalypse* laid down its rules of time and pace.

When St John describes his first vision ('Seven golden candlesticks', etc.), he uses few words, but his intensely melismatic vocal line takes five minutes to journey through the seven Byzantine tones. The Prologue ends in a way which enhances the atmosphere of contemplation. First, a boy treble, taking the part of a disciple of St John, sings 'Alithee' (Greek for 'Indeed'), on the single note D. Then the string quartet undertakes a microtonal exploration, Indian fashion, moving upwards and downwards from the eternity note. 'Alithee' and the microtones will be heard again, between the Ikons, each of which begins with St John's 'I saw'.

Ikon I: The Seven Churches introduces the seven male-voice choirs, each one of which sings *Kyrie eleisons* in its appointed tone, while the associated intervals are sounded on the handbells.

Ikon II: Heaven introduces the Four Beasts around the Throne: four counter-tenors, who chant 'Holy, Holy, Holy', in tight canon, like pealing bells. When we come to Him who sits upon the Throne with a Book in His right hand, the trumpets and trombones assert the intervals which go with the seven tones, and then the choirs unite on the note of D:

The Book is sealed.
Sealed seven seals.

'Who is worthy to open the Book?' asks the First Angel, in Tone I. 'The lion of the tribe of Judah,' cry the twenty-four Elders (bass voices from the seven choirs), making this answer seven times, moving through the intervals which mark the seven tones.

The climax of this Ikon is a sequence of roof-raising outbursts from all the choirs and instruments: 'Worthy is the Lamb' (Tone I); 'Who was slain' (Tone II); 'Honour, glory, blessing' (Tone III); 'Glory and power' (Tone IV); 'To Him upon the Throne' (Tone V): 'And to the Lamb' (Tone VI); 'Unto the ages of ages' (Tone VII).

Ikon III: Six Seals introduces the delinquent sound of the soprano saxophone, which reinforces St John's exclamations as the Seals are opened: 'White horse!' 'Red horse!' 'Black horse!' 'Pale horse! The rider DEATH!' Meanwhile, the strings are insistently plucking the note B, to signal Tone III and Human Calamities. After the sixth seal has been opened, a Lament is sung by the lead singer of Choir VI, while the strings provide a sustained, Satanic G sharp. The solemn ending of this Ikon has St John intoning on D, while the high, trilling trumpets create colossal space around his words:

> And he opened
> The Seventh Seal.
> Heaven silent
> For half an hour.

Ikon IV: The Seventh Seal foretells catastrophes and introduces each one with a trumpet fanfare. The first trumpet, in Tone I, heralds 'Hail! Fire!' The sound of the second trumpet, in Tone II, means 'Third of sea-blood!' The third trumpet, in Tone III, is the harbinger of 'Wormwood! Third of waters bitter!' The fourth trumpet, in Tone IV, proclaims 'Darkness!' The fifth trumpet, in Tone V, warns against 'The bottomless pit unlocked. Locusts!' And here the violins and basses make furious whirling and stinging noises. When we come to the sixth trumpet, in Tone VI, we meet lion-headed horses, breathing fire, smoke and brimstone.

Ikon V: The Messiah opens with the sound of the most splendid trumpet of all: the seventh trumpet, in Tone VII. All the Angels take up its theme, and sing Alleluias. Then comes

> A wonder in Heaven!
> A woman clothed with the sun
> The moon beneath her feet
> On her head a crown of twelve stars.

In Mother Thekla's manuscript these lines are assigned to Choir I, but she was over-ruled by John, who seized his chance to heighten the drama by involving Patricia Rozario. He wrote a fearfully high soprano line for her, in Tone I, marked 'Very pure and full of wonder', to be accompanied only by the drone from the string quartet.

The Woman Clothed with the Sun is followed by Wars in Heaven, massively dissonant: created by the seven solo trumpets, all playing

simultaneously in their seven different tones, while the trombones growl
the tones' distinguishing intervals.

Thrown out of Heaven, Satan brings misery to earth: represented
musically by another cacophony, in which the trombones play the
material previously heard on the trumpets, while the trumpets take over
the intervals previously played on trombones.

The Ikon ends with counter-tenor Angels chanting in canon: a
descending musical phrase, which is in Tone V as required by the words:

Babylon is fallen.

Ikon VI: Six Vials. These are the golden Vials, full of the Wrath of God,
and this Ikon mirrors Ikon IV. The emptying of each Vial is announced
by a trumpet fanfare, underlined by the sound of locusts.

Ikon VII: The Seventh Vial re-introduces the sound of the saxophone
– the alto this time – which makes a solo statement, then becomes the
partner of an entirely new character:

The Whore of Babylon!
Upon a scarlet beast.
On her forehead written:
MYSTERY
BABYLON THE GREAT
MOTHER OF HARLOTS

Mother Thekla's manuscript gives these lines to Choir V, but John found
it more dramatic, and symbolically more powerful, to have them sung
by another solo voice: a mezzo soprano. The singer on the night was
young Ruby Philogene, who took up a position stage left, in a slinky
dress, with the saxophonist standing beside her. She was given the same
melody as her heavenly counterpart, The Woman Clothed with the Sun,
but down an octave, and modified by being switched from Tone I to
Tone V.

In that same Tone, the choirs chant the refrain 'Babylon the great is
fallen'. Then they move to D major to sing Alleluias, while a triumphant
descant dances in and out of all seven Tones.

Ikon VIII: The Last Judgement opens with a massive D major chord.
While some instruments continue to sound it, a contingent of brass is
joined by the organ pedals, to assert the intervals associated with the
Tones.

When the Ikon reaches a peak, the massive chord returns, and the intervals are again spelled out, at half the previous speed, as the choirs sing:

THIS IS THE FIRST RESURRECTION

The next climax is the Second Resurrection, after which, for the very first time, the drone stops. Complete silence. Then an announcement by all the voices on a unison D:

THE BOOK OF LIFE

The chord comes again, followed by another statement of the intervals, four times slower than at the beginning, while the choirs all sing:

THE SECOND DEATH

The drone stops once more, for St John, in Tone VI:

> Whoever is not in the Book of Life
> Is cast into the lake of fire.

Instead of the usual *Alithee*, St John's young disciple responds to his master's grim vision with 'Alithestata' ('Indeed, indeed'), and here the string quartet refrains from any microtonal exploration. Instead, the drone re-starts and we glide straight into Ikon IX: The New Jerusalem. This last Ikon is the one John was working on while waiting for heart surgery. As previously related, he believed the proper response to the New Jerusalem was to let it pulse on the eternity note. Accordingly, St John, The Voice of God, all the choirs, and all the instruments (apart from the organ) work their various ways slowly and quietly through the twenty-four permutations of the rhythmic pattern 4, 3, 2, 1, all ending together, never having wavered from the note of D.

It is left to St John, just with the drone, to bring the Ikon to a close:

> No temple. No sun. No moon.
> God and the Lamb are the Temple.
> Their glory the light.

This compressed biblical text leads directly to the Epilogue, and the high, trilling trumpets which were John's first inspiration. Their 25-note palindrome is delivered in five instalments, separated by tender singing from St John, who repeats the closing words from the Book of Revelation which also come at the end of *We Shall See Him As He Is*:

> Even so, come, Lord Jesus.

After that, in typically inconclusive Tavener fashion, the drone fades away as the members of the string quartet stop playing one by one . . .

Appendix A : Chronological list of Tavener compositions

1961　*Duo Concertant*, for trombone and piano
　　　Portrait d'une Jeune Fille et l'Harpe, for harp, organ, violin
　　　Credo, for tenor solo, chorus, narrator, oboes, brass, organ
1962　*Elegy In Memoriam Frank Salisbury*, for violin solo and string
　　　　quartet
　　　Genesis, for tenor solo, chorus, narrator, brass, percussion, organ,
　　　　piano, string quartet
　　　Piano Concerto (1962–3), for piano solo, horns, percussion,
　　　　strings
1963　*Three sections from T. S. Eliot's Four Quartets*, for high voice and
　　　　piano
1964　*The Cappemakers* (revised 1965), for narrators, soloists, chorus,
　　　　orchestra
　　　Three Holy Sonnets of John Donne, for baritone solo, brass,
　　　　percussion, strings
1965　*Cain and Abel*, for 4 solo voices and orchestra
　　　Chamber Concerto (revised 1968), for small orchestra
　　　The Whale (1965–6), for mezzo and baritone soloists, chorus,
　　　　narrator, orchestra, tape, men with loud hailers
1967　*Grandma's Footsteps*, for musical boxes and instrumentalists
　　　Three Surrealist Songs, for mezzo-soprano, tape, piano, bongo
　　　　drums
1968　*Introit for March 27, the Feast of St John Damascene*, for soprano
　　　　and alto soloists, chorus, brass, piano, vibraphone, organ,
　　　　strings
　　　In Alium, for high soprano solo, Hammond organ, grand organ,
　　　　piano, strings, tape
1969　*Celtic Requiem* (1968–9), for high soprano solo, children's chorus,
　　　　adult chorus, orchestra
1970　*Nomine Jesu*, for mezzo solo, chorus, 2 alto flutes, chamber organ,
　　　　5 male speaking voices
　　　Coplas, for S.A.T.B. soloists, chorus, tape
1971　*Responsorium in Memory of Annon Lee Silver*, for 2 mezzo soloists,
　　　　chorus, flutes

In Memoriam Igor Stravinsky, for 2 alto flutes, chamber organ, handbells

1972   *Variations on Three Blind Mice*, for orchestra

Ma Fin est Mon Commencement, for chorus, trombones, percussion, cellos

Little Requiem for Father Malachy Lynch, for chorus, flutes, trumpet, organ, strings

Canciones Españolas, for 2 high voices, flutes, organ, harpsichord, percussion

Ultimos Ritos, for mezzo solo, 12 basses, S.A.T.B. soloists, 5 male speaking voices, chorus, orchestra, tape

Antiphon for Christmas Morning, for soprano voices

1973   *Requiem for Father Malachy* (revised 1979), for soloists, chorus, orchestra

Thérèse (1973–6), for soprano, bass and 2 tenor soloists, chorus, children's chorus, orchestra

1976   *Canticle of the Mother of God*, for soprano solo and chorus

1977   *A Gentle Spirit*, for soprano and tenor soloists, orchestra, tape

The Liturgy of St John Chrysostom, for priest and chorus

Six Russian Folk Songs, for soprano solo, domra, orchestra

Kyklike Kinesis, for soprano and cello soloists, chorus, orchestra

Palin, for piano solo

Lamentation, Last Prayer and Exaltation, for soprano solo and handbells

1978   *Palintropos*, for piano solo and orchestra

The Immurement of Antigone, for soprano solo and orchestra

1979   *Greek Interlude*, for flute and piano

Six Abbasid Songs, for tenor solo, flutes, percussion

Akhmatova: Requiem (1979–80), for soprano and bass soloists, orchestra

1980   *Sappho: Lyrical Fragments*, for 2 soprano soloists and string orchestra

My Grandfather's Waltz, for piano duet

1981   *The Great Canon of St Andrew of Crete*, for chorus

Trisagion, for brass quintet

Prayer for the World, for chorus

Mandelion, for organ solo

Risen! for chorus and orchestra

Funeral Ikos, for chorus

1982   *Towards the Son*, for 4 bowed psalteries, 3 trebles, orchestra

Doxa, for chorus

The Lord's Prayer, for chorus

Mandoodles, for a young pianist

He Hath Entered the Heven, for trebles with handbells

The Lamb, for chorus

1983   *To a Child Dancing in the Wind*, for soprano, flute, harp, viola

Sixteen Haiku of Seferis, for soprano and tenor soloists, percussion, strings

Ikon of Light, for chorus and string trio

1984   *Little Missenden Calm*, for oboe, clarinet, bassoon, horn

Chant, for guitar solo

Mini Song Cycle for Gina, for soprano and piano

Orthodox Vigil Service, for priests, chorus, handbells

1985   *Eis Thanaton*, for soprano and bass soloists, bass trombones, harp, percussion, strings

Two Hymns to the Mother of God, for chorus

Love Bade Me Welcome, for chorus

Angels, for chorus and organ

1986   *Panikhida*, for chorus

Akathist of Thanksgiving, for soloists, chorus, percussion, organ, strings

Ikon of St Cuthbert of Lindisfarne, for chorus

In Memory of Cats, for piano solo

Meditation on the Light, for counter-tenor solo, guitar, handbells

Magnificat and Nunc Dimittis, for chorus

1987   *The Protecting Veil*, for cello solo and string orchestra

The Tiger, for chorus

Let Not the Prince Be Silent, for double chorus

Prayer (for Szymanowski), for bass solo and piano

Wedding Prayer, for chorus

Many Years, for chorus

The Acclamation, for chorus

God Is With Us, for chorus and organ

Hymn to the Holy Spirit, for chorus

1988   *Ikon of St Seraphim*, for baritone and counter-tenor soloists, chorus, orchestra

The Uncreated Eros, for chorus

Apolytikion for St Nicholas, for chorus

The Call, for chorus

Song for Ileana, for flute solo

A Nativity Carol, for girls' chorus

Resurrection, for soloists, chorus, recorders, brass, percussion, organ, string quartet

Ikon of the Crucifixion, for soloists, chorus, brass, percussion, organ, strings

1989   *The Hidden Treasure*, for string quartet

Lament of the Mother of God, for soprano solo and chorus

Wedding Greeting, for tenor solo and chorus

Eonia, for chorus

Mary of Egypt (finally completed), for soprano, bass and alto soloists, chorus, children's chorus, orchestra, tape loop

Psalm 121, for chorus

Today the Virgin, for chorus

1990   *The Repentant Thief*, for clarinet solo, percussion, strings
        Thunder Entered Her, for chorus, organ, male voices, handbell
        Ikon of the Trinity, for chorus
        We Shall See Him As He Is, for tenor and soprano soloists, chorus,
            trumpets, percussion, organ, strings
        O, Do Not Move, for chorus
        A Christmas Round, for chorus
        Thrinos, for cello solo
1991   *The Apocalypse* (1991–2), for tenor, bass, soprano, mezzo and
            saxophone soloists, 7 male-voice choirs, 7 counter-tenors,
            children's choir, recorders, brass, percussion, handbells, organ,
            strings, string quartet
        The Last Sleep of the Virgin, for string quartet and handbells
        Ikon of the Nativity, for chorus
        Let's Begin Again (1991–4), for bass solo, chorus, orchestra,
            children miming
        Eternal Memory, for cello solo and string orchestra
        Village Wedding, for chorus
1992   *Annunciation*, for S.A.T.B. soloists and chorus
        The Child Lived, for soprano and cello
        Akhmatova Songs, for soprano and cello
        Theophany (1992–3), for orchestra, bandir drum, tape
        Hymns of Paradise, for bass solo, boys' voices, 6 violins
1993   *The Myrrh Bearer*, for viola solo, chorus, percussion
        The Lord's Prayer, for chorus
        Song for Athene, for chorus
        The World is Burning, for bass solo, chorus, tam-tam
1994   *Melina*, for soprano solo

WORK IN PROGRESS
1995   *Agraphon*, for soprano solo, percussion, strings
        Chronia Polla, for men's voices
        Innocence, for soprano and cello soloists, chorus, organ
        Lament for Phaedra, for soprano and cello
        Song of the Angel, for soprano solo and strings
        Svyaty, for Russian choir and cello
        Three Antiphons, for chorus
        The Toll Houses, A metaphysical pantomime

Appendix B : Select discography

This list is of currently available recordings, but does not include the many compilation albums containing one or two Tavener tracks.

Akathist of Thanksgiving
Westminster Abbey Choir, BBC Singers, BBC Symphony Orchestra, Martin Neary
SONY CLASSICAL CD SK 64446

Annunciation · Ikon of the Nativity · The Lamb · A Nativity · Today the Virgin · The Lord's Prayer · Many Years · Wedding Prayer · He Hath Entered the Heven · The Acclamation
Oxford Pro Musica Singers, Michael Smedley
PROUDSOUND PROU CD 136

Celtic Requiem · Nomine Jesu · Coplas
Little Missenden Schoolchildren, June Barton: soprano, John Tavener: organ, The London Sinfonietta & Chorus, David Atherton
APPLE CD SAPCOR 20

Eternal Memory
Steven Isserlis: cello, Moscow Virtuosi, Vladimir Spivakov
BMG CLASSICS 09026 619662

The Great Canon of St Andrew of Crete
The Tallis Scholars directed by Peter Phillips
GIMELL CDGIM 002

Ikon of Light · Funeral Ikos · The Lamb
The Tallis Scholars, Members of the Chilingirian Quartet, Peter Phillips
GIMELL CDGIM 005

Ikon of Light · Two Hymns to the Mother of God · Today the Virgin · The Tiger · The Lamb · Eonia
The Sixteen, Members of the Duke Quartet, Harry Christophers
COLLINS CLASSICS CD 14052

The Last Sleep of the Virgin · The Hidden Treasure
The Chilingirian Quartet with Iain Simcock: handbells
VIRGIN CLASSICS VC5 45023 2

The Liturgy of St John Chrysostom
The Europa Singers, Clive Wearing
IKON RECORDS C IKOS 8E

Mary of Egypt
Patricia Rozario, Stephen Varcoe, Chloe Goodchild, Choristers of Ely
Cathedral, Britten-Pears Chamber Choir, Aldeburgh Festival Ensemble
COLLINS CLASSICS 2CD 70232

Orthodox Vigil Service
Christ Church Cathedral Choir, Francis Grier
IKON RECORDS IKO 16/17

Panikhida · Ikon of St Cuthbert of Lindisfarne · Apolytikion for St Nicholas
· Funeral Ikos
Voces Angelicae, Ivan Moody
IKON RECORDS C IKO 21

The Protecting Veil · Thrinos
Steven Isserlis: cello, London Symphony Orchestra, Gennady Rozhdestvensky
VIRGIN CLASSICS VC 7 59052 – 2

The Repentant Thief
Andrew Marriner: clarinet, London Symphony Orchestra, Michael Tilson Thomas
COLLINS CLASSICS 20052

Thunder Entered Her · The Lamb · The Tiger · Two Hymns to the Mother
of God · Responsorium in Memory of Annon Lee Silver · Song for Athene ·
Eonia · God Is With Us
BBC Singers, Christopher Bowers-Broadbent: organ, Simon Joly
UNITED RECORDING COMPANY CD 88023

Thunder Entered Her · Angels · Annunciation · The Lament of the Mother of
God · Hymns of Paradise · God Is With Us
Winchester Cathedral Choir, David Dunnett: organ, David Hill
VIRGIN CLASSICS VC5 45035 2

To a Child Dancing in the Wind · Lamentation, Last Prayer and Exaltation ·
Mini Song Cycle for Gina · Melina
Patricia Rozario, with accompaniment including John Tavener: piano
COLLINS CLASSICS CD 14282

The Uncreated Eros · Magnificat · Nunc Dimittis · The Lamb · Two Hymns
to the Mother of God · Today the Virgin · God Is With Us · Ode of St Andrew
of Crete · Love Bade Me Welcome · The Tiger · Eonia
Choir of St George's Chapel, Windsor Castle, Christopher Robinson
HYPERION CDA 66464

We Shall See Him As He Is
John Mark Ainsley: tenor, Patricia Rozario: soprano, BBC Welsh Chorus,
The Britten Singers, Chester Festival Chorus, BBC Welsh Symphony Orchestra,
Richard Hickox
CHANDOS CHAN 9128

The Whale

Anna Reynolds: mezzo, Raimund Herincx: baritone, Alvar Lidell: speaker, John Tavener: organ and Hammond organ, The London Sinfonietta & Chorus, David Atherton

APPLE CD SAPCOR 15

Appendix C : Those interviewed

Betty Andersson, *Jean Andersson, Lady Freda Berkeley, Robin Boyle, Michael Buckland, *Brian Chapple, Elizabeth Collins, Rachel Davies, John Drummond, *Mia Farrow, Father Michael Fortounatto, *Annie French, Lionel Friend, *Jenny Frith, *Barrie Gavin, *Sir William Glock, *Francis Grier, Father Sergei Hackel, Pat Harrison, Richard Hickox, *Margaret Hubicki, Lady June Hutchinson, Steven Isserlis, *Guy Jonson, *Bishop Kallistos, Rhonda Kess, *Stan Kitchen, *Lady Margaret Long, Sarah Long, David Lumsdaine, Sheila MacCrindle, Gerard McLarnon, *Margaret Mail, Vicky Maragopoulou, *Pamela Moody, *Braham Murray, Martin Neary, *John Noble, Peter Phillips, Philip Pilkington, *Robert Ponsonby, *John Poole, Dimitri Poulakos, Doreen Pugh, *Kathleen Raine, *George Rizza, Patricia Rozario, Gennady Rozhdestvensky, James Rushton, *John Rutter, Nicholas Snowman, Francis Steiner, *Margaret Steinitz, Brenda Tavener, Kenneth Tavener, Maryanna Tavener, Roger Tavener, *Robert Tear, Mother Thekla, Dr David Thomas, *Sir John Tooley, Penny Turton, Deborah Wearing, *Kenneth Woollam, Sir Magdi Yacoub.

*interviewed by telephone

Appendix D : The eight Byzantine tones

For the purposes of drawing a distinction, one may say that the Russian tones are marked by their melodies, while each of the Byzantine tones has particular modal characteristics. However, this generalization gives no idea of the complexity of the Byzantine tone system. The brief summary which follows has been prepared with the invaluable assistance of David Melling, senior research fellow at Manchester Metropolitan University, who is writing a book on the subject.

Each of the eight Byzantine tones makes use of a cluster of modes. Each of these modes is defined by (a) its characteristic scales; (b) its basic note; (c) its dominant notes; (d) its typical melodic phrases, which give structure to the melodies; (e) its melodic cadences, which serve as musical punctuation of the text; (f) its emotional character.

To identity the notes of the scales, syllables are used, just as 'do' 're' 'mi' are used to name the successive notes of the scale in European music. The syllables used in Byzantine chant are as follows:

> **Ni Pa Vou Ga Dhi Ke Zo Ni**

If we are singing the diatonic scale, they correspond to

> Do Re Mi Fa So La Si Do

The most common scales of the eight tones are listed below. [The numbers in square brackets between the syllables indicate the number of microtones in each step of the scale. Psaltic theory divides the octave into 72 equal microtones.]

TONE I:

Pa [10] Vou [8] Ga [12] Dhi [12] Ke [10] Zo [8] Ni [12] Pa
Basic note   Pa

TONE II:

Ni [8] Pa [14] Vou [8] Ga [12] Dhi [8] Ke [14] Zo [8] Ni
Basic note   Dhi

This tone also uses the scale of Tone VI.

TONE III:
Ni [12]   Pa [12]   Vou [6]   Ga [12]   Dhi [12]   Ke [6]   Zo [12]   Ni
Basic note   Ga
This scale is in effect the piano tuning of the major scale on F.

TONE IV:
Ni [14]   Pa [6]   Vou [8]   Ga [12]   Dhi [12]   Ke [10]   Zo [8]   Ni
Basic note   Vou
This tone also uses a mode with the same scale as Tone II.

TONE V (or PLAGAL I):
Pa [10]   Vou [8]   Ga [12]   Dhi [12]   Ke [10]   Zo [8]   Ni [12]   Pa
Basic note   Ke
This tone also uses a mode with a scale similar to that of Tone I, but with Zo flat.

TONE VI (or PLAGAL II):
Pa [6]   Vou [20]   Ga [4]   Dhi [12]   Ke [6]   Zo [20]   Ni [4]   Pa
Basic note   Pa
This tone also has a mode which uses the scale of Tone II.

BARYS, THE GRAVE TONE:
Zo [12]   Ni [12]   Pa [12]   Vou [6]   Ga [12]   Dhi [12]   Ke [6]   Zo
This scale is in effect the piano tuning of the major scale on B flat.

The Grave Tone also makes use of a mode with the same scale as Tone III, but quite different typical phrases and cadences, and of the following scale on B natural:
Zo [8]   Ni [12]   Pa [10]   Vou [8]   Ga [12]   Dhi [12]   Ke [10]   Zo
This mode of the Grave Tone employs many microtonal variations.

TONE VIII (or PLAGAL IV):
Ni [12]   Pa [10]   Vou [8]   Ga [12]   Dhi [12]   Ke [10]   Zo [8]   Ni
This scale can be thought of as the normal diatonic major scale, as it would be sung by an unaccompanied folk singer.

NOTE: In the music of John Tavener the tones are used creatively and with great freedom.

General Index

Index of Tavener Compositions